GODS OF FLESH / GODS OF STONE

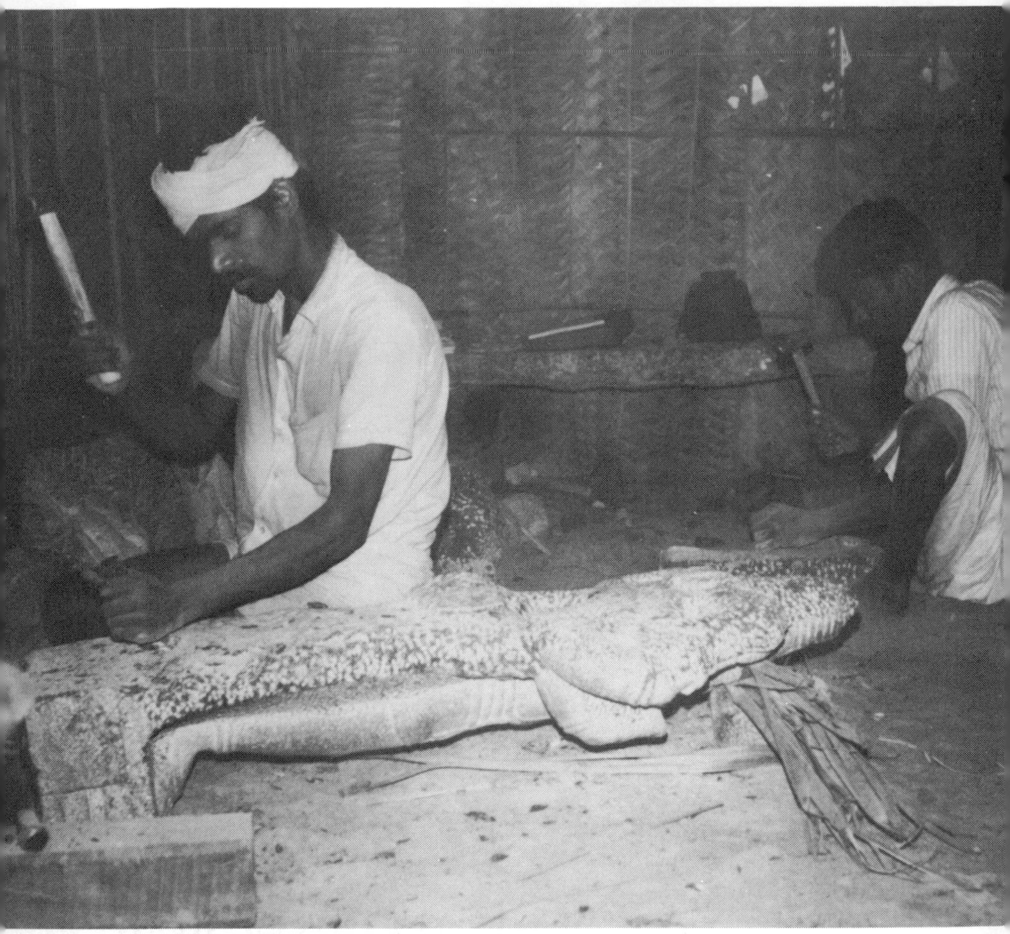

Image-makers at Mahābalipuram, Tamilnadu. By Sally Noble

Gods of Flesh Gods of Stone

The Embodiment of Divinity in India

Edited by

Joanne Punzo Waghorne

and Norman Cutler

in association with

Vasudha Narayanan

ANIMA

Cover photos: Image of Gaṇēśa as Lord of Felicity Installed for a Tamil Wedding. By Sally Noble. / The Image-Body of Śaivite Saint Māṇikkavāsacar in Full State Dress, Carried in a Palanquin During a Procession in Mylapore, Madras City. By Dick Waghorne.

CIP Data

Gods of flesh / gods of stone.

Bibliography: p. 201
Includes index.
1. God (Hinduism) — Addresses, essays, lectures. 2. Gods, Hindu — Addresses, essays, lectures. 3. Hinduism — Customs and practices — Addresses, essays, lectures.
I. Waghorne, Joanne Punzo. II. Cutler, Norman, 1949-
III. Narayanan, Vasudha.
BL1213.32.G63 1984 294.5'211 84-18543
ISBN 0-89012-037-4

Anima Publications is a subdivision of Conococheague Associates, Inc., 1053 Wilson Avenue, Chambersburg, Pennsylvania 17201. Printed in USA.

Preface

THE ESSAYS INCLUDED in this volume originated as oral presentations at two successive workshops of the Conference on Religion in South India (CRSI) a group of scholars and students who meet annually to discuss a chosen topic pertaining to the theory and practice of religion in south India and, increasingly in recent years, in other regions of the sub-continent as well. The first, which met in May 1981 and was organized by Joanne Punzo Waghorne, addressed the topic of "image worship." The second, which met the following year and grew directly out of the first, was organized by Norman Cutler and Vasudha Narayanan and addressed the closely related topic of "the human and the divine." In the original workshop context and in this volume, these essays have been conceived as responses to a central theoretical issue and consequently are closely interrelated. The editors have worked closely with the contributors to produce a multifaceted yet fully integrated critical study of the embodiment of divinity in India.

This volume has come into being through the cooperation and support of a number of individuals and organizations. First and foremost, the editors wish to thank the contributors who cheerfully bore with what must have at times seemed like a never-ending barrage of questions and comments. We wish also to thank the Association for Asian Studies, which awarded the CRSI a subsidy to support publication of work presented at its 1982 workshop, and the Committee on Southern Asian Studies at the University of Chicago, which provided a grant to aid in preparation of the manuscript. Finally, we wish to thank Sally Noble and Dick Waghorne for permission to use their fine photographs in the cover design and frontpiece.

Joanne Punzo Waghorne
Norman Cutler

Boston and Chicago

A Note on Transliteration

MATERIAL TREATED in this volume comes from a variety of linguistic sources, Sanskrit and vernacular, and thus the transliteration situation is a complex one. Terms in Vasudha Narayanan's essay, for example, come from both the Tamil and Sanskrit languages, as well as Maṇipravāḷa, a hybrid of the two, which is the linguistic medium for much Śrīvaiṣṇava discourse. Likewise, Lise Vail's paper includes Kannada and Sanskrit terms. Tamil and Kannada, both Dravidian languages, possess some long/short vowel pairs (*ē/e, ō/o*) which Sanskrit and many Indo-Aryan languages do not (having only *ē* and *ō*, and thus commonly omitting the long mark). To avoid confusion, therefore, throughout the volume Sanskrit *ē* and *ō* are represented with the macron, though this is contrary to the common practice. Otherwise, the standard transliteration system has been employed with the exception of a few words which are commonly used in English (e.g., Brahmin). These latter are not formally transliterated or italicized. Tamil words are transliterated in accord with the system employed by the Madras University Tamil Lexicon, and Kannada words in accord with a complementary scheme. In some cases the names of contemporary sectarian organizations and leaders follow the spelling found in sectarian publications, even if these fail to follow the standard system of transliteration (e.g., Akshar Purushottam Sanstha).

Contents

Introduction

Joanne Punzo Waghorne

SCHOLARS OF RELIGION have long been too outwardly sophisticated to use terms like idolatry, devil worship, or demon possession to describe the multifaceted embodiment of gods in India. Yet in so many introductory texts to Hinduism, mention of these most obvious, even empirically observable, manifestations of religion in India is restricted to a few pages carefully sandwiched between long descriptions of salvation in the *Bhagavad Gītā* and the reforms of Rammohan Roy or tucked into a corner of a chapter on "theism."[1] When the embodiment of god in the divine image or the holy person is mentioned, authors often adopt the stoic guidelines of a teacher forced to explain sex in class — keep it short, keep to the facts, and provide some solid assurances that it is not so mysterious after all. The divine image, for example, is often characterized as an expression of "popular worship" and left to sit alone amid the vast implications of the term *popular*.[2] Recently, the image has even been treated to a bit of Freudian analysis and found to be "oneiric" — fundamentally part of the dream-world brought to near wakefulness as artistic expression.[3] Typically in these "explanations," the embodiment of gods in flesh, stone, metal, or clay is covered by some blanket category as if to hide such shockingly direct experience of god in India. Only very recently have scholars of Hinduism begun to understand and "to see"[4] those fully embodied gods who inhabit small shrines and great temples or who walk as teacher and lord among their devotees; and, in whose living presence most Hindus, modern or traditional, orthodox or tribal, pass their lives.

This recent interest in the many aspects of the concrete and immediate experience of god in India seems almost spontaneous. Suddenly, within the last decade, those weeks devoted to the Vedic sacrifice and the Upaniṣads in religion courses or these endless discussions of caste in anthropology seemed inadequate as a serious reflection of "Hinduism." Those classic textbook "issues" bother few practicing Hindus, whose religious attention has always lain elsewhere. Discussions of the sacrificial origins of *pūjā* are shouted down by the intense expressions of joy when the *utsava mūrti*, the mobile image of a god, is carried through the streets of Madras. A family's careful preparation to receive the Lord Gaṇēśa in his image-body into their own home during the *vināyakacaturthī* muffles worry over the Aryan or Dravidian origin of the rite. The devotee of the god-filled guru has his concentration first on the experience of divinity rather than the issue of this "renouncer's" place in the society. And, when Hindus reflect theologically, questions concerning the nature of such divine embodiment now overshadow issues concerning the nature of *mōkṣa.* All of these unquiet and visible aspects of religion are the subject of this present volume — a joint effort of many scholars to present the embodied god as central to the study of religion in India.

Before these essays unfold and before the revelation of gods of flesh and stone in India begins, a moment of self-examination for both anthropology and the history of religions is in order. Why was such concrete theism condemned as idolatry, shunted aside as popularism, or buried in not-this-but-that explanations for so long? It is not enough to say simply that a Judeo-Christian heritage made the study of "idols" difficult. The axioms and methods of both disciplines have been as intellectually iconoclastic as any hammer in the hand of an image-smashing prophet. The reasons lie deep in the natal years of both disciplines.

Although image worship as a topic has either been condemned or hidden, the comparative study of religions actually began with a closely related set of concepts as the central issue — mana, fetishism, and animism. These terms provided "scientific" language for a serious theological issue — the origin of the concept of god in the history of civilization. Animism/mana, it was argued, were the first primitive notions of independent divine forces which, presumably, lead to polytheism, and idolatry, and finally to monotheism. E. B. Tylor began his famous study of the religion of primitive people with an examination of "how and why they believe in the soul and its existence after death, the spirits who do good and evil in the world, and the greater gods who pervade, actuate, and rule the universe." Animism was the first step toward the concept of god — a primary belief in the independence of some spirit force from pure biological life. For the primitive, however, this soul-force had physical status because this "untaught reasoner" could not distinguish between the categories of rational philosophy and physical science. They tried to "get at the meaning of life by what the senses seem to tell." And this "very evidence of his senses" told the primitive that Life departed in death and must have gone somewhere.[5]

James Frazer preferred the term *magic* to religion for his descriptions of such early proto-science but his descriptions of magic again touched upon the quasi-physical origins of god. Frazer began with "Kings as Incarnate Life-Spirits" and traced these "embodiments" of soul-life-spirits in primitive and classical traditions. Ultimately, of course, Frazer sounded Tylor's own drum of doom for such "a false conception of natural law."[6] Once science and rational philosophy freed humanity from this sad state of unclassified confusion, the primitive quasi-physical conception of god went, or rather should go, the way of the dinosaurs.

A neon sign isn't necessary to point out the impact of such theories for the study of the embodiment of divinity in India. The study of Hinduism was caught in a trap formed by the ironclad axioms of early anthropology. In the march of process, the identification of divine powers with the physical world was seen as an anachronism. It was simply impossible to suppose that religion did *not* move from a vague sense of matter-made-divine toward a separation of such misplaced concreteness, from pure spirituality, with science taking over the role as explicator of the natural world. There could no more be an advanced matter-based religion than there could be a literate duck-billed platypus. India, however, did not quite fit the theory. Hinduism needed serious reinterpretation if it was to fit neatly into this Darwinian mold.

India was not a primitive society. No anthropologist could possibly so classify this urbanized and highly literate culture. But India also was undeniably a society that used its senses to experience god. Its "idolatry" was hard to ignore. By the 1840s, India's bold "idolatry" was *the* major public issue in the debate over the use of public funds to support the East India Trading Company's rule in the subcontinent.[7] As the new "raj," the Company had inherited the old royal duty to administer and to protect, with army and police if necessary, the temples in its domains. Such protection was expensive, and the issue of indirect British support for such idolatry never waned until the end of the century.[8] The "scientific" study of religion in India grew up amid this debate. India's "idolatry" in the face of its urbanity and literacy was always the shadow issue behind the discussions of its ancient religion.

In the midst of this dilemma, the comparative study of religion was born with F. Max Müller as the founding father. Max Müller directly confronted the issue of India's continued use of concrete divinity by arguing that this ancient culture "gives us opportunities for a study of the origin and growth of religions such as we find nowhere else."[9] The reasons for such a claim lay in India's own sense of its religious history. In India no earlier stage of religion was ever discarded; rather, these more simplistic notions of divinity were preserved for the young and by strong inference for all the more "childish" in the society — the masses. Hence, every high caste Hindu moved through carefully determined religious stages from ritualized worship of a concrete god to true Self-discovery. Thus by using the logic of his day, Max Müller subtly "solved" the problem of idolatry in India: all sensual concrete experience of god was the atavism of a primitive stage of religion which served to awaken the child or the childish to an initial experience of God. "Idolatry" therefore, by inference, was not to be condemned, but simply understood as a useful *tool*.[10]

Max Müller's initial solution to the issue of embodied divinity remains in itself the most prevalent survival of nineteenth century theory. Those earlier quoted textbook discussions of image worship in Hinduism betray their ancestry in Max Müller. But the early work of Max Müller, Frazer, or Tylor should not be dismissed as mere nineteenth century *faux pas*. Max Müller may have muddled the discussion of embodied divinity with his insistent Darwinism but he at least, along with the early anthropologist, confronted the issue. There was little doubt for any of these scholars that for the primitives, and by strong inference for most of "uneducated" humanity, divinity had a physical embodiment. Further, they saw that this embodied divinity was the initial data, in fact, the only logical starting point for an empirical discipline. If they were trapped by Darwinism into ultimately denying the continued existence of embodied divinity, they were equally trapped by their own scientism into taking this evidence of god seriously. Max Müller best expressed the paradoxical ground rules of this new scientific discipline:

> I accept these terms, and I maintain that religion so far from being impossible, is inevitable, if only we are left in possession of our senses, such as we really find them, not such as they have been defined for us. Thus, the issue is plain. We claim no special faculty, no special revelation. The only faculty we claim is perception, the only revelation we claim is history,or, as it is now called, historical evolution.[11]

Max Müller's statement applied equally to both the investigator and the living data studied. Both must come to understand religion through, not in spite of, their sense experience. Appeals to revelation and to pure reason were rejected as improper *methods* and improper *data* for the new scientific study of religion.

The scientific study of religion in the nineteenth century then was actually forced by its own logic to propose another new type of divinity into the former theological and philosophical definitions of *god*. Max Müller proposed that god was experienced in stages from "objects tangible, semi-tangible, and intangible."[12] But "god" for Max Müller, as for Frazer and Tylor, existed always in the nexus of the physical, experiential, and mental world of the religious person. The category of "animism" or "intangible object" allowed for the concept of embodied divinity. The paradox for this scientism lay at the point where description gave way to analysis and finally to judgment. The nineteenth century was intellectually and temperamentally unable to ultimately accept a category of Being that was neither physical nor mental, neither simple concrete object nor pure abstract spirituality. The nineteenth century science revered empiricism but it also demanded clear categories. The type of god categorized as animistic was, from this viewpoint, a species doomed by its own internal confusion.

The paradoxical category of the neither-physical-nor-spiritual was simply dropped as a point of discussion in the twentieth century. When the discussion abandoned such scientism, the explanation of "idolatry" became a mute issue. The twentieth century discovered the "symbol" and knew for certain that the dilemma of god's seeming concrete reality was simply a false metaphysical issue.[13] The real issue was not the nature of god but rather the nature of the *meaning* of god. *God* was to be understood as a kind of language by which humanity expressed its deepest concerns. Such theories need not be discussed in detail, for this mode of scholarship has dominated the study of religion since Sigmund Freud. The problem with this twentieth century two-step around concrete divinity is that it denied the possibility that devoted Hindus, themselves, ever actually thought that god had an embodied reality. It was assumed that in making an icon of god, the Hindu was simply making meaning.

With such a legacy of analytical theory from the nineteenth and twentieth century, is it any wonder that the embodiment of divinity in India remained an embarrassment — a topic which is best consigned to "popularism" or quickly discussed as yet another type of "symbol"? The truth may well be that the very concreteness of god in India still demands serious consideration as a challenge to both the theory *and* the descriptive science of religion. The contributors to this volume are convinced that the time is right to take a new look at this type of religious experience that so intrigued and baffled the founders of comparative religion.

The eight essays in this volume, then, represent more than a collection of new information about an old topic. The contributors have approached their material fully aware of the problems of the past. They are asking an old question in a new way. Those clear divisions of matter and spirit that were taken for science have been shattered by a newer science. "Mind" can no longer be defined as purely mental. Our hopes, dreams, and even our very perceptions are shown to be oddly physical — subtle products of a chemical reaction. The very ground on which we stand has been revealed to be a mass of whirling atoms whose matter is also energy. The old category of spirit-in-matter is now not impossible but interesting. It is no longer necessary to ask what is wrong with "idolatry" or what do they *really* mean by image worship. The question now is: How does the process of god embodiment operate and how do the Hindus themselves discuss the subtle relationship between the "ordinary" concrete world of experience and the concretization of god.

The arrangement and selection of essays in this volume was the result of discoveries made within the individual essays and shared among the authors and the editors. It became clear that the embodiment of divinity spread over a wider range of material than was at first suspected. Thus, the making of an icon also involves the divinizing of the "maker." Both stone and flesh serve as vessels for divinity as the process of the transmutation of matter into divine matter occurs. In some cases, primary attention, however, focuses on the god embodied as icon, in other cases the flesh-made-god commands major attention. The essays, therefore, are arranged in a continuum from god embodied as stone-clay-metal-or-wood to divinity embodied in flesh.

The arrangement of the essays was also determined by another discovery. Both practice and proposition were part of each of these god-embodiment traditions in various proportions. Image worship and guru worship belong to traditions of serious theological discussions, both written and oral. Some essays were selected which presented the "outsiders'" anthropological analysis and description, while others present the "insiders'" overt theological and philosophical formulations of their practice. The proportionate attention given to theology and practice varied in degrees, not only in accord with the disciplinary training of the author, but also because the groups studied give variable emphases to these matters. Nevertheless, the relationship between discussion and practice is always a continuum. No tradition lacks either aspect totally.

The single conviction behind all of these essays remains the certainty that the process of the embodiment of god in India is not a mere popular phenomenon nor is it a relic of a by-gone age. These essays seek to present the embodiment of divinity as the central feature of Hinduism *and* as a central feature in the study of religion. The authors and the editors look to the time when Hindu practice and theology may well provide a richer vocabulary and better methods for understanding the nature of religion. Such a perspective could have serious impact on the way both theology and the comparative study of religion proceeds. The current movement in Western theology towards methods of analysis that increasingly present divinity as linguistic constructs are not without critics. Gordon Kaufman's new attempt to define god in the mode of the imagination has met with a criticism for which India's concrete sense of image-making could prove very relevant:

> To put the matter squarely, Kaufman does not really like imagery at all . . . He belongs to that current group of uplifters, who are running around painting fig leaves over our images of God, covering up those embarrassing personal pronouns. In the end, this theology of imagination impoverishes theology by replacing the richness of its imagery with an impersonal conceptuality.[14]

Let the removal of all such "fig leaves" begin from the body of gods in India and beyond.

The wooden icon of Lord Jagannāth is being pulled by hundreds of devotees into one of the large 33-wheel chariots during the annual car festival at Purī. Here the icon is protected by a burlap covering. In 1972 devotees had great difficulty pulling the sacred image of Lord Jagannāth into the chariot. The Rājā of Purī arrived on his elephant, prayed for the forgiveness of his people's corporate sins for that year, and the image was then easily pulled into place. This event was widely interpreted as a miracle among devotees.

1

Creation of the Sacred Image:

Apotheosis and Destruction in Hinduism

James J. Preston

THROUGH THE STUDY of icons and their construction we are able to perceive some of the most vital impulses underlying religious experience. Sacred images are products of the human imagination – they are constructed according to systematic rules, and then they are infused with sacrality and kept "alive" by highly controlled behaviors intended to retain the "spirit in matter." An analysis of this process of constructing sacred images, and the corollary process of their destruction, reveals to us something paradoxical and intriguing about human religion. Somehow the mystery of the invisible becomes more intense and awesome in the attempted act of its creation. This is the substance of revelation – an unveiling of the deity through the construction of its image, and then the discovery, each time anew, that the image is but a phantom of a larger reality beyond human grasp. The outstretched hand gropes in the darkness to touch something forever beyond its reach. The mystery is in the reaching and the eternal frustration of never completely finding.

There is no religion in the world that more fully expresses this process of apotheosis and destruction than Hinduism. The Hindu sacred image (or *mūrti*) is extraordinarily polymorphic and ubiquitous. Such images of divinity are "lifeless" until ceremonies of installation are performed. Thereafter the image *is* the deity, *not* merely a symbol of it.[1] The image and the worshiper are fused together temporarily during *pūjā*, and this relationship is reestablished each time the act of worship is implemented. For Hindus, temple deities are particularly dynamic instruments for participation in the religious life. Such *mūrtis* are treated as persons; in the words of Appadurai and Breckenridge, they are treated as "paradigmatic sovereigns" demanding and receiving all due respect from their devotees, and in turn, redistributing resources to temple, servants, donors, and worshipers.[2] Even though some Hindu sacred images are not usually represented anthropomorphically – such as Śiva *liṅgas* – these aniconic representations receive offerings and are generally worshiped as though they were sacred personages. Non-anthropomorphic tribal icons often become assimilated into Hinduism, overtly retaining their aniconic characteristics, but, in conception at least, these inevitably become anthropomorphized. Thus, for instance, a wooden post (once a tribal goddess) may be decorated with a skirt. And though it has no facial characteristics, it is clearly treated as a Hindu goddess, such as Durgā, with all the associated ceremonial.

Behind the elaborate panoply of sacred images in Hinduism is a profound insight that the image is temporary, incomplete, and inadequate as a full expression of divinity. The destruction of the image is as important as its creation. Unfortunately, there is little scholarly literature on the descent or enlivening of divinity in icons. Our purpose here is to explore this dual process of creating and destroying the *mūrti* in contemporary Orissa. Two traditions will be compared: the *navakalēvara* ceremony at the Purī Jagannāth temple and the construction of street images in the popular religion of Cuttack city. What do these data tell us about the role of sacred images in Hinduism? Are significant changes taking place in the ways sacred images are patronized, constructed, and worshiped? And why are some *mūrtis* periodically destroyed and renewed while others are constructed as semi-permanent monuments?

Hindu Image Makers

Who constructs Hindu icons and how do these become sacralized in their creation? Although there is an enormous literature on Hinduism, curiously little has been written about Hindu sacred images, and especially about their construction. According to the *śāstras*, traditionally the four *varṇas* may practice crafts such as image making, but Śūdras particularly are designated as artisans.[3] It would appear that image makers in contemporary India may be of any caste background. Reports of Brahmin, Vaiśya, and Śūdra image makers have been documented. Most commonly they are Śūdras from either carpenter or potter subcastes. In south India and in Kashi, image makers (*sthāpatis*) are often Viśvakarman Brahmins.[4]

Image makers work in various media — stone, metal, wood, and clay. The icons are created for many purposes. Some are constructed as permanent fixtures; others are deliberately intended to be temporary icons for display only on festival occasions. Usually permanent icons are installed in temples, in neighborhood niches, or along roadsides. Temporary icons are virtually ubiquitous, adorning already established sacred spaces, such as shrines and household altars, and also enhancing otherwise ordinary sites, including places associated with

Life size images of Lord Śiva and his consort Parvatī constructed by the image makers of Cuttack during Durgā Pūjā.

an occupation, places of particular natural beauty and religious significance, entrances to villages, and locations where intense cultural interactions occur, such as village squares, buildings where political parties hold meetings, libraries and schools, marketplaces, and major crossroads.

It is clear from the literature on image makers that their profession is on the wane. This is particularly true for sculptors of stone and metal images who are patronized by temples or royal courts. In some places, sculptors have become so numerous they are unable to practice their traditional caste occupations and are thus forced to find other sources of livelihood. Apparently, only where there has been a dramatic increase in popular street religion does the art of icon construction flourish as an occupation. Festivals like Durgā Pūjā are noteworthy as foci for emerging street ritual, where hundreds of temporary images are displayed, and subsequently merged in a tank or river.

We shall begin our examination of image making with an extraordinary example from Orissa. It has been noted already that temple icons are usually permanent fixtures, requiring no reconstruction, unless the image becomes the focus of either a political change (as in the case of an adopted emblematic deity of a patron) or when some theological transformation in the region requires the modification of the icon (as when Buddhist images become Hinduized). However, in Orissa, we find the unusual case of the periodic renewal of the three wooden images of Jagannāth, his brother Balabhadra, and his sister Subhadrā. Not only are these icons repaired and repainted each year, they are also periodically destroyed and recarved, which is rare for temple icons. This extraordinary, yet orthodox custom of renewing temple icons will be compared with the expanding street ritual tradition associated with the growth of popular Hinduism. Although each of these traditions expresses quite different variants of Hinduism, both share the common thread of *impermanence*, a central theme basic to the underlying Hindu conception of the relationship of divinity to matter.

The Navakalēvara Ceremony[5]

The Purī Jagannāth complex is well known for its eclecticism; temple servants from over eighty subcastes serve the deities. There is relative balance in the distribution of labor among high caste Brahmins and non-Brahmin priests. Similarly, the Jagannāth triad represents an eclectic synthesis of several Orissan sects — Śaiva, Śākta, and Vaiṣṇava in particular. At various stages in Orissan history, different

A typical poster image found in household shrines, on temple walls or in shops. This is an image of the ten-armed goddess Durgā slaying a demon.

religions have reigned supreme: Jainism and Buddhism have played important roles in the early development of Orissan religion, and tribal themes have always been strongly represented in the fabric of the dominant religion, whether Jainism, Buddhism, or Hinduism.

Today Jagannāth is, without doubt, a Vaiṣṇava deity; but most scholars would agree that it was originally a tribal god, made of wood, that eventually was anthropomorphized to become the synthetic focus of divergent Orissan religions under the patronage of the Gaṅga kings (probably in the twelfth century A.D.). Stietencron argues convincingly that there was a pre-existing Brahmanic Vaiṣṇava cult that was merged with a semi-tribal cult of the wooden god Bhairava / Nṛsiṃha under the Gaṅga kings, who extended their power and influence by amalgamating tribal, Śaiva, Śākta and Vaiṣṇava elements into the Purī-based Jagannāth triad.[6]

Eschmann argues that Vaiṣṇavism spread throughout pockets of tribal Orissa in the Nṛsiṃha (man-lion) form which easily accommodated to the corresponding ***ugra***, or furious, characteristics of many local tribal deities (especially in coastal Orissa).[7] Furthermore, this form of Vaiṣṇavism is heavily tantric. Nṛsiṃha also appears in a female aspect as Nṛsiṃhī, an angry goddess corresponding to tribal goddesses who demanded human sacrifice and appear iconographically in the form of wooden posts (Stambēśwarī).[8] Eschmann asserts that Nṛsiṃha worship spread along the coast from south India in the fourth to sixth centuries A.D. and was adopted in Orissa because it was compatible with extant tribal, Śākta, and Śaiva sects. Since Jagannāth is represented as an anthropomorphized post with wide-open eyes (like those of a lion), the connection with Nṛsiṃha has some merit. The images of the deities still have a "tribal" look today. They are "crude" wooden figures similar to the aniconic symbols associated with the tribal Śabaras. A legend explains this "crude" appearance of the Jagannāth triad: When the sacred log (*dāru*) appeared in Purī nobody could carve it. Finally Jagannāth (or in some versions Viśvakarmā) appeared as a feeble old carpenter who consented to carve it, provided no one disturbed his work. Queen Gundicā could not restrain herself, peeped in prematurely, and consequently the figures remained unfinished.[9]

Although Jagannāth is likely a Vaiṣṇavized tribal image, the other two deities in the Jagannāth triad represent the Śākta element, in the form of Jagannāth's sister, Subhadrā, and the Śaiva component, represented by Jagannāth's brother, Balabhadra.[10] Thus, the imagery at the Purī Jagannāth temple displays a rich condensation of previously separate religious fragments, only later unified under a single religio-politico umbrella.[11]

The complex maneuvers of Orissan rājās for ascendancy in the political arena culminated in the twelfth century A.D. with the Jagannāth synthesis formulated by King Cōḍagaṅga. Earlier dynasties were each associated with a particular sect. The final unification of these sects in the Jagannāth cult brought together large, previously competing, geographic territories into a single political unit.

Not only is synthesis seen in the iconographic and political sphere, it is also evident in the prominence of non-Brahmin priests serving at the Jagannāth temple. Of course, this phenomenon is not peculiar to the Jagannāth temple alone in Orissa. Non-Brahmins play important roles in many Orissan temples.[12] At the famous Liṅgarāj shrine in Bhubaneswar, for instance, members of the Śūdra Baḍu subcaste are assigned important duties that bring them into intimate contact with the deity. They alone are allowed to bathe Liṅgarāj, to adore him, and carry his movable image (*calanti pratimā*) in procession outside the temple.[13] These Śūdra temple servants are considered to be Śabaras — once forest-dwelling tribals of south India who migrated to Orissa and whose deity was the goddess Stambēśwarī (wooden pillar).[14] A comparable non-Brahmin Śūdra caste known as Daitās play an important role at the Purī Jagannāth temple, particularly in the construction of the sacred image. They also trace their origins to tribal Śabaras, and are believed to be the only ones capable of carving the sacred images. There is an interesting tie of fictive kinship here, a tie that legitimates the involvement of Daitās in the important renewal ceremony known as *navakalēvara*. As original descendants of the tribal Śabaras, the Daitās claim Lord Jagannāth to be a close relative.[15] Thus, they assert it is their rightful duty to dress the images, to move them in procession on festival occasions, to repair them annually, and to periodically renew the sacred images. Indeed, for two full weeks each year, just after the bathing ceremony, the deities are worshiped by the Daitās alone (and not the Brahmins) in a style all their own.

The *navakalēvara* ceremony is a highly secret ritual of renewal of the sacred images, requiring the total replacement of the three icons (Jagannāth, Subhadrā, and Balabhadra) every twelve to nineteen years as determined astrologically.[16] This ceremony of renewal is performed for several reasons: (1) to demonstrate the fundamental belief that sacred images are transitory and perishable; (2) to continue a tribal tradition (still extant) whereby sacred posts are periodically renewed; (3) to continue a practice that originated during the Marātha occupation of Orissa when the Jagannāth images were hidden (probably buried) and then exhumed and recarved.[17]

The famous car festival at Purī held each year during the Monsoon season. At this time the three wooden images of Jagannāth, Balabhadra, and Subhadrā are removed from the temple and taken on a journey down the streets of Purī for public display. This represents one of the most attractive festivals in India for pilgrims who come in the millions to witness the event.

The ceremony begins six weeks before the famous chariot festival (unless the wooden images remain intact). This is an expensive and elaborate affair which is performed only when necessary. If the wooden images have started to show signs of serious decay, then and only then is the ceremony of new embodiment (or renewal) performed. *Navakalēvara* must occur in a year with two Āṣāḍhas (the lunar month of June/July) either twelve or nineteen years from the last time the icons were renewed. The ceremony must take place at least every nineteen years, no matter what the condition of the wooden images may be. *Navakalēvara* involves five phases: (1) a search for the *dāru* (divine wood or log) which is ceremonially brought to the temple at Purī; (2) the carving of the new images in secret by the Daitās; (3) consecration of the images and the insertion of the "life-substance" (*brahmapadārtha*); (4) burial of the old icons of the Jagannāth triad, their funeral, and purification rites of the Daitās; (5) the final cleansing of the new images by the Brahmins. Each phase is discussed below in greater detail. *Navakalēvara* is too complex to treat in its entirety; thus, of necessity, the sketch presented here is but an abbreviated composite, omitting numerous intriguing nuances.

Forest Rites: Vanayātrā

A party of Daitās and Brahmins sets out from Purī for the Maṅgalā temple in Kākaṭpur village (about thirty miles away) where there is a dense forest of Nīm trees that are used in constructing the new sacred images. The goddess Maṅgalā is bathed in an elaborate ceremony; then she is offered garments and *mahāprasād* from the Purī temple. The principal non-Brahmin priest prepares himself to receive (often through a dream) information concerning the location of the *dārus*, or trees, to be used for the sacred images. These trees must possess certain characteristics. The formulas for selecting the proper *dārus* are extremely complex. For example, the appropriate tree must have bark of a certain color, its location should be near a burial ground (for Balabhadra's image); a snake should live near the tree, etc. A separate tree must be selected for the icon of each of the three deities. When at least five of these conditions have been met, temporary shelters are built around the trees, Brahmins perform a fire sacrifice, and the trees are cut down. Finally, Viṣṇu is asked to assure the party, through a dream (containing either good or ill omens), that the *daru* is acceptable.

Cutting the trees involves elaborate purificatory rites. Axes of gold, silver, and iron are smeared with sandal paste, vermillion, and covered with flowers. The *bhūtas* (or spirits) living on or near the trees are then propitiated with offerings of grains and spices, and Viṣṇu is asked to command them to leave. Next the axes are smeared with clarified butter and honey, and, to the accompaniment of Vedic chants and loud music, the carpenters (*mahārānās*) cut down the trees. Each log is cut carefully to the prescribed length. The remainder of the tree is buried on the spot.[18] The logs are then stripped of bark, wrapped in silken cloth, and taken to Purī in procession, accompanied by the party of priests and temple servants. At Purī the *dārus* (logs) are welcomed by the Rājā of Purī and purified of any evil they may have contracted in transport.[19]

Carving the Images

The next stages of the *navakalēvara* ceremony occur within the temple. In the first phase (lasting two weeks), the images are carved and the *brahmapadārtha*, or "life-substance," of the old statues is transferred to the new ones. In 1568 A.D. when Orissa was overrun by Muslims, the wooden images of the Jagannāth triad were taken to Bengal and burnt. According to the temple records, a man from Orissa recovered the "life-substance" (presumably ashes or pieces of wood) from the image and returned it to Orissa where it was secretly worshiped until new images were carved and installed in 1590. During the next sixty years the priests of Purī temple had to flee at least twelve times to escape the iconoclasm of the Muslim generals of

Cuttack. Often the images were buried, or hidden in mud thatched houses. According to Tripathi:

> It was most probably in this turbulent period of political insecurity that the ceremony of *Navakalevara* attained more or less a regular character. The introduction of a regular *Navakalevara* might have had a psychologically advantageous aspect as well. It shows to the priests and the devotees alike that the images of Jagannāth, etc., are, by their very nature, a transitory and perishable object. They are the wooden forms of the immortal deities, to be discarded and buried, as it is every 12 years or so. Of importance is only the continuity of the divine substance, the *Brahmapadārtha*, and the fact that the new images be constructed exactly in the same manner as the previous ones.[20]

The images of the Jagannāth triad are carved in secret by the Daitās in a specially constructed enclosure within the temple. No other castes, Brahmins notwithstanding, are allowed to see or hear the act of carving. It is believed that anyone who observes or hears this sacred act of creation will become deaf or blind. To prevent this from happening, even accidentally, the sound of carving is drowned out by continuous loud music. We do not know the fine details of the carving itself, but there are specific, and quite exact measurements for each image. The wooden icons consist of five clearly discernible parts: face, neck, heart, waist, and feet. The two male deities are given arms. A cube-shaped cavity, considered to be the place for the "soul" of the deity, is made in each of the three images. Here mysterious objects are placed by the Daitās. The "soul" or "life-substance" is highly secret. People have speculated that the object is either a Buddha's tooth,[21] a piece of the original Jagannāth image buried during the Marātha period, or perhaps tantric *yantras* inscribed on metal plates.

Whatever it may be, the "life-substance" is treated with great ritual caution in the *brahmapadārtha* ceremony (transfer of "life-substance") that occurs when the carving of the wooden images has come to completion. At this time, the rough new wooden images of the three deities are placed in front of the old ones. All the lights in the temple are put out. The chief Daitā then opens the lid of the cavity of the old images, and blindfolded, with hands wrapped to the elbows so he can neither see nor feel the *brahmapadārtha*, he transfers the "soul," or "life-substance," from the old to the new icons.

This delicate and vital ritual is performed entirely by the non-Brahmin Daitās, a remarkable, and intriguing feature of the Jagannāth tradition. The Brahmins, however, are not entirely excluded from the carving rituals. They create the lids for the cavities containing the "life-substance." Curiously, the Brahmins consecrate this lid, but not the entire image or even the "life-substance" itself.

Burial and Purification

When the "life-substance" is removed, the old images are considered dead, and are taken to a cemetery located within the temple compound where they are buried alongside other wooden images of previous years. Here a pit is dug, lined with red velvet, and the "dead" images are lowered into it. This aspect of the *navakalēvara* ceremony reflects the fundamental Hindu principle of reincarnation; the external shell is mortal, but the soul or essence-of-being is immutable, immortal, and continually seeks new forms.

The typical dashboard of a Hindu-owned taxi displaying a variety of deities. Hindu sacred images are not only impermanent, they are also portable. Niches for the divinity are found in every locus of Indian life. These portable icons particularly flourish in places of occupation and where there is some risk, danger, or "luck" necessary for success, such as taxis, shops, and in the offices of bureaucrats.

After the images of the deities have been buried, the Daitās weep and mourn for their dead "clansman." The Daitās believe they are blood relatives of Jagannāth. Thus, they treat his death as one of their own, remaining in a state of ritual impurity for ten days. During this time the Daitās eat frugally, bathe, cut their hair and nails, and whitewash their homes. Finally, when the period of mourning has ended, the Daitās celebrate with a feast.

This act of fictive kinship, posited upon a blood relationship between the Jagannāth triad and the non-Brahmin Daitās of Purī, is not contested by temple authorities. To the contrary, the temple is expected to pay for some of the mourning rituals, and since the Daitās are close relatives of Lord Jagannāth, they are entitled to his property as heirs. This requires the temple to pay the Daitās a redemption of about 5,000 rupees (1969). They are also allowed to take "relics" from the dead images of the deities, such as cloth, resin, and sandal paste used as decorations. These materials, considered to have medicinal and miraculous qualities, are sometimes sold by the Daitās to pilgrims.

Preparing the New Images

During the burial phase of the *navakalēvara* ceremony, nothing is done to the new images; all attention is given to the process of mourning and purification. When the funeral phase is finished, the new images become the main focus of attention. Despite the fact that the new icons have been completely carved, the "life-substance" transferred, and the lids consecrated by the Brahmins, they remain essentially embryonic, because the wooden structures are considered to be unfinished skeletons of the images. Thus the final two weeks of the *navakalēvara* ceremony are devoted to infusing the images with "flesh" and "blood." This process is completed by Daitā Mahāpātras, temple servants of the Kāyastha caste.

A stylized Orissan painting of Lord Jagannāth. Note the distinct "tribal" quality of the image, reminiscent of the wood or stone icons found among the tribal peoples of Orissa (Usually Jagannāth appears alongside his brother Balabhadra and sister Subhadrā.)

"Flesh" and "blood" are given to the wooden skeletons by the layering of various symbolic substances; (1) cloth strips = skin, (2) red yarn or cloth = blood, (3) resin = flesh, (4) perfumed oil = marrow, (5) sandal paste = fat, and (6) rice or wheat starch = semen. These layers are renewed each year after normal decomposition. They represent the body of the deity and must always be present when the images are viewed by the general public.

Next the Citakāras, or painters, apply paint to the images except for the pupils of the eyes, a final task reserved for the Brahmins. This final touch is carried out in a solemn ceremony within the inner sanctum.

Now the sacred images have been completely renewed; the only thing that remains to be done is to bathe the new images. This is carried out by the Brahmins, the intention being to free the images from contamination incurred through contact with the carpenters, sculptors, and painters. The next day the deities are taken out of the temple for the famous car festival which ends the *navakalēvara* ceremony.

According to Tripathi, this elaborate rite of renewal represents the superimposition of Brahmanic Hinduism on a cult of purely tribal origins.[22] Obviously, certain aspects of the ceremony feature the Brahmins, such as the forest sacrifice. But most of it is heavily dominated by the Daitās, who fell the trees, bring the logs to the temple, carve them, and transfer the "life-substance." The Brahmins are not allowed to enter the place where the deities are carved, nor to see or touch the unfinished wooden images, even to consecrate them. They may handle the images only on the last day. Furthermore, much of what we see in the *navakalēvara* ceremony is found among contemporary Orissan tribal peoples (such as the Khonds) in their renewal rites for sacred images.[23]

Although the Daitās play a central role in the periodic renewal of the Jagannāth icons, their function during the remainder of the year is minimal. They have little to do with the performance of routine *pūjās*. During the car festival they sing to the deities and perform other traditional customs. Also, they dress the images, assist in their annual repair, and spend two weeks each year worshiping them with special tantric rites (from which Brahmins are excluded). Otherwise, if it were not for the *navakalēvara* ceremony, the Daitās would have no significant role at the Jagannāth temple. The periodic recreation of the sacred images preserves their art and function as caretakers of the deities. Unlike other artisans involved in the creation of sacred images in Orissa, the Daitās are also priests who are closely involved in the Purī Vaiṣṇava tradition. Their restricted role in the ritual of Jagannāth does not diminish their overall importance as members of an eclectic array of service castes assigned to the deities at the shrine. Orissan Hinduism typically employs ritualists of multiple castes in its many religious centers which are associated with different sects. Non-Brahmin priests are ubiquitous in Orissan Hinduism; most of them, however, are not artisans. The Daitās are unique in that they are both priests and temple artisans.

We shall shift our focus now to the creation of sacred images constructed for display in popular Orissan street festivals. Here we see a change of patronage for the art of sculpture, away from temples and courts, towards a corporate form of patronage involving many segments of the community. Once again the impermanence of these images, which are destroyed and recreated each year, ensures work for the image makers. In this case, however, and in contrast with the Jagannāth *navakalēvara* ceremony, the artisans may exercise their interpretive skills with some freedom, and they may cater to particular demands imposed by different patrons from a wide spectrum in the population.

Popular Street Images[24]

In recent years, popular religion has flourished in urban India. Orissa's largest cities have exploded with street festivals involving large numbers of temporary clay images.[25] These popular extravaganzas are also found extensively in West Bengal and other parts of eastern India. The art of image making has expanded rapidly in this climate of growing popular religion. Business for image makers is particularly intense during Durgā Pūjā, Saraswatī Pūjā, Kālī Pūjā, and Viśvakarmā Pūjā.

Traditionally, image makers in Orissa have been Kumbhāras (or potters), but caste affiliation is not very strict. Both Brahmin and untouchable image makers have been observed in this part of India.[26] In urban areas, such as Cuttack, image makers live in their own neighborhoods, a tradition consistent with the old craft guild pattern of settlement found throughout India. Kramrisch notes that such craft guilds sometimes occupied whole villages to the exclusion of other groups. They also were often affiliated with the courts and lived adjacent to the palace.[27] Today these image makers have little work as sculptors of permanent temple images. If it were not for the rise of popular street religion, their art would disappear and, as has happened to other castes, their traditional occupation would be replaced as a source of income by jobs in the commercial or bureaucratic sector. Interviews with Cuttack's image makers reveal how very lucrative this occupation has become in recent years. Indeed, the art of image making has attracted apprentices from other castes who are eager to share in the new prosperity.

There are various ways to construct temporary festival images. Some are made from plaster molds. These are usually small and less ornate than the larger, life-size images fashioned from wooden models overlaid with mixed layers of bamboo, straw husks, jute thread, and mud from the Mahānadī River. Finally, a coating of slip (claypaint) is applied before the image is painted. Some icons are fired to make them more permanent, but most are easily disposable, an important characteristic in a festival tradition that emphasizes the impermanence of the sacred icon.

The image makers of Cuttack follow local traditions which are not documented in the classical *śāstras*. Some of the beautiful life-size images of Saraswatī, for instance, are decorated in Orissan filigree silver. These expensive statues are sometimes so costly, only very wealthy merchants, or the Indian government, can afford to purchase them. Not all the twenty families of image makers in Cuttack adhere to the Orissan style; today there is considerable influence from Bengal. One of Orissa's most celebrated image makers learned the art by observing his father who had originally studied sculpture in Calcutta. According to the Kumbhāras interviewed, today's aspiring image makers often go to Shantineketan in West Bengal for instruction in the art.

The style of images among some artists remains relatively unchanged and true to the *śāstras*. Others, especially the more successful image makers, introduce numerous innovations. Such changes are requested by patrons. Especially popular are images of Śiva and Saraswatī as portrayed in Hindi films. Typical changes include modern hairstyles, tight fitting saris, and rich pastel colors currently in vogue. Some artists refuse to meet these demands, claiming such "modern" departures from traditional forms do *not* inspire genuine religious devotion. Those artists who do tolerate innovations get their ideas from numerous sources, including the India-wide poster tradition depicting gods and goddesses of all kinds in scenes from the epics and *purāṇas*. Some of Cuttack's artists copy these poster images; they also get ideas from image makers they meet in other parts of India when they travel to government supported craft fairs. Most interesting, however, are innovations of a more personal type. Several image makers interviewed said they felt free to include new ideas revealed to them in dreams, but such personal innovations appear to be mostly minor changes of style, deviating little from the popular tradition.

The creation of a popular street image involves a whole family of image makers and numerous outside hired assistants. They work from early morning until late at night trying to meet the demands of patrons during the busy festival season. Today, image makers in Cuttack engage in few religious rituals while constructing the icons, and they do not feel much spirituality regarding their occupation. This is not to suggest that image making has been secularized due to a diminished value placed on the sacred images constructed. The piety associated with the occupation, which was experienced by the parents of the image makers, is simply impossible to reproduce in the context of the flurry of activity surrounding the creation of popular street images. These artisans are proud of the beauty of their images, but popular demand has made the occupation a "big business." Thus, a shortage of time and a changing patronage have conspired to attenuate the ritualization of image making, rendering the task of creating the sacred image less pious than it was previously.

The upsurge of popular image making is related to a change of patronage for the art of sculpture. Temples and courts in Cuttack no longer act in their traditional role as chief patrons for the construction of sacred icons. The new patrons represent a wide range of segments in the community – government institutions,[28] rich merchants, groups of students, and neighborhood associations. This broad spectrum features educated bureaucrats and merchant classes, who have the cash to support the carnival-like atmosphere of popular street rituals like Durgā Pūjā. Merchants act as patrons, in part, to advertise their business enterprises as the images are carried through the streets of the city. Many of them are Marwaris, Bengalis and Gujaratis who have traditionally worshiped the goddess as their *iṣṭa dēvatā*. Among newly educated bureaucrats, the motivation for patronizing image makers is different. The new bureaucratic elites display their power as patrons of popular art in order to establish legitimacy in their new roles as urbanites and professionals. Government officials who occupy prestigious positions are often enthusiastic contributors to the creation of popular sacred icons. They live in expensive houses, often have access to the scarce luxury of government supplies, possess private cars (along with driver), and exercise their power by grant petitions to the many people who flock to their offices, and even stand outside the gates of their homes, reminding one of the atmosphere at a princely court. The only thing missing is the customary sacred sanction associated with such power. Thus, the bureaucratic elites often extend their prestige and influence by engaging in a tradition which is deeply embedded in the old *dharma/rājā* configuration; they donate large sums to temples, assist in the construction of new neighborhood shrines, and display their devotion by patronizing the creation of popular street icons during important festivals. Since a *pūjā* pandal involves several images costing between 2,000 to 3,000 rupees, the investment of merchants and high government officials can be considerable. Students, lower level bureaucrats, and neighborhood associations, on the other hand, share resources, involving more modest investment on the part of individuals. This corporate form of patronage for sacred image construction is a relatively new phenomenon.

Especially revealing is the patronage of popular images by neighborhood associations. Such corporate patronage often cuts across caste, occupation, and interest groupings, since members of increasingly heterogeneous neighborhoods come together, take up a collection, share food, and identify themselves as a single unit through the sacred image. One aspect of Durgā Pūjā is the friendly competition that arises between neighborhoods which strive to create the best image (as determined in a contest financially supported by the Rāṇī of Darpani). These same neighborhoods rush to be first in the destruction of the images during the *bisurgan*, or immersion phase of the festival.[29] The ritual reaches a crescendo when the icons are dumped into the Mahānadī River. At this time the crowd often becomes excited, there are scuffles among drunken youths, and screams of delight as the images are destroyed. The immersion of the clay deities is a joyous act involving no remorse for the destroyed images, which are considered "lifeless" at this point in the festival.

The *bisurgan* ceremony is important for the image makers because it keeps their art alive. Though some artists express sadness to see certain, particularly beautiful works of art go under the murky waters, they universally agree that preserving the statues would be disastrous for their trade. Although some outstanding specimens may be saved for craft exhibits, no one thinks of saving the images from year to year. Their impermanence is celebrated for its assurance of future image construction.

The increase of popular street ritual extends beyond the commercial interests of rich patrons. These events are fun and entertaining, and there is a certain amount of pride attached to competing for the best image. But more important is another result of street rituals mentioned earlier — namely, that people from diverse traditional backgrounds temporarily regroup as a single unit on such occasions, despite their relative isolation at other times of year in the confines of neighborhood, family, and caste.

Incarnatus Dei

The Hindu embodiment of divinity in a material icon is not a final act to be enshrined forever; rather it is a process that continues to evolve as the many conceptions of divinity change through time. There can be no doubt that sacred images have been used as monuments by royal patrons seeking to establish their power in a particular region. Yet, even such monuments were relatively impermanent as royal courts shifted sectarian patronage. Nor is this a system of anarchistic image construction. Clearly, Hindu sacred images require precise traditional dimensions to be recognized as legitimate representations of the deity. The sheer variety of images available within Hinduism offers such a broad scope for creative activity it would appear, at first glance, that the creation of sacred images is wide open to free expression. Freedom in the creation of sacred images is not located so much in the vast scope of forms taken by the divinity, but rather in the constant cycle of creating and destroying these icons.

The common element in the two thriving traditions of image construction discussed here is *impermanence*. In both the *navakalēvara* ceremony and the street rituals of Cuttack, sacred images are temporary; they decay, being deliberately made of perishable materials, or they are intentionally destroyed. Here we see the fundamental vision common to Hinduism wherever it is practiced, that shape and form are mere passing phenomena, like human lives, eventually merging back into the oneness at the core.

The more permanent *mūrtis* constructed for temples, often carved in stone or cast in metal, are also proliferated, redesigned, and somewhat impermanent. Yet patronage of such orthodox sacred images is declining rapidly. Several studies of urban centers in India reveal the decline of artisans supported by patrons of orthodox images. Jindel's work on Nāthdwārā's artisans (Rājasthān) decries their financial hardships due to inadequate sculpture assignments from the temple. Here 51 painters of wall murals have been forced to turn to other occupations; the 400 enamelers are in similar trouble.[30] In Kashi, active patronage of dancers and musicians has not extended to sculptors and painters. The Ganda Brahmin sculptors of Kashi have little prospect of earning a living through their traditional occupation. According to Saraswati, this decline extends even to the *quality* of work done by these artisans. "Today there is no sculptor in Kashi with sufficient knowledge of the *Shilpashastras*."[31]

On the other hand, in Kashi itself, temporary images are being made increasingly for the popular street worship of Durgā. In 1972, Vidyarthi reports, as many as fifty Durgā images had been purchased by various merchants and clubs.[32] And Babb calls attention to the upsurge of popular religion in Raipur city (Madhya Pradesh). Here the festival most often associated with street ritual is that of Gaṇēśa. As in other cities, each neighborhood erects temporary shrines for clay images of the deity. There is the usual *pūjā*, distribution of *prasād* among neighborhood members, the procession to the tank on the outskirts of the city, the immersion of the images, and the city-wide competition for best decorated image. Babb notes similar village processions of clay images of Śiva, Parvatī, and Lakṣmī on several different festival occasions.[33]

Clearly something is changing. While some image makers are being unionized and trained in public schools, as recorded by Singer in Madras (to fix prices and attain government grants), others are changing trades for want of support from traditional patrons.[34] But in some places new patrons, particularly in recently urbanized areas like Bhubaneswar, have widened the access of the general populous to the creation of images. Though some might see these street images as irreligious, they unify people in new ways. Freeman observes that in Bhubaneswar, during Durgā Pūjā, multicaste neighborhoods organize and compete with one another, and that the image serves as a focus of this new sense of group identity.[35]

Throughout Orissan history, the image has been employed as an instrument of change as new patrons manipulated sacred icons in their respective religious political arenas. In Hinduism, the specific object of worship at the operational level can retreat to its "nominal phase" (Babb's terminology), to be reconceived and once again elaborated when it becomes embedded in a specific temple or episode of *pūjā*.[36] This interpenetration of divinity with the material world reflects a principle of "cosmic implosion" that is embedded in the nature of Hindu image making. The cosmos implodes in a particular space and time, becomes a focus of worship, and then withdraws. The *pūjā* itself reflects this principle; the priest purifies himself so he can become the temporary locus where the deity can descend. And the image — at first internal — is subsequently projected outward, in particular forms.

In a brilliant treatment of spirit possession in African and Afro-American traditions, Sheila Walker expresses an intriguing insight into how the sacred image becomes introjected, then projected outward, and how the possessed individual is considered momentarily identical with the divinity. From childhood the devotee ". . . day after day from his immediate environment [receives] a series of reactions and sensory-motor reflexes which give him a particular consciousness of his religion. He constructs within himself images of the deities which constitute a mystical thought system completely integrated into his personality."[37] "In possession the subject can both participate in the omnipotent god image and achieve passive and aggressive mastery over the whole community of spectators. He is totally dependent upon them but they must accede to his every wish because he is now a god.[38]

This dialectic between the particular concrete outer image, or *mūrti*, and the internal "nominal image" is also found in the Hindu tradition. Indeed, it is a characteristic of the image making process in general. This point is articulated most elegantly by Octavio Paz in the following passages: "Man himself, split asunder since birth, is reconciled with himself when he becomes an image, when *he becomes another*."[39] Man searches "... for that other who is he himself. And nothing can bring him back to himself, except the mortal leap: love, the image..."[40]

The construction of Hindu images suggests that the icon is more than a focus of divinity; it also has a significant place in the social system, as it accumulates the labor and energy of numerous castes involved in its construction, worship and destruction. Hindus are image makers *par excellence*. Even if the external image is removed or destroyed by enemies, the image making *process* continues to thrive. Though the new images associated with popular Hinduism may be unorthodox, even gaudy by some standards, they do not necessarily signify the decline of a tradition (as some informants insisted). For it is the process of creating the sacred image, not the form of that image, which is the principal cornerstone of Hinduism — and unless the image is destroyed it cannot be created again.

A final question remains unanswered: How is the social use of the icon related to its changing theological nature? We have already noted in this essay that: (1) Icons are impermanent and express a deep sense of the nature of human existence. (2) Sacred images are instruments of sociocultural change as evidenced in the patronage of icon construction.[41] The well documented, increasing popularity of street images, particularly in urban India, is due to a combination of social factors already mentioned: a shift of patronage to a much broader base, identification of newly urbanized people through the creation of their own sacred images, and a strong economic impulse stimulated by wealthy merchants who gain commercial advantage by competing in these festivals. In addition to these social factors, the theological emphasis on the impermanence of the street images also plays a role in their popularity. It is not as though urban Hindus in Cuttack city are turning away from their more stable temple images; on the contrary, at the time of Durgā Pūjā, the shrine of Cuttack's tutelary deity Caṇḍi is more heavily attended than at any other time of year (approximately 70,000 people attend during the last five days of the festival). Instead, urbanization seems to be increasing the ways in which people may participate in festival activities. An older conservative piety is giving way to a popularization of religion in all domains, suggesting strongly that modernization does not necessarily result either in increased secularization or in Sanskritization. In Cuttack city people at all levels in the social spectrum have found various ways to participate in festival activities. The increasing availability of cash, along with weakening caste obligations and identification with neighborhood groups, making friends through common occupations, and exposure to heterogeneous special interest groups, give many people access to new avenues for expressing religiosity. However, it is not as though urbanization displaces orthodoxy; instead it provides a broader spectrum for the operation of the Hindu iconic imagination. Thus, the impermanence of the popular street images carries with it the potential for reactivating older tribal forms of the "homeless" and templeless divinity.

The theological emphasis on impermanence witnessed in the street festivals of India may even represent an expression of the impermanence associated with urban life. We need not, however, speculate too ambitiously on this point, since impermanence is a fundamental principle of Hinduism expressed even in the iconography of the more stable temple icons. While we have illustrated the principle of impermanence in the orthodox tradition of the construction of the Jagannāth icons, we have also noted the uniqueness of *wooden* images in contemporary Hindu temples. Nevertheless, despite the special case represented by the *navakalēvara* ceremony, virtually every Hindu temple icon participates in the principle of impermanence. *Svayambhū* (self-generated) Śiva *liṅgas* are ubiquitous in India. Often temples are built around these stones, invariably described by devotees as being in a process of change, growing larger or changing shape. And it is rare to find an orthodox temple image that is not adorned in different clothes throughout the annual cycle of festivals. The goddess at the Caṇḍi Temple becomes all major Hindu goddesses during the sixteen days of the Daśaharā festival (including Durgā, Saraswatī, Kālī, and Lakṣmī). Not only is the icon at the Caṇḍi Temple dressed as one of these goddesses on each night of the ceremony, special foods are offered and the *pūjā* itself changes to match the appropriate rites associated with each deity. Then, of course, we cannot forget another vital dimension of impermanence crucial in the history of Hinduism; royal patrons reconstructed icons, sometimes radically changing the associated theology, in order to attain suzerainty over a particular territory.

The history of Orissan Hinduism is a study in impermanence marked by various *rājās* competing for power through identification with one sect or another, shifting patronage whenever necessary to attain the political support of different segments of the population.

While, no doubt, a qualitative difference in the expression of impermanence is displayed when an icon must be destroyed and recreated periodically, it should not be forgotten that impermanence is assumed in the most stable iconic Hindu traditions. Even the more stable icons that do not require periodic reconstruction are only activated through the performance of *pūjā* by a priest. This suggests still another kind of impermanence associated with icons. Indeed, the further study of this whole process of apotheosis and destruction (and the corollary principle of impermanence) in all its manifestations, should yield profound insights about the root paradigms operative in Hinduism.

The principle of *impermanence* ensures the dynamism of Hinduism; the infinite takes form then vanishes. The invisible is made visible in stone, wood, or clay, then withdraws with decay, or is buried. Thus, spirit in matter never becomes completely crystallized. The immensity of divinity becomes manifest anew for each occasion, and the mystery is retained despite its brief partial revelation.

No rational analysis can totally solve the mystery of the icon. Our *rationalism* has not penetrated to the heart of that deep impulse in the human spirit which must create images of the sacred other. Nor do we understand why such images are destroyed, transformed and reworked to re-emerge generations later as reminders of primal experiences that will not be set aside. This process of creation and destruction of sacred images, this powerful act of imagination, challenges us to ask why humans must insist over and again that the invisible should be, *must* be, made visible.

Pūjā performed at the domestic altar established during *Vināyakacaturthī* in Ahmadnagar, Maharastra. Photo by Paul Courtright.

2

On This Holy Day In My Humble Way

Aspects of *Pūjā*

Paul B. Courtright

MOST SIMPLY and comprehensively the word *pūjā* means worship. It derives from a word in Sanskrit meaning to adore or respect. Unlike simple prayer or praise, however, the offerings and carefully articulated gestures and words of the *pūjā* move beyond an attempt to communicate with a distant deity. Whether as a simple act of private devotion or as a multi-leveled communal performance, *pūjās* bring together the human and the divine worlds at specific times and places by actualizing the presence of a deity in a physical form that in some way "embodies" the reality of that deity. All these events, in turn, rest upon a network of shared beliefs, assumptions, myths, and ritual formulations. Hence *pūjā*, the basic formal means by which Hindus establish relationships with their deity, embodies the very reality that it seeks to adore. Or put another way, *pūjās* create or invoke their own worlds of meaning.

At the center of the phenomenon of *pūjā* is a transaction that takes place between worshiper(s) and the deity(ies). The latter is represented by an object, image, or abstract design in which the deity is understood to take his or her "place" during the course of the rite and for some specified time thereafter. The former adopts the posture of the host, servant, and devotee. Through the performance of *pūjās* the deity and the devotee realize a special intimacy with one another: the deity receives homage and food, and the worshiper gains spiritual and existential enhancement. The prevailing metaphor for *pūjā* is hospitality and servitude. Both deity and devotee become dependent upon one another and receive benefits from their mutual interaction in various ways.

This essay will describe one particular example of *pūjā* and explore ways to interpret the transactions and religious realities which are brought into being through the performance of *pūjā* in a specific

---

This topic is treated in the author's forthcoming book, *Gaṇeśa: Lord of Obstacles, Lord of Beginnings* (New York: Oxford University Press).

context. The *pūjā* in question is performed for or offered to Gaṇēśa, the elephant-headed son of Śiva and Pārvatī, on the occasion of his annual festival which begins on the fourth day of the bright half of the Hindu month of Bhādrapada (August / September). This *pūjā* is particularly popular in the state of Maharashtra, located in the western region of India. The descriptive detail and analysis that follows has been drawn from texts in common use and from observations made in that region.

My approach will concur with that of Ákos Östor who observes that *pūjās* are "legitimate forms of analysis" and should not be reduced to simple functional vehicles for determining social status and relationships.[1] *Pūjās* must be treated as distinct *religious and symbolic* units which require an analysis that seeks to understand the elaborate and ingenious worlds of meaning that flow in and out of their performance. My goal, then, will be to describe the ritual and engage in exegetical analysis of important symbols and episodes that contribute to the larger meaning of Gaṇēśa's *pūjā* and reflect the religious realities that come into being during its performance.

The Pūjā to Gaṇēśa on Vināyaka Caturthī

There are many contexts for the worship of Gaṇēśa, as there are for worshiping other deities in Hinduism. Acts of private prayer and meditation, communal singing of devotional songs, calendrical rites and vows, pilgrimages to sacred shrines, and annual public festivals — all these make up the whole fabric of means by which Hindus articulate their relationship to this god.

Gaṇēśa is often said to be the most popular deity in the Hindu pantheon. He receives so much attention because it is he above all who creates obstacles to and removes them from new undertakings. He also ensures that worshipers have access to other deities, success, and well-being. Hindus honor Gaṇēśa before commencing *pūjās*, life-cycle ceremonies (*saṃskāras*), pilgrimages and other journeys, courses of study, writing letters, opening businesses, or simply beginning the routines of daily life. One may worship him with a brief Sanskrit formula (*mantra*), "Homage to Lord Gaṇēśa," or with much longer and more elaborate prayers, such as the *śrīgaṇēśa atharvaśīrṣa* in which Gaṇēśa is identified with the very source of the universe itself, the ultimate *brahman*.[2] Whatever other deities a Hindu may worship, be they deities of the household shrine (*kuladēvatā*), the guardian deities of the village (*grāmadēvatā*), or that god or goddess who has the special place of honor in a devotee's affections (*iṣṭadēvatā*), Gaṇēśa is worshiped first. He stands at the doorway and allows the devotee access to other deities and whatever blessings may flow from them. Consequently Gaṇēśa looms large in a Hindu's worship, no matter what his or her allegiance to other deities. Orthodox Brahmins of the Smarta tradition, popularized by the eighth-century theologian Śaṅkara, worship Gaṇēśa as one of the five-fold divinities, the *pañcāyatana*. These deities, who also include Śiva, Viṣṇu, Sūrya, and Dēvī, are worshiped in the household shrine on specific occasions. In most households, among upper caste Hindus, Gaṇēśa's image is found on the southern side of the family altar, protecting the other gods and the household from inauspicious influences emanating from the dangerous south, the abode of demons.[3]

Gaṇēśa's image may be seen nearly everywhere in India in a variety of forms. He may appear, like his father Śiva, as a rough stone covered with red paint located near the boundaries of the village or at the intersections of roads. He may be found atop the doorways of homes and shops, in niches at the thresholds of temples or in small shrines situated just inside the doorway. Thus the devotee encounters Gaṇēśa before he reaches the main deity in the center of the shrine. Framed copies of inexpensive lithographs of Gaṇēśa adorn shops and tea stalls along with other deities the proprietor may venerate. School children frequently write the Gaṇēśa *mantra* on the tops of examination papers, and books on religious subjects often include the same *mantra* at the top of the title page.

Because Gaṇēśa is associated with thresholds and is known as the remover of obstacles, poets and devotees have composed many invocatory prayers to this god, and appropriately, these are found at the beginnings of texts or dramas. These verses celebrate the elephant-lord's auspicious form and call upon him to lend his benevolent presence and grant success to the matter at hand.

In Maharashtra the most popular devotional song, or *āratī*, to Gaṇēśa is attributed to the seventeenth century saint Rāmadāsa, reputed by some to have been the spiritual preceptor to Śivājī, the founder of the Maratha empire and the father of contemporary Maharashtrian cultural identity. The song vividly describes Gaṇēśa's physical form and conveys the experience of the auspicious visual apprehension (*darśana*) of the deity.

> Maker of happiness, remover of miseries, whose grace extends love to us and does not leave a trace of obstacle remaining, you have a layer of red lead over your whole body and a necklace of pearls shines brightly around your neck.
>
> Victory to you, victory to you. O god of auspicious form, at your sight are all desires of the mind fulfilled.

O son of Gaurī, you have a jewel-studded ornament, ointment of sandalwood paste, red powder and saffron, and a diamond-inlaid crown. They all look beautiful on you. Anklets with tinkling bells make a jingling sound around your feet.

Victory to you, etc.

You have a large belly, you wear a yellow silk garment, and have a snake for a sacred thread. Your trunk is straight, your tusk broken, O three-eyed one. This devotee of Rāma, waits for you in his home. O god who is revered by all the great gods, be gracious to us in times of difficulty and protect us in times of calamity.

Victory to you, etc.[4]

In addition to these invocational *mantras*, songs, and prayers, which are recited according to the individual's inclinations, calling upon him for protection from obstacles, Gaṇēśa enjoys special worship at fixed times during the Hindu religious year. Each lunar month of the year is divided into two parts: a bright half (*śuklapakṣa*) when the moon waxes, and a dark half (*kṛṣṇapakṣa*) when it wanes. The bright half brings with it ascent and auspiciousness, and Hindus regard it as an appropriate time to begin new undertakings in the confidence that they will prosper. The dark half is inauspicious, a time of decline, when the possibilities of chaos and failure are greater and new projects should be avoided if possible. It is also the more appropriate time for prudential and renunciatory forms of religious expression.

The fourth day of the dark half of the month is called *saṃkaṣṭacaturthī*, the "dangerous fourth," a day when it is particularly inauspicious to begin any new undertaking. A vow to worship Gaṇēśa on this day during the dark half of each month may be performed in hope of averting difficulties and obstacles.[5] Such a vow includes offering *mōdakas* or sweet flour balls and other sweets to Gaṇēśa, fasting, worship, feeding one's preceptor and/or twenty-one Brahmins. Tradition has it that because Śiva undertook this vow to honor Gaṇēśa on this day he was able to defeat the terrible demon Tāraka.[6] Because Gaṇēśa's character is ambivalent (he both creates and removes obstacles), devotees fast and worship him on *saṃkaṣṭacaturthī*, the fourth day of the dark half of the lunar month, a day of concentrated inauspicious power. As the creator of obstacles, an attribute especially associated with his Vinayāka form, Gaṇēśa must be propitiated in order to avert calamity, just as demons would be given food at the beginning of the sacrifice in order to satiate them and to keep them from stealing the offerings intended for the gods. Gaṇēśa is also worshiped on this inauspicious day because he is the one empowered to overcome dangerous obstacles, to render powerless that time which is, according to the structure of temporal movement, inauspicious and harmful. The basic ritual posture for the devotee is to seek protection by demonstrating devotion to the deity by offering *mōdakas* and by keeping an ascetic regimen, and to receive the benefits of Gaṇēśa's obstacle-removing power in the broadest contexts of life.

The fourth day of the bright half of the month is called *vināyakacaturthī*, or "Gaṇēśa's fourth." In contrast to *saṃkaṣṭacathurthī*, this day generally reflects Gaṇēśa's benevolent side, his power to grant success in undertakings. On this day it is auspicious to begin new projects. The mood is happy and energetic. Throughout the year on *vināyakacaturthī* Gaṇēśa receives special recognition in the forms of offerings, prayers, and songs. When *vināyakacaturthī* falls in the month of Bhādrapada (August/September), the most important annual festival honoring Gaṇēśa takes place in Maharashtra. It is sometimes said that *vināyakacaturthī* is Gaṇeśa's birthday, his day of auspicious beginnings. On this day his image is installed and worshiped in homes. Bhādrapada *vināyakacaturthī* is the most auspicious day associated with Gaṇēśa; it is the day designated for the commencement of his festival and all that it entails.

On *vināyakacaturthī* Hindu householders establish and consecrate a clay image of the god on the domestic altar. At this time the image is endowed with life; it is worshiped as an honored guest in the home for a period of time varying, according to the family's preference, from one to ten days; and finally it is taken out of the home and immersed in a nearby river or other water source where it quickly dissolves. This immersion may be a fairly private family affair, or, as is frequently the case in both villages and cities, it may coincide with the grand and raucous public immersion procession (*visarjana*).

This pattern of domestic worship or *pūjā* is an ancient one, and resembles procedures common to the worship of other gods. Purāṇic texts offer instructions as to how Gaṇēśa's *pūjā* is to be performed on this most sacred of his days, what items are to be offered, and what benefits (*phala*) such as wealth and success in endeavors may be expected by those who perform the worship properly. As a ritual process *pūjā* draws upon the symbolism of the Brahmanical sacrificial tradition with its prominent use of Vedic *mantras* and the cosmogonic hymn to Puruṣa, the *puruṣasūkta* (*Ṛg Vēda* 10.90). It incorporates elements of traditions of hospitality, highly valued in the *dharma* and *gṛhya* texts, in which the deity is shown signs of honor much as a guest would be honored in the home. The *pūjā* also incorporates aspects of ceremonies associated with the installation of deities in temples, as well as principles of internalization and manipulation of the cosmos through the use of *mantras*, a pattern typical of the tantric tradition. There is a wide range of such ritual performances, some very simple, others extremely complex.

The analysis here draws upon two textual sources (Javadekar and N. Jośī); both are popular ritual manuals available to anyone wishing to perform the rite in his home. Both draw on the Vedic tradition of Puruṣa and the *upacāras* or ways of service followed in temple installation and rituals of worship. The *pūjā*, as I saw it performed among Deśastha Brahmins of Ahmadnagar District in Maharashtra, was a rather more elaborate performance, making use of a family priest (*purohita*) who chanted much of it in Sanskrit while giving instructions to the head of the house (*yajamāna*) in Marathi. Ritual manuals recommend the services of a Brahmin priest, but if no priest is available or if the worshiper cannot afford to hire one, the rite may still be performed with the aid of the manual and some coaching from a Brahmin priest. Recently cassette tape recordings of the *pūjā*, recited by a Brahmin priest, have appeared for sale at the time of the festival.

Possible *pūjā* formats are many, varying according to the intensity of a worshiper's devotion or his ability to purchase the necessary ritual items and to pay priests who assist in the ritual performance. Still, underlying this variety there is a common goal: to bring about an enhanced level of intimacy between the worshiper and the deity. This intimacy is realized through a series of transactions or exchanges. The worshiper prepares a sacred arena, provides a clay image (*mūrti*), and establishes the deity's presence in that image by invoking the life-force (*jīva*) and vital capacities (*indriya*) into it. This process of invocation includes the transfer of his own *jīva* and *indriyas* into the image. It is as though Gaṇēśa were condensed from his dispersed universal presence in the cosmos into a particular, immediate, and accessible form, sharing a time and a place with the devotee. The worshiper then honors Gaṇēśa-in-the-image by bathing, feeding, clothing, and giving the god gifts, and by entertaining him with songs; in short, honoring him as the most valuable and royal of guests.

Gaṇēśa reciprocates by using his obstacle-removing powers to watch over the family and kin group during the coming year. After he has enjoyed the offerings of food, he returns them to the family where they are shared as his "left overs," sanctified by contact with his divine presence. By consuming this special food, the devotees take into themselves a tangible existential enhancement made possible by contact with the deity. This sacred food is called *prasāda*. The word is

The devotee transfers his own life-force into the image (*prāṇapratiṣṭhā*) during the crucial moments of the Gaṇēśa *pūjā*. Photo by Paul Courtright.

derived from the prefix *pra* and *sāda* meaning "grace sent down." It is the edible symbol of Gaṇēśa's "real presence" in the image, and an assurance to those who eat it in the company of the god that their undertakings will be successful and suffer no obstacles.

In this way the *pūjā* creates its own reality. It marks off this occasion of enhancement temporally by fixed calendrical times and spatially by an altar and home purified of contaminants and destructive influences. Through special speech, gestures, forms of nourishment and ornamentation, the human and divine meet each other halfway, giving and receiving mutual support.

How does this religious reality come about? What are the means by which the *pūjā* creates a "world" of its own within yet transcending the world of ordinary experience? What methods or strategies are employed and what assumptions about reality are necessary for this special divine-human interaction to take place? A useful way to address these questions is to examine the constituent episodes and transactions that make up the ritual, pausing along the way to exegetically examine the ones that precipitate major turns in the ritual process.

The specific name of the *pūjā* to be analyzed here is the *śrīpārthiva-mahāgaṇapati-pūjā*, or "the auspicious worship of the great Ganēśa in earthen form." The *pūjā* exhibits a three-fold dynamic form: an entry, a liminal or transformational phase, and an exit into the world outside the ritual. This three-fold scheme has been identified in a variety of ritual situations by Van Gennep and Turner.[7]

Before the ritual can begin, the space of the household and the persons of the worshipers must be in a maximal state of purity. This is achieved by cleaning and whitewashing the home, or more often, the altar area of the house. Worshipers bathe; the *yajamāna*, or male head of the household, wears a silk lower garment, usually red, and a silk scarf around his shoulders. The clay image, which has been fashioned by a sculptor, usually of the smith caste, is brought into the home and placed on the family altar. At the time it is placed on the altar it is inert substance, a mere curio. It possesses no special sanctity until it is established with life-breath, or *prāṇa*. The altar is marked off as a sacred zone with patterns of colored powdered chalk. The women of the household draw these ornate boundaries for the ritual within which all ritual events take place. They also prepare the special foods, leaves, spices, flowers, waters, fragrant substances, and other ritual paraphernalia and place them in front of the altar in various containers in a manner that brings to mind the formal arrangement of items for a meal.

The family brings the image into the home and places it on a low table on the family altar. The composition of the altar is pervaded by the symbolism of kingship. The low table (*cauraṅg*) resembles a throne. The deity is guest, king, and lord; to receive him into one's home is the ultimate expression of hospitality. Behind the image is placed a picture of Gaṇēśa's self-created (*svayambhū*) forms as they appear in the eight major Gaṇēśa shrines (the *aṣṭavināyakas*) in Maharashtra. A brass lamp is lighted next to the image. The patron sits facing the image and the Brahmin priest, who, sitting to the right of the image, recites the Sanskrit *mantras* and, should he require it, instructs the patron in the appropriate gestures and utterances he is to make at each stage of the *pūjā*. Family members and guests sit behind the patron, also facing the image, as a sort of audience to the proceedings that follow. The ritual involves the contributions of three different persons or roles: the priest, who provides the sacred speech and instructions for the proper moves at each step of the rite so that it can be effective; the patron, who performs the gestures of offering and service and gains the benefits of the rite for himself and his family; and finally, Gaṇēśa himself, who receives the family's hospitality and in return enables the household members to achieve greater intimacy with him. This exchange is substantiated through the god's gift of sanctified food (*prasāda*) which the family consumes at the end of the rite.

The *pūjā* formally begins at the time designated by the priest according to calculations based upon the ritual calendar (*pañcāṅga*). The patron sips water (*ācamana*), regulates his breath (*prāṇāyāma*), and then addresses Gaṇēśa and all the other gods in an honorific manner (*namaskāra*). Then the patron, or the priest on his behalf, announces to the deity, who is about to appear in the image, the nature of his commitments to the rite, and his intentions to perform it properly. This is called the *saṃkalpa*, and, according to one version of the ritual manuals for this *pūjā*, it is to be recited as follows.

> On this holy day in my humble way, with as much preparation as possible, in order to gain the fruits designated in the revealed texts (*śruti*), the remembered texts (*smṛti*), and the traditional texts (*purāṇa*), and in order to obtain sons, grandsons, wealth, knowledge, victory, success, fortune, life, and all other wished-for things in this as well as in future births, and in order to propitiate the deity Siddhivināyaka (i.e., Gaṇēśa), I shall perform the worship of Gaṇapati, reciting verses from the hymn to Puruṣa and from texts of the tradition, while performing the giving of water (*arghya*), [Here the list of sixteen traditional *upacāras* or "ways of service" — to be described later — is enumerated.][8]

The *saṃkalpa* expresses the intentions of the worshiper and defines the relationship between him and the deity, sets the limits on what is to take place within and beyond the boundaries of the rite, and articulates the goals of the worshiper to the deity. If the ritual performance is completed according to the proper conventions, and if the worshiper is filled with faith in the deity, then the goals or fruits that are expected to follow should be realized.

Once the intention of the worship has been declared, the patron, with the help of the priest, performs a series of preparatory gestures which sacralize the various implements to be used, as well as the user, for the central transaction of the ritual, the *prāṇapratiṣṭhā* in which the clay image is invested with vital breath. First, the patron calls upon the goddess Bhū (Earth), in whom the world is supported, to support the patron; while touching the ground three times with his left heel he commands the demons and harmful spirits (*piśāca* and *bhūta*) to flee from the sacred space of the ritual so that Gaṇēśa's worship may be accomplished without obstruction. Calling on all gods to protect the rite, the patron symbolically measures out the sacred arena on which he sits by placing the span of his thumb and forefinger on the ground in front of the image. This set of gestures is called *āsanavidhi*, the preparation and purification of the patron's seat.

Reciting verses from the *puruṣasūkta* (*Ṛg Vēda* 10.90), along with single-word *mantras*, the patron touches his heart, head, the tuft of hair on the crown of his head, his chest, both his eyes and the subtle third eye between them, and then claps his hands three times. This series of gestures is called *ṣaḍaṅganyasa*, the "investing of the six limbs." Through these actions the patron identifies the various parts of his body with those of the deity and the universe — bringing into a single center the macrocosm and microcosm. A similar series of identifications takes place in the *puruṣasūkta* itself when the dismembered pieces of the cosmic progenitor, Puruṣa, are distributed from the sacrifice to make up the universe. In this way the patron becomes redefined, brought out of the merely human realm into the sacred arena which he will share with Gaṇēśa for the duration of the rite. Like the deity he has invited, the patron is now homologous with the cosmos. A similar process follows with respect to the major implements used in the *pūjā*. The water vessel (*kalaśa*), whose contents will bathe and nourish Gaṇēśa during the ceremony, is identified with the pitcher of the Vedic sacrifice (*Ṛg Vēda* 9.17.4) and becomes symbolically transformed into the cosmos itself. The priest recites:

> Viṣṇu resides at the mouth of the pitcher, Rudra in the throat, Brahmā at its base, and the group of mother goddesses in the middle. All oceans and the earth with its seven continents reside in its interior. The *Rg Vēda, Sāma Vēda, Yajur Vēda*, and the *Atharva Vēda*, along with the appended texts (*vēdāṅgas*) dwell in the vessel. In it resides the *gāyatrī* chant with Sāvitṛ as its deity, which brings peace, prosperity. May those who remove all sins come here for the worship of this deity. O Gaṅgā, Yamunā, Gōdāvarī, Sarasvatī, Narmadā, Indus, and Kāvērī rivers, come and be present in this water.[9]

A similar pattern is followed for consecrating the other ritual implements: the conch, bell, and lamp. The patron places on each of these items flowers and *akṣata. Akṣata* is the term used for unbroken rice grains into which red powder is rubbed. It is used in many ritual settings and is not unique to the worship of Gaṇēśa. It symbolizes, like the rice thrown at weddings in Western cultures, food and seed, the emblems of nurture and generation. When rubbed with red powder, its generative potential is enhanced. This is in keeping with the symbolism of the colors red and white in combination.[10] Throughout the ritual, when the deity is offered any food, clothing, or ornaments, he is again sprinkled with *akṣata*. In this transaction the patron is the giver of this power-bestowing substance and Gaṇēśa is the receiver. This is a reversal of the conditions of the world outside the rite in which the deity is the giver of success and the patron the receiver.

After a transitional gesture of purification (*śuddhikaraṇa*) the patron offers sacred *dūrvā* grass. He then sprinkles himself and the ritual enclosure with water. The moment for the "establishment of the image in its vital breath" (*prāṇapratiṣṭhā*) has now arrived. Some texts omit the *prāṇapratiṣṭhā* part of the rite, replacing it with a shorter and simpler *sthāpana* or "placing" of the image on the altar after the manner of a king's enthronement.[11] Traditionally a Brahmin priest is necessary for rites involving the investing of breath. Before describing the specific ritual transactions pertaining to *prāṇa*, a brief exegetical excursus into the symbolism of the breath is in order.

The compound word *prāṇapratiṣṭhā* is made up of two words: *prāṇa*, "breath" or "vitality," and *pratiṣṭhā*, "establishment" or "support" from *prati* "toward" or "upon" and *stha*, "stand firmly" or "abide." The term *pratiṣṭhā* expresses the pervasive Indian religious and existential impulse, from the Vedic period forward, for what Jan Gonda terms the "firm and ultimate ground to rest upon, an imperishable and immovable support of existence, for sky and earth, for themselves and the universe."[12]

The precise character of this support (*pratiṣṭhā*) is alternatively understood, according to different taxonomies of reality, to be identified with a foothold, food, earth, the master of the house, Vedic metres, the womb, layers of the sacrificial altar, speech, *brahman*, space, and breath.[13] That which is established or grounded is a stabilizing power — a power which maintains the conflicting powers of the cosmos in a state of balance. It is a matter of life and death, for the dead are those who are *apratiṣṭhā* — without support — those who have no bodies and stand nowhere. The descendants of the dead must give them support by providing them with "bodies" made of rice flour (*piṇḍa*) that both feed them and place support beneath them, thus giving them status in the cosmos. A person's own standing can be upset by means of a curse, but it can also be recovered through other compensatory rites. To be grounded is to have a world and be secure in the midst of flux, to have power over threatening forces; indeed, to achieve profound rest and well-being. This notion of ground, support or standing firm, is an expression of the ultimate soteriological goal of Brahmanical Hinduism, that of *mōkṣa* or release, and it is the basis of the ritual episode we are considering. The vehicle for this support is the vital breath (*prāṇa*), which is brought into the image by means of sacred speech (*mantra*), and the conduit is sacred *dūrvā* grass, which links the patron, who already possesses *prāṇa* as a condition of being alive, and the image.

In the *Chāndōgya Upaniṣad* the story is told of the time the five senses quarreled over which of them was supreme. Unable to resolve their differences they approached Prajāpati, the lord of the universe. He told them, "He, who upon departing from the body, leaves it looking the worst, he is the best among you."[14] Speech, sight, hearing, and mind left the body in turn; but, however limited it became from the loss of one of the senses, it nevertheless remained alive because it possessed *prāṇa*. "Then," the text continues, "*prāṇa* prepared to depart, tearing up the other senses like a spirited horse might tear out his tethering stakes. Then they gathered around him, saying, 'Stay with us, don't leave. You are the best among us.'"[15] Then all the senses took their firm support, their *pratiṣṭhā*, in *prāṇa*. In the homology of the cosmos to the *ātman*, the author of the text sees the air as the *prāṇa* of the universal self (*brahman*), just as Vāyu, the wind, came forth out of the *prāṇa* of Puruṣa.[16] Hence, *prāṇa* is that upon which both the cosmos and the individual stands. The breath is the sacrifice of one's own self to *brahman*; it is the sacred oblation, the equivalent of *sōma*.[17] *Prāna* is the primal animating power upon which the self and the cosmos find their mutual support, their *pratiṣṭhā*.

The *prāṇapratiṣṭhā* proceeds as follows: first, the priest recites a verse identifying the *bījā mantras*, or "seed syllables" — condensed and potent sounds — which serve as the vehicles for placing the *prāṇa* in the image. As the priest recites the *mantras* the patron touches two sprigs of *dūrvā* to the image. Then the priest says, "This *prāṇa* is the *prāṇa* of the god." In this way the distributed *prāṇa* of the cosmos, not insignificantly including that of the ritual patron, becomes condensed into the inert clay image bringing it to life. A similar pattern is followed in invoking animating life (*jīva*) into the image. At this moment the separation between the patron and the deity in a religious sense dissolves and they share common support in *prāṇa*. This is a moment of profound metaphysical and religious significance, and is the crux of the liminal phase of the rite.

The two vehicles for this transfer of *prāṇa* and *jīva* into the image are *mantra* and *dūrvā* grass, sound and material substance. *Mantra* can be seen as *prāṇa* condensed into speech, a conveyer of sacred power. According to Gonda, a *mantra* is a "word(s) believed to be of 'superhuman origin,' received, fashioned and spoken by the 'inspired' seers, poets and reciters in order to evoke divine power(s) and especially conceived of as creating, conveying, concentrating and realizing intentional and efficient thought, and of coming into touch or identifying oneself with the essence of the divinity which is present in the *mantra*."[18] It is as though *mantra* is that speech/sound appropriate to the realm of *brahman*, in which self and god, knower and known, giver and receiver of *prāṇa* recognize their fundamental indivisibility and eternality. This reality is actualized when the *mantra* is recited.

The *dūrvā* grass acts as a conduit through which passes the animating power of the *prāṇa*, activated by the *mantra*, from the patron to the image, from giver to receiver. *Dūrvā* is thought to be especially favored by Gaṇēśa and some claim it has medicinal properties in addition to its religious ones. It resembles sacred *kuśa* grass which is used in Vedic sacrifice. According to one version of the myth of the churning of the ocean, when Garuḍa rescued the *amṛta* from the thieving hands of the demons, he flew up with the vat in his claws and some of it spilled out, falling on some *dūrvā* grass below. Hence *dūrvā* became the receptacle of the immortality-bestowing ambrosia, the spilled leftovers of divine creative power.[19] By virtue of this contact with the original and uncompromised substance of the universe, *dūrvā* has acquired important capacities for transmitting the power of *prāṇa*.

Within the framework of assumptions of the ritual, the patron first reconstitutes himself as the divine Puruṣa and then brings the distributed *prāṇa* into the deity, whereby it comes to reside in the image. This process constitutes a kind of symbolic dismemberment reminiscent of Puruṣa's sacrifice, but with the divine-human hierarchy inverted. Gaṇēśa, who receives his own *prāṇa* through the mediating efforts of the patron, is dependent upon his largesse. He thus is committed to return the favor by benevolently using his power to remove obstacles for the patron and his family. Both patron and divinity participate in a carefully bounded and prepared divine world, contributing to one another's identities and sharing in common awareness and power. The image of Gaṇēśa, in a sense, comes "alive."

Some informants claimed that the image actually changes, it becomes lustrous, its colors becoming more radiant. Others said they actually saw it enlarge slightly. This perceived transformation of the material form of the image does not take place for the devotee in any other context than that of religious belief and expectation. Is it a matter of magical or alchemical change? As one informant put it, "Of course, magic is not magical to the magician." The ritual effects a transformative relationship between devotee and deity if a devotee is prepared for such a "heightened" event. Other Hindus adopt a more skeptical attitude, and suggest that such claims of the material transformation of the image belong to the realm of superstition. The most important event in the ritual, they argue, is the increase of *bhāva*, or religious sentiment or experience. This increase in *bhāva* can be achieved without the use of images (*nirguṇa*), but for some, the presence of a tangible image (*saguṇa*) can be a useful aid to religious realization.

The *pūjā* provides a locus for the intersection of the divine and the mundane. The sacred, in the form of the enlivened image, becomes the cosmic center expanding in all directions and redefining the limits of the real. From the perspective of ordinary experience outside the assumptions of the rite, the enlivening of the image is the liminal episode, when the power of the divine presence converges with the ritual enclosure which is so vulnerable to contamination. From the perspective of the intentions of the rite itself, that which appears so transitory from the outside — the enlivened deity — is *the* secure and grounded center of the cosmos. That some devotees "see" the image become lustrous and enlarge bears witness to their faith and the grace of the deity.

With the *prāṇa* now established in the image, so far as the intention implicit in the ritual is concerned, Gaṇēśa's full presence has been made manifest. Dwelling in his image, he has, along with the patron whose breath he also breathes, passed from inert matter into living presence. This phase of the *pūjā* most clearly articulates the transformational character of the ritual. Those polarities which may have seemed most separated, earth and deity, have now become one another. After the investiture of *prāṇa* the image is not to be moved until the *uttarapūjā* or final worship when the *prāṇa* is released from the image and dispersed again into the cosmos as a whole. Once the breath is established, the traditional sixteen *upacāras* or "ways of service" are performed. These, like the breath-establishment, are rooted historically in traditions of domestic worship and later elaborated upon from procedures employed in the worship of images in temples. They call for bathing, feeding, and caring for the deity in the same ways an honored guest is cared for. Among the sixteen *upacāras* two are central: *abhiṣēka*, sprinkling the image with sacred water; and *naivēdya*, offering of food. In both cases a transaction between devotee and deity is highlighted. In return for purifying and feeding the god, the worshipers receive general well-being or success and *prasāda* — food returned by the deity and filled with grace.[20]

The *upacāras* are preceded by a meditation (*dhyāna*) in which the patron contemplates the fully enlivened image from the perspective of their mutual support in *prāṇa*. Then follow the series of honorific gestures (*upacāras*), each accompanied by the recitation of a stanza of the *puruṣasūkta*. Recitation of the *puruṣasūkta* establishes the homology between the image, Puruṣa, and the cosmos. With each recitation the patron places a few grains of *akṣata*, unbroken rice-grains, and *dūrvā* grass at the feet of the image. A series of *upacāras* invoke the deity's presence (*āvāhana*), offers the deity a throne (*āsana*) and water for washing the feet (*pādya*), an oblation of water (*arghya*) to be poured over the betel nut at the foot of the image. The betel nut serves as the symbol of Gaṇēśa for the purposes of any lustrations required in the *pūjā*, because the fluids poured over the clay image would cause it to dissolve or to become disfigured. Next a sip of water (*ācamana*) is offered to the deity, and then the betel nut is bathed with the five sacred fluids (*pañcāmṛtasnāna*). These five nectars are: milk, curd, clarified butter, honey, and sugar; each poured in turn and followed by the sprinkling of a few grains of *akṣata*. These substances, and the waters of bathing that also are poured during the ritual collectively make up what is called *tīrtha*. (The same word is used to denote a sacred spot in a river and a crossing-place between the human and divine realms.) In the ritual it is the patron who gives the deity these perfect fluids for his bath, while in the world it is the god who provides the bathing places (*tīrthas*) for his devotees in the forms of rivers having sacred qualities. After the image is bathed in sacred fluids it is rinsed with water (*abhiṣēka*), thus completing the bathing portion of the *pūjā*.

At this point in the rite the image is dressed and adorned with jewels and perfumes. It is given a garment (*vastra*), upper garment or sacred thread (*upavastra*), scented sandal paste and other fragrant substances (*gandha*), offerings of flowers, and incense. Also, a lighted lamp is waved in a circular pattern in front of the deity (*dīpa*). These first fourteen of the sixteen *upacāras* serve to honor Gaṇēśa's form through bathing, dressing, and ornamenting the deity's body much as one would honor a guest. The imagery of kingship weaves itself throughout these honorific gestures and offerings, suggesting that the deity, like the human king, is the most honored of guests. Each of the fourteen steps is accompanied by a verse from the *puruṣasūkta*, declaring the homology between the cosmos and deity at each episode of the rite.

Next comes the offerings of food (*naivēdya*). The foods offered are *sāttvik*, that is, most pure. Offerings of fruit, *mōdakas* or sweet wheat flour balls especially favored by Gaṇēśa, various sacred leaves, betel nut, and a coin, are presented by the patron to the image while the priest recites the verse from the *puruṣasūkta*. The patron pays homage to the *prāṇa* present in the offerings. This festive meal, offered to the deity and sanctified by its proximity to his image, will be returned to the worshipers at the end of the *pūjā* as *prasāda*, or food of grace, and is shared by the members of the patron's family in the presence of the deity.

Following the feeding portion of the *pūjā*, the patron performs a symbolic circumambulation (*pradakṣiṇā*) around the deity and makes one final gesture of honoring the image (*namaskāra*). The patron stands in front of the image and turns around three times to his right, reciting a verse from the *purusaṣūkta*, and then says, "Sins I have committed in this birth and previous births now vanish with each step of my circumambulation to the right."[21]

After these formal *upacāras* have been completed and the image suitably bathed, dressed, adorned, fed, and honored, the patron's family collectively participates in the *pūjā*. As a lamp is waved before the image by the patron, the whole family sings a popular devotional song or *āratī* in Marathi, such as the one by Rāmadāsa quoted earlier. Camphor is then lighted and burned before the image and passed among the worshipers, who pass their hands through the flame and smoke and bring their hands close to their eyes and foreheads in order to take in the purifying properties of the flame which has been sacralized by its proximity to Gaṇēśa. The patron offers an additional twenty-one sprigs of *dūrvā* grass, various leaves and flowers, and prayers. The prayer (*prārthanā*) has a much greater devotional tone and reflects a more intimate and emotional attitude to the deity than the more formal and transactional language of the earlier episodes in the *pūjā*. Addressing Gaṇēśa as the "protector of the poor, reservoir of compassion," the patron says, "Highest lord, you are my refuge, there is no refuge apart from you. Take compassion on me and protect me . . . the worship I have given you without mantras, rituals, or devotion, may my devotion to you become perfected."[22]

At this point, as the ritual draws to a close, attention shifts to the priest who is now worshiped. The patron offers the priest a portion of the *prasāda*, specifically ten of the twenty-one *mōdakas* offered to Gaṇēśa earlier in the *pūjā*. He offers further gifts of a seat, flowers, betel nut, sandal paste, oblation, and a small amount of money (*dakṣiṇā*). With the *pūjā* now completed (its performance takes approximately forty-five minutes), the family and assembled relatives share in the *prasāda* after which they may partake in a festive meal. The priest frequently departs at this time to perform the rite elsewhere for another client family.

As long as the image remains in the household shrine, it will be worshiped in the morning and evening with simple recitations, devotional songs, offerings of fresh flowers, incense, and ritual lamps, as required by the ethos of service and hospitality. The image may not be moved, nor may the ritual space which surrounds it be violated by polluting objects. When the number of days for Gaṇēśa's visit have passed (for most families the "visit" lasts from one and a half to ten days), a simple ritual (*uttarapūjā*) of divesting the image of its special status is performed. The ritual begins with offerings of food, flowers, and prayers. Then, with sprigs of *dūrvā* grass dipped in honey, the patron symbolically closes the eyes of the image and thereby disperses the *prāṇa* from the inert clay. The patron recites a sort of benediction, "May all groups of deities now depart, having accepted this worship of the earthen image of Gaṇēśa in order that all desired objectives (of the rite) may be realized and that they may return again."[23]

Then members of the family, alone or in procession with others, take the image to a nearby water source and immerse it. It dissolves quickly and returns to its formless state. This final rite is called *visarjana* (literally, "sending forth") or immersion. The *visarjana* brings full circle the process begun with the forming of the clay image and its installation in the home. The life of the image moves from formless clay to iconographic representation to animation and empowerment to dispersion and return to formlessness. In this respect it replicates the cosmological cycle itself. As the devotees lower their clay image of Gaṇēśa, now emptied of his *prāṇa*, into the water, they shout in unison the familiar stanza in Marathi, *Gaṇapati Bāppā Morayā, Pudhacyā varṣī lavkar yā!* ("Gaṇēśa, Lord of Morayā [Morayā Gosavī, the founder of the lineage of Gaṇēśa saints in Maharashtra], come again early next year!")

Conclusion

The domestic *pūjā* to Gaṇēśa follows a three-part processural pattern: (1) the deity becomes present in the form of the image, (2) he graciously resides in the household for a period of time, (3) he returns to a primordial cosmic state when the image is immersed. This process takes place in the context of a highly developed ceremonialism that draws upon ancient traditions of hospitality to guests for its dominant symbolism and ritual actions. In this ritual context the deity and patron, together with his priest, engage in a complex relation of interdependence. The patron provides the deity with breath, life, and food; the deity reciprocates by giving the patron and his family the grace of his presence and general well-being. As we pointed out in the beginning of our discussion of this *pūjā*, the pattern of worship outlined here is not unique to Gaṇēśa; rather it represents one group of variants — taking into account the differences to be found among forms of Gaṇēśa *pūjās* — of a large and pervasive form of Hindu religious ritual life. *Pūjās* to Durgā in Bengal, Sarasvatī in Uttar Pradesh and Bihar, among other deities in India, employ disposable clay images. These *pūjās* also stress the cycle of hospitality, auspicious presence, and distribution of that divine presence into the cosmos as a whole. As Durgā *pūjā* does for Bengalis, Gaṇēśa *pūjā* presents a microcosm of the rhythms of the macrocosm: from formlessness into form with its animating power followed by a dissolution back into formlessness; creation, maintenance, destruction and the hope of new creation. At the level of popular religious practice, the *pūjā* is an occasion for heightened awareness of Gaṇēśa and all the joy and hope associated with his obstacle-removing capacities. As the deity takes his place within the immediate and mundane frame of reference of the family, he enables family members to step out of the mere immediacy of their domestic world and share a time of special and transcendent intimacy with their god. As the image of Gaṇēśa sinks into the water and returns to its undifferentiated state, the devotees experience a mixture of sadness and relief — relief that the more intense ritual demands of the deity's visit have been completed and sadness that the special presence he brought into the home is over. It is out of this complex religious and emotional mood that they are able to say, with an attitude of hope mixed with certainty, "Gaṇēśa, Lord of Morayā, come early next year!"

Empty palanquin awaits the divine image the night before a procession. Kapālīśvara Temple, Mylapore, Madras City. Photo by Dick Waghorne.

3

Arcāvatāra: On Earth as He Is in Heaven

Vasudha Narayanan

THE PERPLEXING NATURE of a deity manifesting itself in material form has been a sensitive topic of theological discussion, especially in the context of the bhakti movements in south India. The Śrīvaiṣṇava community believes that the Lord is present on this earth in a temple in the same manner as he is in heaven. This community, which acknowledges the supremacy of Viṣṇu and his consort Śrī, became organized as a distinct religious group about the eleventh century A.D. during the lifetime of its most articulate theologian and spiritual preceptor (*ācārya*) Rāmānuja. While the Śrīvaiṣṇavas emphasize the inner experience of God, they never adopted the near iconoclasm of sects like the early Vīraśaivas.[1] Instead, the Śrīvaiṣṇavas developed a theology that articulated an essential relationship between the external manifestation of the Lord in the temple and the inner embodiment of God within the devotee's own heart.

For Śrīvaiṣṇavas, the songs of the *āḻvārs*, the Tamil Vaiṣṇava mystics who lived between the sixth and ninth centuries A.D., are preeminent, revealed scripture. (*Āḻvār* means literally "those who are immersed," in this context, in the love of God.) The first Śrīvaiṣṇava preceptor, who lived not long after the last of the *āḻvārs*, introduced the hymns into temple and home worship. The twelve Tamil mystics sang about Viṣṇu primarily in his manifestation as an image (*arcā*) enshrined in a temple. In total, the *āḻvārs* sang about 108 such manifestations (by traditional reckoning) and these poems became the inspiration for the writings of later preceptors and theologians. Today, the Śrīvaiṣṇava community considers both the poems of the *āḻvārs* and the writings of the *ācāryas* to be canonical. The hymns of the *āḻvārs* and the writings of the well-known preceptors who lived during the formative years of the community are essential for a full comprehension of the complex Śrīvaiṣṇava understanding of the Lord in the form of an image on earth.

Worship of the deity in the temple has been central to the Śrīvaiṣṇava tradition from the time of the *āḻvārs*. This chapter will focus on the nature of Viṣṇu's manifestation in the temple: the permanent descent of the deity as an image (*arcā avatāra*) which makes possible the ascent of man to heaven, the celestial realm of Viṣṇu known as *vaikuṇṭha*.

While the image of the deity may be made of earthly material, the pious Śrīvaiṣṇava believes that this is the real body of the Lord. Far from regarding the image as a body made of stone or hewn out of rock, the Śrīvaiṣṇava understands the image to be made of a non-earthly transcendental substance which is unique to the deity and is made perceivable on earth only by virtue of God's desire to be accessible to his devotees. This manifestation of the Lord, however, does not exist in contradistinction to, nor is it lesser than his manifestation in the heart of the devotee. The outer and inner experiences of the Lord are both exalted in Śrīvaiṣṇava theology. Nevertheless, the Śrīvaiṣṇava ultimately understands the external manifestations in temples to be superior to all other forms of God.

Śrīvaiṣṇavas distinguish two forms of Viṣṇu. First, he is seen as having an all-pervasive form: the entire universe is his body and he is the inner soul of everyone and everything. In addition, Viṣṇu has his own divine auspicious form (*divya maṅgala vigraha*).[2] This divine form is the locus of all the worlds, according to Śrīvaiṣṇava theology.[3] The divine auspicious form manifests itself in five different ways, and the fifth of these manifestations is the *arcā* or "material" image. The other four manifestations are:

1. The supreme (*para*) form. This is the eternal, unchanging form of Viṣṇu seen only in heaven. A vision of this form engenders bliss in the devotee.

2. The emanations (*vyūha*). There are three primary emanations called Saṃkarṣaṇa, Pradyumna and Aniruddha, which are said to preside over the functions of creation, preservation, and dissolution of the worlds, respectively. Iconographically this form is represented as Viṣṇu reclining on a five-headed serpent, called Śeṣa, on an ocean of milk. This is the posture of several images of Viṣṇu found in temples.

3. Manifestations at particular times (*vibhava*, sometimes called *avatāra*). These include specific "historical" descents of the Lord onto earth as Rāma, Kṛṣṇa, etc. Some holy men, such as Vyāsa, are also held to be partial incarnations of Viṣṇu.

4. The Inner Controller (*antaryāmin* or *hārda*). This is the special subtle form of the Lord which resides within the hearts of humans.[4]

5. The last, and the most important form of Viṣṇu, for Śrīvaiṣṇavas, is his permanent descent into the world as an image which can be worshiped. This image is an actual and real manifestation of the deity, neither lesser than nor a symbol of other forms. It is wholly and completely God, though it does not exhaust his essence.

In Śrīvaiṣṇava iconography, images of Viṣṇu are found in four postures: standing, sitting, striding, or reclining, and even the earliest Tamil mystic Poykaiyāḻvār speaks of various temples where Viṣṇu is depicted in these postures. In Śrīvaiṣṇava theology these four postures of the *arcā* are understood to represent the other four forms of Viṣṇu. Their significance can be summarized as follows:

Posture	*Form of Viṣṇu*	*Location*
sitting	*para*	*vaikuṇṭha*
reclining	*vyūha*	'Sea of Milk'
striding	*vibhava*	earth
standing	*hārda*	the human heart

The *arcā* is seen as an embodiment of the other four manifestations. In some Śrīvaiṣṇava holy places, for instance in Tirunīrmalai, *arcāvatāras* in all four postures are present. Tirumaṅkaiyāḻvār speaks of these:

> ... The Lord is in Tirunaraiyūr, Tiruvāli, Kuṭantai, Tirukkōvalūr: he stands, sits, reclines, and "walks" as Trivikrama in these places; this Lord abides continuously in Tirunīrmalai.[5]

It should be stressed that, for the Śrīvaiṣṇava, the distinction between the manifestation of the Lord in the temple and within one's heart is not total, nor is one manifestation in any way lesser than the others.

Just as the Lord graciously descends from heaven and manifests himself in a temple, he appears in the worshiper's heart. Tirumaḻicaiyāḻvār expresses this idea as follows:

> The days are gone when I saw at Ūrakam, the standing Lord. At Pāṭakam I beheld my father sitting. At Vehkā, he reclined. I was not "born" then (Tamil: *aṉṟu nāṉ piṟantilēṉ*). But no, the thought will never depart, that he stands, sits and reclines — in my heart.[6]

Periyāḻvār draws a direct parallel between exterior worship in a temple (Tamil: *kōyil*) and the interior worship of the *hārda*:

> Build a shrine (Tamil: *kōyil*) in your heart, install the Lord who is called Mādhava (Tamil: *Mādhava eṉṉum teyvattai nāṭṭi*); offer him the flower called love ...[7]

Thus a Śrīvaiṣṇava theologian writes: "*Hārda* is a nonmaterial (*a-prākṛta*) form of the Lord present in the human heart like the *arcā* in the temple.[8]

The Classifications of the Arcās

Arcās can be classified as "immovable" and "movable." The primary image (*mūlavar* or *mūla mūrti*) of the deity in the innermost chamber of the temple (also called *garbha gṛha* or the "womb house") is regarded as immovable, and the smaller images used for processions and for various celebrations are called the "festival images" (*utsavar* or *utsava mūrti*). A third kind of *arcā* is the *śālagrāma*, a small, dark colored fossil of a fish which is used in Śrīvaiṣṇava home worship. The immovable image is said to be of five kinds according to Śrīvaiṣṇava theologians. This classification can be depicted:

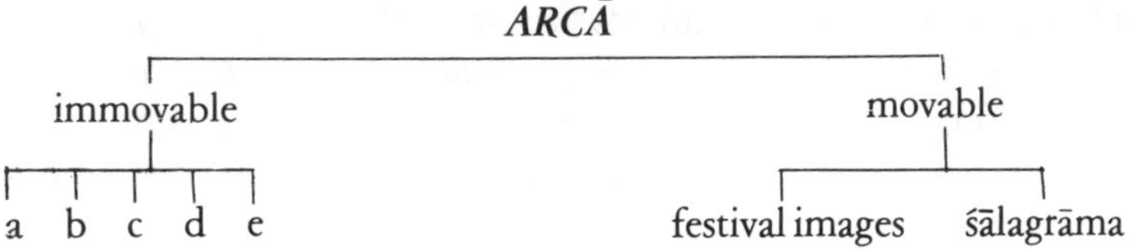

a. spontaneous manifestation[9]
b. appears to divine beings (*divya*)
c. appears to very holy people (*ārṣa*)
d. appears to men (*mānuṣa*)
e. appears to devotees of Viṣṇu

The movable images are small and are usually made of metal. These are used for processions and for particular rituals. These images may sometimes have an identity which is distinct from that of the immovable image, in which case they are given a separate name. In Rājamaṉṉarkuṭi, for instance, the immovable image is called Vāsudēvaṉ. This is a depiction of the "supreme" or *para* form of Viṣṇu, and he is represented here with his celestial consorts Śrī Dēvī and Bhū Dēvī. The movable image, however, is better known, and it is the name of this image (Śrī Rājagōpālaṉ: "King of the cowherds") that is associated with the shrine. This image is identified with the Kṛṣṇa *avatāra* of Viṣṇu. The Lord, thus depicted, is accompanied by his earthly consorts. Other well-known movable images in Śrīvaiṣṇava history are found at Śrīraṅgam and at Melkote.

The *utsava mūrti* at Melkote provides a delightful example of just how mobile such movable images can be. The image used for festivals at Melkote is called "Precious Son" (Tamil: *celvap piḷḷai*; Sanskrit: *sampatkumāra*) and has a distinctive history. The story is rather unusual and is reported in a thirteenth-century biographical work, the *Guruparamparā prabhāvam* or the "*Glory of the Succession of preceptors*:"

> Rāmānuja had the immovable primary image consecrated by Śrī Raṅgarāja Bhaṭṭar in the manner dictated by the *Pāñcarātra Sātvata Saṃhitā*, but was sad because there was no movable image with which he could celebrate continuous festivals for Tirunārana . . . [here a list of festivals follows]. Thinking of this, Rāmānuja slept; the Lord Tirunārāyaṇa graciously came into his dream and said, "My festival form called Rāmapriya

> is now in Delhi; he is delighting in his sport [The exact Maṇipravāḷa phrase "*līlai koṇṭāṭi eḻuntaruḷiyirukkirār*" is actually a delicate way of saying "consorting with."] in the house of the Turkish King (*Turuṣka rāja*). Go there and bring him home."
>
> Uṭaiyavar (Rāmānuja) woke up early in the morning, told his dream to other devotees and eagerly proceeded to Delhi. The ruler of Delhi received Rāmānuja graciously and with honor. He then asked, "Please tell us your reason for coming." Uṭaiyavar replied, "The Lord of our temple, Rāmapriya is here. Please give him to us." The king said, "Surely. You may search the lockers where we have all the gods we have plundered." Rāmānuja searched them and could not find any form comparable to Tirunārāyaṇa. Not having found Rāmapriya, he wearily lay down. That night Rāmapriya came to him in a dream and said "Why do you look weary? I am receiving worship from the daughter of the king; I am in her inner chambers. Come there and fetch me." Rāmānuja related this to the king. The king however said, "if the Lord is so infatuated with you, he will come to you on his own." Rāmānuja requested that he be allowed to see the Lord and touch his feet; this request was granted and the king and Rāmānuja went to the daughter's inner chambers. There the Lord saw Rāmānuja and jumping up ... with all his golden bells and ornaments tinkling, ran out and sat on Rāmānuja's lap, in front of everyone ... Rāmānuja ecstatically embraced the Lord crying, "Are you my precious son?" (Tamil: *eṉṉuṭaiya celva piḷḷaiyō?*). Since that day, Rāmapriya has been called "Precious Son." Seeing this, the king fell at Rāmānuja's feet and with all honors sent "Precious Son" off with him ... everyone called the Lord, the son of Rāmānuja ...[10]

According to oral tradition, the Muslim princess (Tamil: Tuluka Nācciār), unable to bear separation from Rāmapriya, followed the Lord to Tirunārāyaṇapuram where she is still honored in the temple ritual. Because she is from "north India" she is served wheat bread (*rōṭṭi; chappāti*) every day instead of rice, which is the customary diet in south India.

The movable and immovable images within each temple can thus have a distinct personality, as do each of the manifestations of the Lord at the various places (*divya dēśa*) in which the images reside. But Śrīvaiṣṇava texts also insist that Viṣṇu is fully present in every temple. In theological terms, the same Lord is said to reside in the many holy places with no difference in status among these local manifestations, just as the manifestation of Viṣṇu as *arcā*, as present in the heart (*hārda*), and as incarnate in the world (*avatāra*) are ontologically equivalent. There is just one Viṣṇu with one eternal form (the *Viṣṇu Sahasranāma* or "the thousand names of Viṣṇu" refers to him as the "one with an eternal form")[11] who manifests himself in a manner that is fitting to particular occasions. However, in oral tradition, each *arcā* is given a distinct personality. These are comparable to the differences ascribed to Viṣṇu's Rāma, Kṛṣṇa, or Narasimha *avatāras*, for example. The distinctive personalities of the local manifestations are revealed in the stories recorded in the history of each holy place (*sthala purāṇa*).[12] Such histories create a sense of continuity; they fix events both in mythical and historical time. One may observe in them at least three different strands which are brought together to give an aura of legitimate sanctity to each holy place and to the *arcā* with which it is associated:

(a) The origin of the *arcā* is recounted in a "purāṇic" or epic history. This may involve the appearance of the deity on its own (*svayam vyakta*) or its appearance before holy people. This strata of legend is usually located in mythic time. It is important because it lends an aura of scriptural approval from the Sanskrit tradition, and most Śrīvaiṣṇavas consider this to be necessary for religious legitimation.

(b) The deity is associated with a Tamil mystic (*āḻvār*). That is, the *arcā* is usually praised by one or more of the *āḻvārs* in the hymns of the Tamil canon.

(c) The deity is associated with a Śrīvaiṣṇava preceptor (*ācārya*).

The sacredness of the place Tirupati,[13] for instance, is a well-represented theme in Sanskrit scriptures. Nine of the twelve Tamil mystics sang of the Lord as an *arcā* here, and several of the Śrīvaiṣṇava *ācāryas*, including Rāmānuja, resided here for extended periods of time. According to oral tradition, this manifestation of the Lord is the younger brother of Viṣṇu at Tiruviṇṇakar (Oppaliyappaṉ Sannidhi), a place located about three hundred miles south of Tirupati. Legends and rituals at Tiruviṇṇakar reinforce the idea. Thus, while the theological tradition may conceive of the one "full" Lord who appears in several places and is "complete" in every sense, the oral bhakti tradition of popular piety respects the individual personality of each *arcā* and treats each as a distant person. Often several stories are interwoven, thus creating a cumulative significance for the *arcā*. Such stories attend both to "purāṇic" origin and to associations with the Śrīvaiṣṇava Tamil mystics and later preceptors. They establish connections between local deities and high gods and thereby establish a unique history and personality for each *arcā* which provides both a mythological basis for its distinctive appeal and a rationale for particular rituals associated with a temple.[14]

A third kind of "image" is also worshiped in the temple, but even more commonly in homes. This is the *śālagrāma*, the fossilized remains of a fish which is found in the Himalaya mountains.[15] At the home shrine, the *śālagrāma* is placed upon a small silver casket shaped like Ādiśēṣa, Viṣṇu's serpent-bed. For Śrīvaiṣṇavas, the *śālagrāma* is Viṣṇu, who has graciously come to reside in the devotee's home. It is the object of household worship (Tamil: *tiruvārātaṉai*). The importance of the *śālagrāma* in the Śrīvaiṣṇava's home cannot be overemphasized. *Śālagrāmas* are smooth and round, of various colors and sizes. The color and size of a *śālagrāma* are important and connote specific qualities. Some colors and sizes are believed to have a destructive influence in a family, whereas others are said to have beneficial effects.[16]

A Śrīvaiṣṇava scholar summarizes the importance of the *śālagrāma* as follows:

> The lord's presence in the *śālagrāma* is of utmost importance in home worship. Where twelve *śālagrāmas* grace a home with their presence, that home becomes a holy place (*kṣētra*). These cannot be polluted by touch (*sparśa dōṣa*). These houses are more important than the places where the Lord appears by his own volition (*svayamvyakta sthala*). If the place where the Lord appears by his own volition becomes polluted, perhaps by discontinuance in worship; one has to re-consecrate and do other rituals to purify the temple again, but even if the worship (Tamil: *tiruvārātaṉai*) of a *śālagrāma* stops for a day or two, there is no harm done. The Lord is continuously present in them. In Viṣṇu temples, even if there are no images or *arcās*, they must have some *śālagrāmas* at least.[17]

Śālagrāmas are generally worshiped singularly or in groups of four, six, or in larger even-numbered groups. One should never buy or sell a *śālagrāma*; one may only give or receive it as a gift. Giving a *śālagrāma* to another person brings good fortune to the giver. Śrīvaiṣṇavas usually give one to a daughter when she is married. This is kept in the home shrine of the family she marries into, and such a gift is said to promote marital happiness.[18]

Since the *śālagrāma* is in essence an *arcā*, many restrictions pertaining to ritual purity govern their treatment in the home. In a home which houses a *śālagrāma*, dietary rules are strictly enforced. Furthermore, *śūdras* are not allowed to touch *śālagrāmas*, and women cannot go near them when they are menstruating.

The *śālagrāma* is worshiped in much the same way as an *arcā* in a temple. Every morning when worshiping the *śālagrāma*, the devotee chants from the works of the *āḻvārs*;[19] the *śālagrāma* is bathed and adorned with sandalwood paste and flowers; and the water used for bathing is later distributed as *prasāda* and drunk by devotees. Also, all food cooked in the house is offered to the *śālagrāma* before it is consumed by the human occupants.

Viṣṇu incarnates as an *arcā* in a temple; he is present as a *śālagrāma* at home. Both the temple *arcā* and the household *śālagrāma* are full and complete manifestations of Viṣṇu, but we can note some differences between them. The temple *arcā* is believed to have a specific history as is noted in the *sthala purāṇas*; moreover, in most instances, the *arcā* is an anthropomorphic representation of the deity. The *śālagrāma* is "abstract" in form; as noted earlier, it is usually smooth and round, and it is not carved in any way. Individual *śālagrāmas* are never given particular names as are the temple *arcās*. Rather they are usually classified by the number of swirls on the fossil and thus identified.

There are several myths that explain the origin of the *śālagrāma*,[20] but none give specific case histories for individual *śālagrāma* icons. Like the divine fossils themselves, these myths are generic rather than specific. All attest to the living presence of Viṣṇu in these river stones and emphasize that these rocks were indeed once animate beings. In one case, the *śālagrāma* is traced to the Lord's manifestation as a tree. "A *ṛṣi* called Salangayana did *tapas* to see the Lord. The Lord appeared to him as a *śāla* tree and said, 'This place will be called Śālagrāma. I shall continuously reside here to shower grace on my devotees. I am the tree that you see.'"

Another myth more literally describes the *śālagrāma* as Viṣṇu turned to stone:

> A king called Jalandara, who was a good warrior, received several boons. His wife Tulasi was Viṣṇu's devotee; she was also devoted to her husband. In a certain war between the *dēvas* and the *asuras*, Jalandara helped the *asuras*, caused grief to the *dēvas*, and was eventually killed by Viṣṇu. Viṣṇu, however, moved by the prayers of Tulasi, took the form of Jalandara and lived with her for a while, accepting her favors. In time, Tulasi heard that her husband was killed by Viṣṇu and cursed the Lord, who had taken the form of her husband. "Since you, pitiless like a rock, killed my husband and lived in disguise, you will become like a rock," she cried.
>
> The Lord heard this with happiness. He said, "as you said, I shall become a mountain on the banks of the Gandaki. Worms called *vajrakīṭa* which have diamond-like teeth will bore marks on the stone. These marks will be my symbols — the cakra, etc. Those who worship these stones in places where there is tulasi (leaves) will be dear to me.

One finds other, more complex origin myths,[21] but the point is clear. For the Śrīvaiṣṇava the *śālagrāma* is not merely a petrified fossil; it is fully God, made of a pure, transcendental, non-material substance called *śuddha sattva* — the material of Viṣṇu's own body. Viṣṇu rules the world from heaven; as a primary or movable *arcā* in a temple he rules the villages and towns; as a *śālagrāma*, he rules the devotee's home.

The Paradox of Non-Material Matter

The paradox of the *arcā* in the Śrīvaiṣṇava tradition is that, while this manifestation of the deity is so obviously made of stone or metal, it is believed to be *a-prākṛta* or non-material. The deity's body in heaven, in the ocean of milk, in the incarnate form, as well as in the *arcā*, is said to be formed of *śuddha sattva*. This *sattva* or "purity" is not on par with the three qualities (*guṇa*) which constitute all living creatures and material things.[22] *Śuddha sattva* is a "super" substance, transcending anything found on earth. It is pure, unadulterated *sattva*, and is described as being "luminous." Only heaven, the deity's auspicious body (*divya maṅgala vigraha*) and the bodies of his attendants are made of this stuff. In Śrīvaiṣṇava metaphysics, this substance belongs to a typology:

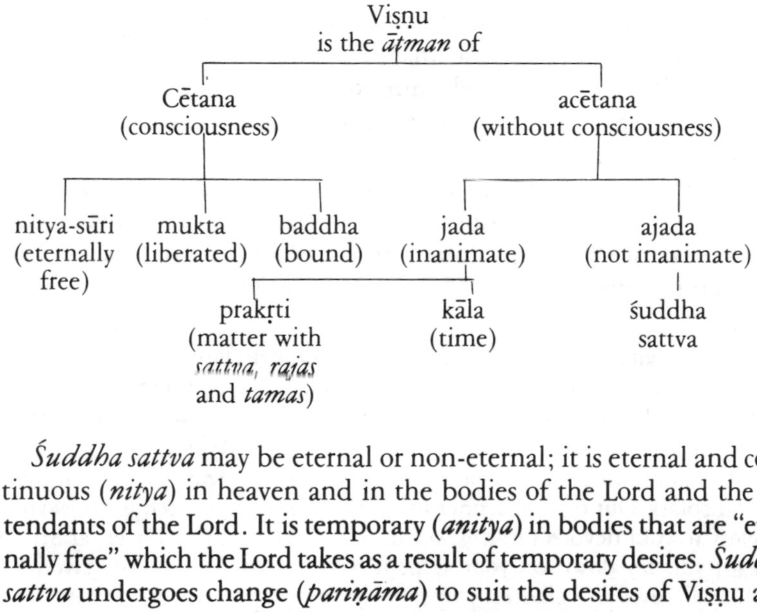

Śuddha sattva may be eternal or non-eternal; it is eternal and continuous (*nitya*) in heaven and in the bodies of the Lord and the attendants of the Lord. It is temporary (*anitya*) in bodies that are "eternally free" which the Lord takes as a result of temporary desires. *Śuddha sattva* undergoes change (*pariṇāma*) to suit the desires of Viṣṇu and serves as an accessory for his enjoyment. Human beings are able to do loving service to the body thus assumed by the Lord.[23] One should think of the deity only as having a form made of this *śuddha sattva* and not otherwise.

Śāstras dictate exactly how an image is to be made and indicate what material is to be used. Even Naṭātūr Ammāḷ, a Śrīvaiṣṇava *ācārya*, who lived during the early thirteenth century, said:

> Śaunaka says: "The *arcāvatāra* is to be worshipped. One is to make an image (*pratimā*) with gold or silver or any other metal. The Lord is to have a pleasing face, and beautiful eyes. ... this will be filled with *brahman* ..."[24]

However, when the Lord graciously descends to earth, the *arcā* is considered to be made of *śuddha sattva*, and Dēśika reiterates this several times. Piḷḷai Lōkācārya takes a different view. While discussing another very sensitive issue — the birth or caste of a devotee — Piḷḷai Lōkācārya and Maṇavāḷa Māmuṉikaḷ (A.D. 1300) say that placing importance on the caste of a devotee is as reprehensible as the questioning or analyzing the elements which compose the *arcāvatāra*. Both are as despicable and as vulgar as regarding the reproductive organ (*yōni*) of one's own mother as a common sex object.[25]

We are confronted with a paradox: what appears to non-Hindu eyes as the most gross and material representation of the deity is understood by the Śrīvaiṣṇava to be a divine, auspicious form, composed of a non-material substance that exists only in heaven and in the Śrīvaiṣṇava temple on earth. The image must not be regarded as a material object. It is a personal god, luminous, and complete with all auspicious qualities; it is transcendent and supreme, yet easily accessible — a bit of heaven on earth.

The *arcā* is often referred to as the ultimate means by which the Lord makes himself accessible to humanity. Śrīvaiṣṇava theologians often speak of the inaccessible supreme being who deigns to come down and manifests himself. Kurattāḻvāṉ, a close associate of Rāmānuja says:

> That divine being, of whom the Upaniṣads declare there is no equal, adorns the Hasti Hill. . . . That great being, who is distant to even the minds of the yogis who have conquered their senses, who is not known even in the Vēdānta, stands manifest on the Hasti Hill. ...[26]
>
> O handsome Lord of the forested hills [i.e., The Lord at Tirumāliruñcōlai]. Out of your tender love (*vātsalya*), you wanted to show your glory to your devotees in this world. So, in the midst of a river, at Śrīraṅkam you lay down on your serpent Śēṣa, so you can be perceived by [human] eyes and glances. ...[27]

In a renowned *sūtra*, Pillai Lōkācārya speaks about the accessibility of the Lord as *arcā* using a vivid metaphor:

> The Lord as an Inner Controller (*antaryāmitvam*) is like water deep down in the earth; the Emanation (*vyūha*) is like the sea of milk; incarnations and manifestations on earth (*vibhava*) are like rivers in flood, but incarnations as images (*arcāvatāras*) are like deep pools [that are easily accessible].[28]

The bodies of water correlated with the first three forms are unpredictable or inaccessible to an ordinary person; floods, for instance, may come occasionally, but later, people may be without water. But the *arcā* is like a pool, always accessible, always within reach.

Apart from accessibility (*saulabhya*), the *arcā* manifests several other divine auspicious attributes. Piḷḷai Lōkācārya speaks about these attributes of the *arcā* and their effect on humanity:

> . . . the fullness of auspicious attributes is seen in the *arcāvatāra*. The mystics (*āḻvārs*) took refuge with the Lord in the form of an *arcā*. Attributes like accessibility (*saulabhya*, which help one take refuge in the Lord, shine here in the *arcā* like light in a dark room.[29]

> Commentary: Over and above attributes like supremacy (*paratva*) the Lord has attributes like accessibility (*saulabhya*) that are seen completely in the *arcā*. . . . The Lord himself has said in the *Padmā Saṃhitā*: "No one can adequately describe the attributes of an *arcāvatāra* . . . It is with this *arcā* form that is perfect with all auspicious attributes that one can take refuge. We see this in the actions of Nammāḻvār[30] . . . the *arcā* displays attributes like accessibility (*saulabhya*), which help us to be attached to the Lord; excellence of disposition (*sauśīlya*) which prevents us from fear when we behold the Lord's supremacy; mastership (*svāmitvam*), which builds our confidence in him; and tender motherly love (*vātsalya*), which prevents us from trembling when we behold our shortcomings.[31]

Thus, the *arcā*, because it has attributes that induce humans to take refuge in the Lord, functions both as a means and as an end. Piḷḷai Lōkācārya and his commentator Maṇavāḷa Māmuṉikaḷ explain this in some detail. It is by incarnating as an *arcā* that the Lord reforms an individual who is involved in worldly affairs and who is unconcerned with God and with scripture. The *arcā*, by virtue of its beauty, causes people to be attracted to the Lord and later induces them to take refuge with him. Taking refuge with the Lord is the very path that scripture advocates as the best means to obtain the Lord. Thus, the *arcā* serves both as the means (*upāya*) and the goal (*upēya*); it is also the object of a devotee's enjoyment. The *arcā* (1) by its beauty induces a taste (*ruci*) for the Lord, (2) by virtue of its auspicious attributes serves as the means (*upāya*) because it engenders an attitude of surrender on the part of the individual, and (3) is the goal (*upēya*) and the object of the devotee's enjoyment (*bhōgyam*).[32]

The *arcā* symbolizes the accessibility of the deity to the human devotee; it also reminds him of their mutual relationship. This can be perhaps understood by considering a ritual which is performed at Tirupati (in Andhra Pradesh). (By extension, this ritual is celebrated in all the temples where the *arcā* of Viṣṇu is called Vēṅkaṭēśvara.)[33] The ritual is *Kalyāṇa utsavam* or the celebration of the auspicious wedding between Viṣṇu and his consorts Śrī and Bhū. *Kalyāṇa utsavam* differs from other ritual wedding celebrations such as that of the deities Mīnakṣī and Sundarēśvarar in Madurai. While the latter is an annual occurrence, the *kalyāṇa utsavam* is celebrated almost every day in Tirupati, upon the request of devotees. In this ritual a priest acts out the part of the Lord as a bridegroom, and all the ritual acts of an actual wedding are performed. The ritual, as interpreted by Śrī-vaiṣṇavas today, highlights Viṣṇu's accessibility. The devotee plays with the deity (as manifested in the *arcā*) and thus reenacts and participates in this most auspicious event, the marriage of Viṣṇu to Śrī and Bhū. Such a reversal of the human-divine relationship is typical of bhakti.[34] The human is not an instrument of the Lord's sport (*līlā*). To the contrary, the Lord, through his manifestation as the *arcā*, participates in the sport of the devotee.

The *arcās* of Viṣṇu, Śrī and Bhū, and the ritual of the wedding also represent the several relationships of the deity to the world. By assuming the form of the bridegroom of Śrī, Viṣṇu reminds the human that he is the bridegroom for every soul[35]; as the consort of Bhū, Viṣṇu can be seen as the support of the earth and as a friend to all humanity. The *arcā* form of the Lord thus simultaneously represents Viṣṇu's supremacy and his accessibility, but it is the latter attribute that is most important to the Śrīvaiṣṇava. Piḷḷai Lōkācārya sums up the Lord's accessibility thus:

> ... The Lord, though omniscient seems ignorant, though omnipotent seems as if powerless, although self sufficient, seems otherwise. Although he is the protector, he seems to be the protected one, exchanging his Lordship to be one who is extremely accessible ... he is thus graciously present in all temples and homes. This is the glory of the *arcāvatāra*.[36]

The temple and the *arcā*, therefore, are not comparable to heaven; they are, in the devotee's eyes, superior to it.

Appendix: The Origin of the *Śālagrāma*[37]

Once upon a time, Brahmā was worrying about how sinners could be saved. At that time, beads of sweat formed on his cheek. These sweat drops fell on the ground and from them arose a girl. Since she was born from a person's cheek (*ganda*) she was called Gandaki. She performed intense *tapas*. Brahmā, pleased, asked her to state her wish. Gandaki wished that all the *dēvas* be born from her womb. Brahmā hesitated. Angered, Gandaki cursed: "Since you tried to cheat me of what I merited, let all *dēvas* be born as worms." The *dēvas*, incensed, cursed back: "Unmindful of our greatness you cursed us because of your pride; you will become an unintelligent (i.e., inanimate) being."

Confusion prevailed. The *dēvas* went to Brahmā, who went to Śiva, and then everyone went to Viṣṇu.

Viṣṇu said, "O *dēvas*, two of my devotees will become an elephant and a crocodile and then receive *mōkṣa*. From their bodies, worms called *vajrakīṭa* will come forth. This Gandaki will be born as a river, more famous than the Ganges. Ten *yōjanas* from this place there is a spot called *cakratīrtha*. I shall reside there. The image there is called Dvāraka Cakra. You *dēvas* will hide on the rocks and hills of this area and live in the river. Thus Gandaki's wish will be fulfilled. Those who know this and worship the *śālagrāma* and the Dvāraka Cakra will attain *mōkṣa*.

In time, Kartama Prajāpati's wife Dēvahuti gave birth to two sons, Jaya and Vijaya. Both were steadfast in dharma. They meditated on the eight-syllabled *mantra* (*"Aum namō Nārāyaṇāya"*); they were extremely friendly with each other; they worshiped the Lord regularly. Once, a king called Maruta invited them to perform a sacrifice. The two conducted the sacrifice well. Receiving the king's gifts they came home, intending to worship the Lord individually. In partitioning the gifts, a quarrel ensued; the elder wanted the gifts divided equally, the younger wanted each one to keep what he was given. The older brother angrily cursed the younger, "Out of greed you wanted the money. You shall, therefore, become a crocodile" [which is a symbol of greed]. The younger brother cursed back: "Since you speak out of madness, you will become a rutting elephant."

The two returned home, bitter. During the time of worship, the Lord said, "Even though my words may be proved false, those of my devotee are always true. You will have to experience the effect of your curses. Due to my grace, you will have impressions of your former births and will eventually attain me."

Later, Jaya and Vijaya were born as an elephant and a crocodile and lived in and near the Gandaki and its environs. One day the elephant came to pluck a lotus from the Gandaki, and the crocodile caught its foot. The elephant called out "Ādimūlam!" and the Lord ran to the elephant's aid, killed the crocodile with his discus, and granted *mōkṣa* to both of them. Since the Lord's discus touched them, all the stones in the hill bore the mark of the discus (*cakra*); the whirls remain on them to this day. This place is called Hari Kṣētra. Since there are *śāla* trees nearby, this place is called Śālagrāma (the village Śāla). The Gandaki river flows here. The *dēvas* by the command of God, became worms called *vajrakīṭa* and live within the stones which have been marked by Viṣṇu's discus. These stones are called the "*śālagrāma* image."

Then Gandaki continued her *tapas*. The Lord asked her to state her wish. She said, "If it is true that you can be pleased and will grant wishes, I ask you, please live within my womb." The Lord acceded to her wish and said, "I shall pervade the *śālagrāma* and dispel the sins (*pāpa*) of my devotees. Because of this, you will become important. Having said this, he resided continuously in the *śālagrāma*

The *utsava mūrti* (right) of Kapālīśvara flanked by his divine bride at the annual celebration of their marriage. Mylapore, Madras City. Photo by Dick Waghorne.

The devotional bathing (*abhiṣēka*) of the image-body of Kṛṣṇa by a member of the Hare Krishna movement in America. Photo courtesy of ISKCON.

4

The Devotee and the Deity: Living a Personalistic Theology

William H. Deadwyler, III
(*Ravīndra-svarūpa dāsa*)

IN JULY OF 1973 the London *Guardian* published on its front page a photograph of the kind of wooden chariot traditionally used at Jagannātha Purī in Orissa since time beyond memory to carry the divine images of Jagannātha, Balarāma, and Subhadrā in an annual parade. In the *Guardian* photograph, however, the tall cloth dome of the chariot rose up next to a famous London landmark. The caption explained: "ISKCON Ratha-yatra is rival to the Nelson Column in Trafalgar Square."[1]

I think the iconography of the photograph rather neatly expresses a type of historical reversal we have seen at least once before, where links originally forged for colonial domination become in time avenues through which the culture of the dominated invades that of the dominator. At one time, a visit to exotic, far-off Orissa for the Jagannātha chariot festival seems to have been almost obligatory for Christian travelers, who were then able to compose horrific eye-witness accounts calculated to induce pious *frissons* in their readers thus confronted by a spectacle that was perceived as the veritable epitome of heathen idolatry in all its pomp and savage ostentation.[2] Who would have imagined then that this same festival would one day be imported into the very heart of the old Empire?

Indeed, Western devotees of Jagannātha now annually celebrate the *ratha-yātrā* festival in major cities throughout Europe and the Americas, bearing public witness to the fact that the practice of *arcanā* — the temple worship of the image of God — has taken root in the West. How has it come about that the practice that at one time appeared so alien if not repulsive to the Judeo-Christian spirit has now become sufficiently intelligible and attractive to induce many Westerners to embrace it themselves?

I confess to being one of those Westerners. I joined the International Society for Krishna Consciousness in 1971 while pursuing graduate studies in religion at Temple University, and the following year, as president of the Philadelphia temple, I was able to preside over the

the installation of the Jagannātha deities there and to organize the first *ratha-yātrā* festival on the east coast of the United States. This, then, is the confession and apologia of an American image worshiper.

The International Society for Krishna Consciousness — known colloquially as "the Hare Krishna movement" and acronymically as ISKCON — is a contemporary continuation of the Gauḍīya Vaiṣṇava tradition; and it is the founding *ācārya* of ISKCON, His Divine Grace A. C. Bhaktivedanta Swami Prabhupāda, who introduced and established the practice of deity[3] worship in the West. While other representatives of Hindu traditions have come West, both before and after Prabhupāda, they have almost exclusively propagated an intellectualized form of spirituality based on the monistic teachings of the *advaita-vedānta*. Restricting practice to various techniques of yoga and meditation and minimizing or entirely eliminating ritual, they have accommodated themselves as much as possible to prevailing Western cultural forms. Prabhupāda, however, in transplanting a bhakti tradition, necessarily proceeded quite differently; and ISKCON soon came to exhibit that exotic and outlandish appearance — a piece of medieval India set incongruously in twentieth century America — that has startled and puzzled so many. People visiting a temple for the first time or overtaken on the streets by a *ratha-yātrā* procession found themselves caught up in another world, overwhelmed by an intense and continuous assault on the senses — the sounds of voices chanting, drums beating, cymbals clashing, and bells ringing fill the air, while the devotees, wrapped in flowing robes, dance before brightly-lit images dressed elaborately in layers of shimmering, jewel-encrusted brocades and draped lavishly with glittering ornaments and long garlands of flowers. And all the while a heady aroma compounded of flowers and incense saturates the atmosphere. Westerners wonder: What does all this attention to visible and tangible externals, all this intense appeal to the senses, have to do with the spiritual? What is the need for people raised in one culture to adopt the exterior forms of another? What has possessed them to do so?

Because of the very nature of bhakti itself, Prabhupāda did what no other Indian missionary to the West had done before: he brought over and established not just an intellectual system or selected portions of a tradition but rather a comprehensive and inclusive spiritual culture, the whole tradition, complete and entire.[4] For bhakti, as Prabhupāda transmitted it, is meant to bring about the total sacralization of life, without any residue or remainder. One of the most important and central practices institutionalized in ISKCON for this end is *arcanā*.

Gauḍīya Vaiṣṇavism originated as a distinctive tradition with Śrī Caitanya Mahāprabhu (1486-1534) in Bengal. While Caitanya himself composed only a few verses, he ordered some of his intimate followers — led by Sanātana Gōsvāmī and Rūpa Gōsvāmī, two brothers who before joining Caitanya were ministers in the government of the Nawab Hussain Shah — to compose literary works that would explicate and elaborate his teachings, thus establishing a sound scholarly and theological foundation for his movement. Rūpa and Sanātana were joined by four others *sannyāsī* followers of Caitanya (Jīva, Gōpāla Baṭṭa, Raghunātha dāsa, and Raghunātha Baṭṭa). The works of the six *gōsvāmīs* of Vṛndāvana, as they are called, together with the *Caitanya-caritāmṛta*, a Bengali biography of Caitanya by their disciple Kṛṣṇadāsa Kavirāja, are the major canonical texts of Gauḍīya Vaiṣṇavism.[5] In the eighteenth century, Viśvanātha Cakravartī and Baladēva Vidyābhūṣaṇa wrote important theological works; the latter contributed the official Gauḍīya Vaiṣṇava commentary on the *Vēdānta-sūtra, Gōvindabhāṣya*.

Plans to spread Gauḍīya Vaiṣṇavism to the West were actually begun in the last century by Bhaktivinōda Ṭhākura (1838-1914). He had received a Western education, saw Gauḍīya Vaiṣṇavism in a global context, and was the first *ācārya* in the tradition to write in English. While serving as a magistrate for the British government in Orissa and Bengal, he expounded the teachings of Caitanya in over 100 works and labored to revitalize Gauḍīya Vaiṣṇavism as a preaching movement that would one day reach beyond India. His efforts were continued by his son Bhaktisiddhānta Sarasvatī (1874-1937), who established the Gauḍīya Maṭha mission with over 60 temples throughout India and who dispatched *sannyāsī* missionaries to London and Berlin in the 1930s. They did not meet with success, however, and it was not until another disciple of his — Bhaktivedanta Swami — founded ISKCON that Gauḍīya Vaiṣṇavism began to fulfill the expectations of Bhaktivinōda Ṭhākura.

In bringing Caitanya's movement to the West, Prabhupāda drew heavily on the work of his predecessors. The organizational structure of ISKCON itself is modeled on the Gauḍīya Maṭha of Bhaktisiddhānta. Prabhupāda also followed Bhaktisiddhānta in basing his preaching efforts on book distribution. In his books, Prabhupāda endeavored to transmit the rich intellectual and spiritual heritage of Gauḍīya Vaiṣṇavism to the West. His commentary on the *Bhagavad*

Gītā closely follows that of Baladēva Vidyābhūṣaṇa, and his commentary on the *Śrīmad Bhāgavatam* relies heavily on those of Sanātana Gōsvāmī, Jīva Gōsvāmī, Viśvanātha Cakravartī, and Baladēva Vidyābhūṣaṇa.

While Caitanya's movement, as Prabhupāda thus received and transmitted it, gives special attention to the chanting of the names of God (particularly in the form of the Hare Kṛṣṇa *mantra*) as the only means of deliverance efficacious in this age, it also recognizes the importance of *arcanā*. Not only had the six *gōsvāmīs* of Vṛndāvana preached and written books, but they had also caused temples to be built, installed deities, and arranged for their worship; Bhaktisiddhānta later did the same. When Prabhupāda began to propagate Kṛṣṇa consciousness in America, at first he simply engaged his followers in chanting Hare Kṛṣṇa, but when he judged his disciples to be somewhat purified by chanting, he introduced *arcanā*. In March of 1967, approximately one year after he had attracted his first committed followers, Prabhupāda installed the deities of Jagannātha, Balarāma, and Subhadrā in San Francisco. The installation ceremony was extremely simple, as was the form of worship he instituted.[6] But as his disciples became more capable, Prabhupāda gradually raised the standards of *arcanā*, and in June of 1969 the first ISKCON Rādhā-Kṛṣṇa deities were installed in Los Angeles.[7]

Deity worship is now established in all ISKCON temples, and it rules and regulates the life of the devotees. Most temples have three sets of deities on the altar: Gaura-Nitāi, Rādhā-Kṛṣṇa, and Jagannātha, Balarāma, and Subhadrā. The first are the forms of Caitanya (who is also called Gaurāṅga and Gaurahari) and his principle associate Nityānanda.[8] Rādhā-Kṛṣṇa are the major deities worshiped by Gauḍīya Vaiṣṇavas, but we also worship the Jagannātha deities because Caitanya, who resided at Purī during the final eighteen years of his life, regularly worshiped at the Jagannātha temple and participated prominently in the *ratha-yātrā*. Some temples also have *śālagrāma-śilās*. The form of worship has been standardized in ISKCON temples according to the procedures established for the Gauḍīya Maṭha by Bhaktisiddhānta Sarasvatī and codified in a handbook called *Arcana-paddhati*, which in turn is based upon the *Hari-bhakti-vilāsa* of Sanātana Gōsvāmī.[9]

What I would like to do here is convey as lively an understanding as possible of what it is really like for a devotee like myself to worship and serve the image of God in the temple. One who wishes to understand and enter sympathetically into this form of spiritual life must comprehend *arcanā* both intellectually (or theologically) as well as practically. To put it another way, one will have to appreciate the *darśana* of the deity in both of the two major senses of the term: as the philosophy that justifies and makes intelligible the worship, and as the concrete acts of association with the deity. The two kinds of *darśana* are related to each other in an interestingly reciprocal way.

Darśana literally means "seeing," but a devotee who "takes *darśana*" — as the idiom goes — of the deity does not engage in an ordinary act of apprehension. As Diana Eck puts it, *darśana* is sacred perception — "the ability truly to see the divine image."[10] At the same time, the word *darśana* is used to mean a philosophy or theology, but this, as Srivatsa Goswami explains, does not designate some cognitive system remote from our experience, but rather "that *by which* we see.[11] Prabhupāda has said, in this connection, that a devotee of Kṛṣṇa is one who sees by means of scripture ("*śāstra-cakṣus*"),[12] or through eyes enlightened by transcendental knowledge ("*paśyanti jñānacakṣuṣaḥ*").[13]

I, and others like me who have taken to deity worship, have become convinced that God can indeed be manifest to the senses in a concrete, tangible form. In doing so, we have had to overcome certain ideas about God bequeathed to us by our own Judeo-Christian heritage. These ideas make it difficult for most Westerners to understand the divine image. Of course, there are the strong Old Testament proscriptions against idol worship, promulgated to keep the followers of Yahweh from bowing down before the Baals and Ishtars of their neighbors, but more significant for the classical Judeo-Christian idea of God is the later intellectual interpretation of divinity in terms of a negative theology derived from Greek speculative metaphysics, with its disdain for the particular and the sensual. This resulted in an understanding of God as a being who by his own intrinsic nature cannot possibly be concretely depicted.

Aristotle and Plato both located that which is unchanging and undecaying — and hence divine — in the mental realm. Aristotle conceived of God as unalloyed *nous*, as detached, disincarnate intellect, while Plato thought of the supreme as pure abstract intelligible essence — in other words, as an object of intellect, a universal. Western religious thought has continued this tendency to conceive of the spiritual in mind-oriented terms. In an address to Unitarian ministers, William James set out what he considered the "essential features" of the idea of God. One of them was that God "must be conceived of as a mental personality." While James supported his definition with characteristic care, he did not consider it necessary to give any justification at all for the adjective "mental."[14] That, apparently, was beyond dispute.

At the same time, Western theologians have tended to be wary of unequivocally applying any positive characterization to God at all. While Plato thought of the divine as an intelligible essence, the Hellenistic-Jewish philosopher Philo of Alexandria understood God to be so unlike anything in the world that His nature is "unnameable," "ineffable," and "unintelligible."[15] And Aquinas says that "we cannot know what God is, but rather what He is not."[16] This approach to divine transcendence gives negative theology a decisive edge over positive. Even positive characterizations of God amount to a concatenation of abstractions — "good," "wise," "just," "powerful," and so on. (Aquinas tells us that "the less determinate the names are . . . the more properly are they applied to God."[17]) And the meanings of even these abstractions are subverted by being intended only analogically or as descriptions not of God but of his effects.

Someone educated in this tradition is likely to see the image of God in the Vaiṣṇava temple — formed as it is like a human being and even clothed, ornamented, and garlanded — as the product of an unsophisticated mentality, as the object of a primitive form of worship by a people whose development of a properly spiritual idea of God was somehow arrested or retarded and who have no due regard for the divine transcendence. William Crooke, for example, writing for Hasting's *Encyclopedia* on "The future of idolatry" in India, credits Christianity and Islam for having "done much to suggest purer conceptions of Godhead" to Hindus and goes on to quote A. C. Lyall:

> Idolatry is only the hieroglyphic writ large, in popular character; it came because unlettered man carves in sticks and stones his rude and simple imagination of a god; and this way of expressing the notion by handiwork continues among even highly intellectual societies, until at last the idea becomes too subtle and sublime to be rendered by any medium except the written or spoken word.[18]

Another impediment to understanding *arcanā* comes from India itself. Indian apologists, who have attempted to defend image worship to Europeans, have almost all been proponents of *advaita-vēdānta*. Their understanding is cognitively about the same as that of Christian critics: sincere worshipers of divine images are indeed spiritually impoverished and theologically unsophisticated. For the image is *māyā* and the worshiper is in illusion. According to Śaṅkarācārya, when *brahman* is an object of knowledge, it is realized as *nirguṇa*

— unqualified by names, forms, attributes, or relations, and it is not different in any respect from the knower. When *brahman* is an object of ignorance, however, it appears as *saguṇa*, as the personal Lord and creator of the universe, and as distinct from the worshiper. "As long as it is the object of nescience," Śaṅkarācārya says, "there are applied to it the categories of devotee, object of devotion, and the like."[19] Thus, a spiritually enlightened person knows that God is ultimately to be understood through negative theology. It cannot be represented by words, let alone by images. Nevertheless, these followers of Śaṅkarācārya give qualified approval to image worship: it is a step on the way, for all paths lead to the same place (that is, to *advaita-vēdānta*). Indeed, from this lofty point of view, both the God of Vaiṣṇava devotion, which can be depicted by a visible image, and the more abstract God of Christian worship, which can be represented only by words, are equally illusory, and there is no need for individious comparisons. In either case, one is dealing with symbols and mundane representations of that which is beyond thought and speech.

However, Indian apologists who explain away the *arcā-mūrti* as a symbol misrepresent actual conviction and practice, as Christian anti-imagists have recognized. The Rev. W. Ward, a Baptist missionary at Serampore, acknowledges one such account as "the best apology I have obtained for the worship of idols," but goes on to note:

> The Hindoo is taught, that the image is really God, and the heaviest judgments are denounced against him, if he dare to suspect that the image is nothing more than the elements of which it is composed. The Tŭntrŭsarŭ declares, that such an unbeliever will sink into the regions of torment. In the apprehensions of the people in general, therefore, the idols are real deities; they occupy the place of God, and receive all the homage, all the fear, all the service, and all the honors which HE so justly claims. The government of God is subverted, and all the moral effects arising from the knowledge of his perfections, and his claims upon his rational creatures, are completely lost.[20]

Similarly, J. N. Farquhar quotes with approval an Indian reformer and iconoclast:

> Whatever the apologist . . . may say, as for instance that . . . Idolatry is only keeping in view a concrete thing for concentration in worshipping the One True Spiritual God; the stern and incontrovertible fact remains . . . that the idolater *does* believe that some of the idols are the actual incarnations of God, called *Archavataras* (incarnations for worship), and not mere symbols. . . .[21]

Vaiṣṇavas do conceive of God in a very concrete and specific way (so that it is possible to depict him by an image), but I want to argue here that the Gauḍīya Vaiṣṇava tradition offers theological grounds for doing so that are hardly naive, grounds that take us beyond the negative theology of both Christians and *advaitins* and further into transcendence.

First, let me quote a few verses from the *Brahmasaṃhitā* (5.29-33) to put directly before us the sort of conception I am talking about:[22]

> I worship Govinda, the Primeval Lord, the First Progenitor Who is tending the cows, yielding all desires, in Abodes built with spiritual gems, surrounded by millions of Purpose-trees [*kalpa-vṛkṣa*], always served with great reverence and affections by hundreds of thousands of Laksmis or Gopees.
>
> I worship Govinda, the Primeval Lord, Who is Adept in playing on His Flute, with blooming Eyes like lotus-petals, with Head decked with peacock's feather, with the Figure of Beauty tinged with the hue of blue clouds, and His unique Loveliness charming millions of Cupids.
>
> I worship Govinda, the Primeval Lord, round Whose Neck is swinging a garland of flowers beautified with the Moon-locket, Whose two Hands are adorned with the Flute and jewelled ornaments, Who always revels in Pastimes of love, Whose Graceful three-fold-bending Form of Shyama-Sundara is eternally manifest.
>
> I worship Govinda, the Primeval Lord, Whose Transcendental Form is full of bliss, truth, and substantiality, and is thus full of the most dazzling splendour. Each of the Limbs of that Transcendental Figure possesses in Himself, the full-fledged functions of all the organs, and eternally sees, maintains and manifests the infinite universes, both spiritual and mundane.
>
> I worship Govinda, the Primeval Lord, Who is inaccessible to the *Vedas*, but obtainable by pure unalloyed devotion of the soul, Who is without a second, Who is not subject to decay and is without a beginning, Whose Form is endless, Who is the beginning, and the eternal Purusha; yet He is a Person possessing the beauty of blooming youth.[23]

As these *ślokas* indicate, God is conceived in a way that is rich in specific and variegated features; he is a person with a body of particular color, characteristic posture, and decorated with specific ornaments. He dwells in the overflowing profusion of a spiritual abode. The contention, then, is that God has — *really* has — name, form, qualities, relations, and activities, and that all of these are "transcendental" — of a quite different nature from the names, forms, qualities, relations, and activities of the material world.

Although there is variety in God, it is a variety without duality. The spiritual nature of God's form is indicated by its absolute unity. Unlike conditioned creatures, in Kṛṣṇa there is no difference between soul and body, between the limbs and their proprietor, between the attributes and the entity possessing them, and every part of God's body has all the functions of the whole. Kṛṣṇa's body, Bhaktisiddhānta Saraswatī says, is made of "concentrated" *brahman*.[24]

This sort of concrete depiction of God, of course, leads critics, whether of Western or Eastern extraction, to charge those who uphold it with projecting mundane ideas onto spiritual nature. Our response is to assert that Kṛṣṇa's form is not anthropomorphic; rather, the human body is theomorphic, modeled on the veritable spiritual form of God. But the other side balks at the notion of "spiritual form" or "spiritual body." The idea strikes them as an oxymoron. They have been habituated in understanding spirit as something in abstraction from, or in opposition to, what is concrete and specific — as something remote, in particular, from the body and its senses.

The pursuit of spirit through negation is, I believe, a generic phase or moment in the human religious enterprise, and can be found, integrated in different ways, in all major religious traditions. The phase has two sides: that of the subject (the aspirant) and that of the object (the goal, the divine). The subjective side is characterized by an asceticism of bodily and sensual denial or withdrawal; correlative to that on the objective side is the characterization of the divine by progressive abstraction or negation (the *via negativa*).

The phase of negation is, of course, a reaction against materialism, a rejection of life in pursuit of (temporary) happiness through the enjoyment of the senses. The objective side of materialism is often a denial of the divine altogether, but there have also been what we may call materialistic religions, in which *dēvatās*, demigods, or similar beings are propitiated through worship or sacrifice for worldly ends. The phase of negation began among the Greeks when Xenophanes rejected the all-too-human gods of traditional Hellenic religion. Early Christians similarly engaged in polemics against the polytheism and idolatry of the pagans, while often attributing divine inspiration to Greek thinkers (especially Plato) who indulged in negative theology.[25]

According to this paradigm of generic religious phases, the deprecations of Vaiṣṇava image worship by Christians on the one hand and by followers of the *advaita-vēdānta* on the other have this in common: the judgment by both of them comes, each in its own way, out of adherence to a version of the negative phase and views the representation of God in a concrete form as a product of the prior materialistic phase it has rejected. I am persuaded that these evaluations of the Vaiṣṇava idea of God are mistaken on the grounds that the idea belongs, in truth, to a higher third, and final, stage.

A recurring feature of Prabhupāda's writings and lectures is the criticism of the first two phases; both are represented in the Indian context with particular distinctiveness, the first by the *karmīs* who seek material well-being by performing the Vedic sacrifices or worshiping the various *devatās*, the second by the *jñānīs* or Māyāvādīs who pursue liberation according to the philosophical tenets of the *advaita-vedānta*. But Prabhupāda's criticism was only apparently aimed at particular historical traditions; the real targets were the generically human spiritual conditions that lay behind these historical manifestations. One of Prabhupāda's first disciples has described his realization of this:

> When Śrīla Prabhupāda first began lecturing in New York in 1966, he would often attack the Māyāvādī impersonalists in his talks, and not understanding this I joked with a friend: "Māyāvādī? When was the last time you saw a Māyāvādī?" None of us could understand who Śrīla Prabhupāda was talking about: we all thought that the Māyāvādīs were a little group of philosophers in India against whom Śrīla Prabhupāda was waging theologic battle. But actually we were all Māyāvādīs.[26]

While Prabhupāda's criticism may appear polemical or apologetical, its ultimate purpose was therapeutic. If his disciples were to come to the stage of pure bhakti, devotional service, we would have to be purged, as it were, of two kinds of spiritual impediments: desire for material enjoyment and desire for liberation by means of philosophical speculation. Had not Rūpa Gōsvāmī defined pure bhakti as favorable devotional service to Kṛṣṇa that has no tinge of *karma* and *jñāna*?[27] In other words, one cannot attain the final, highest phase of religion without being freed from even residual adherence to either of the first two phases.

In bhakti there is neither engagement of the senses in material objects, as in the first phase (*karma*), nor negation of the senses through denial, as in the second phase (*jñāna*). Rather, the senses are directed toward spiritual or transcendental sense objects, primarily the name, form, qualities, and activities of God. The Māyāvādīs protest that name, form, and the like are features of matter, not spirit, and they should not be projected onto transcendence. The implicit reasoning behind their protest is that *if* God were to have name, form, qualities, and so on, *then* necessarily they would be material. But the idea that all names are material names, all forms material forms, all determinate qualities material qualities, etc., is an illegitimate generalization, and to assert that these things cannot be features of spiritual reality is to project mundane conceptions of name, form, qualities, etc., onto the condition of transcendence. In India, Vaiṣṇava bhakti has defined itself in rather stark opposition to the *jñāna* of the Māyāvādīs, and thus I will develop my argument over and against the uncompromisingly negative theology of the *advaita-vēdānta*.

In *jñāna*, then, the goal is to distinguish the absolute from the relative by negation. Yet we must note that the process of negation has its own inherent limitation and is incomplete by itself. If "form," for example, is a material idea, then so must be "formless," for the predicate depends upon and requires "form" for its meaning. It is therefore as relative, and as material, as that which it denies. Accordingly, the absolute defined only by negation can be only a relative material conception of the supreme.[28]

One cannot, then, rest with negations. I have suggested that the quest to comprehend God is a process of spiritual development having three phases of *karma, jñāna,* and *bhakti*. Interestingly, these three phases are related in the dialectical pattern of thesis, antithesis, and synthesis. Negation is not the ultimate but the penultimate step, and it requires sublation. Thus "form" and its negation, "formless," point to a final synthesis, having, from a material point of view, the contradictory feature of being simultaneously with and without form. Now this sort of impetus to go beyond negation makes its appearance regularly enough in impersonal speculative literature, usually in an attempt to transcend mind or intellect altogether in a nonrational, supracognitive act of "realization." But it is not necessary to regard the union of "form" and "formless" as intractable mystification without utterable content. Let us be more precise about the beginning and define *form* explicitly as "material form." Thus, its negation, *formless*, means "no material form." Now we can see our way clear to the final synthesis, the affirmation that sublates the negation; "spiritual form." This is the higher unity of "form" and "formless": there is form but no [material] form.

The procedure I have used with reference to the object can also be applied to the subject. Any action of the conative and cognitive senses can be called *karma*, but the word is used particularly to designate actions that bind the subject to the material world (see *Bhagavad Gītā* 8.3). These are the sorts of actions, impelled by worldly desires, that characterize the phase of *karma*. In *jñāna*, the subject aims at the total elimination of all action. Thus Śaṅkarācārya says in his *Bhagavad Gītā* commentary that "avidya and kama (nescience and desire) constitute the seed of all action,"[29] so that when a person

> has learned to look upon all this dual world as a mere illusion, as though it were night, when he has realized the Self, his duty consists not in the

performance of action, but in the renunuciation of all action. . . . When the knowledge of the Self has been attained, neither organs of knowledge nor objects of knowledge present themselves to consciousness any longer.[30]

In bhakti, devotional service, this duality between action and inaction is transcended, and sensory experience is neither enjoyed nor renounced. As Rūpa Gōsvāmī says, quoting the *Nārada-pañcarātra: hṛṣīkēṇa hṛṣīkēśa-sēvanam bhaktir ucyatē* — "bhakti means serving the master of the senses (i.e., God) by means of the senses."[31] When the senses are used solely to serve God, there is action which is at the same time inaction, as the *Bhagavad Gītā* states.[32] In other words, devotional service consists of spiritual acts, acts that are karma-less. The impetus for these actions is not *kāma*, which is the desire to gratify one's own senses, but *prēma*, the selfless desire to please the transcendental senses of Kṛṣṇa.[33]

So far I have tried to show that the spiritual nature of God does not preclude his being a transcendental object of the senses, and that spiritual life does not entail on our part the suppression of the senses. I now must explain how Gauḍīya Vaiṣṇavism conceives of the nonduality of God and the relation between God and the world.

For the Gauḍīya Vaiṣṇavite, nonduality means not denying variegatedness. Absolute unity transcends the opposition between unity and diversity, the one and the many, by including diversity; unity conceived as a denial of diversity is material unity. The divine unity extends to the relationship between God and the world. The existence of a real world does not mean that there is something other than God which limits him. God is still *advaya*, one without a second, because God includes the world, while at the same time transcending it. "All beings are in Me," Kṛṣṇa says in the *Bhagavad Gītā* (9.4), "but I am not in them" (*mat-stāni sarva-bhūtāni na cāham tēṣvavasthitaḥ*). Gauḍīya Vaiṣṇavism explicated this statement by the doctrine of *acintya-bhēdābhēda-tattva*, the principle of inconceivable oneness and difference. This holds that while nothing is different from Kṛṣṇa, Kṛṣṇa is different from everything. "In a sense, there is nothing but Śrī Kṛṣṇa, and yet nothing is Śrī Kṛṣṇa save and except His primeval personality.[34] The phenomenal world of spiritual and material beings — *parā* and *aparā prakṛti* in the terms of the *Bhagavad Gītā* (7.5) — is, in a sense, Kṛṣṇa because it is made of his energies.

These three ideas — that there is variegatedness of form, name, and qualities in transcendence, that there is an absolute unity which includes diversity, and that there are spiritual activities of the senses — form the theological grounds for worshiping God in the form of an image in the temple.

First, if God is a transcendental person, complete with form, limbs, color, and a host of other specific features, then a veridical image of God is possible. The contention, then, that any specific image of God must be *by that very fact* an imagination constructed on the basis of worldly experience is simply false. It is possible to make an image of God that actually *is* an image of God.

Secondly, the nondual nature of God (as including diversity) implies that even though there may be both object and the representation of that object (say, in sound or in stone), the object and its representation are at the same time one. On the basis of this conception of the absolute nature of God, for example, the Gauḍīya Vaiṣṇava theology of the Holy Name is constructed. Simply put, Kṛṣṇa *is* his name, and anyone who utters that name at once directly associates with Kṛṣṇa. The name of Kṛṣṇa is thus considered to be an *avatāra* of Kṛṣṇa in the form of sound. In a similar way, the image of Kṛṣṇa in the temple *is* Kṛṣṇa himself. It does not symbolize Kṛṣṇa or represent Kṛṣṇa; it *is* the full and complete presence of Kṛṣṇa, the *arcāvatāra*. This is the implication of nonduality.

Thirdly, there is no reason why a form made of stone or wood or metal cannot serve as an instance of God's presence. God and his energies are one, and from the absolute standpoint the duality of matter and spirit does not exist; there are just varieties of spirit. As there is a sense in which God is everything, God can manifest himself in matter. He can, so to speak, turn matter into spirit. Thus, even though God is not stone or wood, he can perfectly well appear *as* stone or *as* wood.

Everything spiritual and material is a transformation of the substantial potency or energy of God. Although Kṛṣṇa's energy is actually one, it acts in three principle ways: As the internal energy (*antaraṅga-śakti*), it manifests the transcendental kingdom of God, the spiritual world; as the external energy (*bahiraṅga-śakti*), it produces the material world; and as the marginal or borderline energy (*taṭastha-śakti*), it generates the multitude of individual souls, *jīvas*, which are called "marginal" because they can dwell in either the internal or the external potency.[35] Although the products of the internal and marginal potencies are called "spiritual," and the products of the external energy are called "material," in the final consideration *everything* is spiritual, since everything is related to Kṛṣṇa as an emanation of his energy. *Spirit* means "connected with God," and *matter* means "separate from God." Since, in reality, nothing is unconnected with God, there is no matter. But the external potency is conventionally called "material" because it has the power to delude the souls trapped within it into thinking that it is unconnected. In the external potency, we can consider ourselves and the people and things around us in a manner unrelated to God. Thus the illusion of matter arises. This illusion arises for souls who desire the ontological impossibility of independence from God. Kṛṣṇa can also dispel that illusion for those who desire it, and in that case he causes the same energy that acted to separate them from him to act now to unite them with him. Thus Kṛṣṇa, by his omnipotence, changes external into internal energy. Prabhupāda uses the example of the electrician who by proper adjustment can employ the same electrical energy to heat or to cool.[36] When "matter" is used to connect the living being to Kṛṣṇa, then it is acting as internal energy or as spirit. Thus, when God, out of his kindness, takes the form of an image in the temple and makes himself visible to the materially limited senses of the worshiper, God has, in effect, transformed matter into spirit.

Accordingly, Prabhupāda repeatedly stresses that

> the Lord in His *arcā-mūrti*, or form made of material elements, is not material, for those elements, although separated from the Lord, are also a part of the Lord's energy, as stated in *Bhagavad-gītā*. Because the elements are the Lord's own energy and because there is no difference between the energy and the energetic, the Lord can appear through any element. Just as the sun can act thrugh the sunshine and thus distribute its heat and light, so Kṛṣṇa, by His inconceivable power, can appear in His original spiritual form in any material element, including stone, wood, paint, gold, silver and jewels. . . . The *śāstras* warn, *arcye viṣṇau śilā-dhīḥ*: one should never think of the *arcā-mūrti*, the Deity within the temple, as stone, wood, or any other material element. . . . To an ordinary person, however, the Deity will appear to be made of stone, wood or some other material. In the sense, since all material elements ultimately emanate from the supreme spiritual entity, nothing is really material.[37]

Gauḍīya Vaiṣṇava theology thus holds that when ignorance is removed the illusion of matter disappears, but this does not mean that the phenomenal world vanishes; rather, the phenomenal world is correctly perceived as spirit, as the energy of God simultaneously one with and different from him.

God descends as the *arcāvatāra* at the request of his pure devotee to aid those less advanced in the removal of their ignorance. In his *arcā* form God graciously comes to dwell among us, to be visible even to materially limited senses, and to allow the devotees to become totally absorbed in body, mind, and senses in the devotional service of the Lord. The devotees on their part must carefully serve the deity with great reverence and attention. In a letter to a disciple concerning worship of the deity, Prabhupāda wrote:

> So do it nicely. I have invited Kṛṣṇa, and He may not be insulted by disrespectful behavior. I have introduced this system of Deity worship amongst the nonbelievers, the atheists, the *melecchas*, the *yavanas* and I pray to Kṛṣṇa that I am inviting You to come, so please, because You are seated in their hearts, please give them the intelligence to serve You so that You may not be inconvenienced. ... Never think of the Deity as made of stone or wood. Every worshiper must remember that Kṛṣṇa is personally present. He is simply kindly presenting Himself before us in a way so that we can handle Him. That is His mercy, otherwise He is unapproachable.[38]

The presence of the deity makes the temple quite literally the house of God, and the devotees dwell with the Lord in his house as a staff of servants wholly dedicated to the pleasure of their resident master. The devotees worship and serve the deity in the same way that retainers, ministers, and domestics used to serve and pay homage to the king in his palace. The deity is regarded as the factual owner and proprietor of the temple. (At Jagannātha Purī the Balarāma *mūrti* is the *legal* owner of the temple and its lands — Balarāma because he is the elder brother.) The life of the temple revolves around the deity, and the day is regulated according to the service of the deity.

The *arcā-mūrti*, residing as the lord of the temple and the master of the devotees, creates, by his tangible presence, a sacred precinct about him in which devotees live with their lives centered around God. Although not every devotee may perform the specialized service of a *pūjārī*, all devotees living in the temple cannot help but be perpetually mindful of the deity, in the same way that a staff of dedicated servants are conscious of the master for whom their various tasks are performed and around whom the entire household is organized. All food the cooks prepare in the temple kitchen is offered exclusively to the deity, while all his servants eat only their master's left-over table scraps, that is to say, the deity's *prasāda*. Even the temple's account books are regularly set before or read to the deity for his approval. The daily schedule of the deity's rising and retiring, enjoying offerings of food, *ārati*, and *kīrtanā*, establishes the rhythm of the life of the temple. As a temple resident I may spend most of the working day typing in my office, but I am always aware when the Lord is awake and when taking rest, and I can hear the conch-shell blowing and bell ringing for each *ārati*. Although the deity resides in the center of the temple, his presence intensely pervades his whole household.

God's descent as the *arcā-mūrti* manifests not only God but God's spiritual abode as well, as the temple itself becomes the image or replica of *vaikuṇṭha-lōka*. The temple is no less than the kingdom of God on earth. Just as in *vaikuṇṭha-lōka* God is eternally served in different ways by liberated devotees in spiritual bodies (*siddha-dēha*), so the presence of the *arcāvatāra* here below gives devotees in the material world the same opportunity to serve the Lord with their material bodies.

Indeed, such service is said to transmute the devotee's material body into a spiritual one. Just as an iron put into fire gradually becomes warm, then hot, then glows cherry red, and thus acts completely like fire, so the material body, mind, and senses of a devotee become progressively spiritualized by constant intimate contact with the deity.

The appearance of God in his *arcā* form enables the devotee to absorb God with every sense. Daily taking in the deity's *prasāda* and performing *kīrtana* for the deity, daily seeing the attractively decorated body of the deity, daily smelling the incense and flowers offered to the deity, daily massaging the body of the Lord with fragrant oils and dressing the Lord, making the garlands, sewing the clothes, or cooking the food offered to him, the devotee meditates steadily on God. The yogi achieves one-pointedness of mind by shutting down the senses; the devotee, by engaging all of them. As a result, his mind and sense become more and more purified (*anartha-nivṛtti*), and in time the presence of God in the *arcā-mūrti* becomes fully manifest to him.

The idea that a devotee in the liberated, spiritually perfect state has spiritual senses is a corollary of the Vaiṣṇava concept of a personal God. If God is a person possessing spiritual form, attributes, and qualities, the only way of apprehending and appreciating these features is through senses capable of doing so. Moreover, if the eternal dharma of the soul is to serve God, the soul must have the instruments, i.e., the senses, required to render that service. Finally, God manifests the richness of his supremely personal nature by sustaining different kinds of relationships with his innumerable devotees, who serve him variously as their master, friend, child, husband, or lover. The *Caitanya-caritāmṛta* describes how the bliss of both Kṛṣṇa and his devotees increases perpetually in these reciprocal exchanges of love.[39] In this way Kṛṣṇa eternally enjoys relationships in his own transcendental society. The concept of Kṛṣṇa is preeminently a social conception of God: his spiritual form and senses are the media for his interactions with others — the liberated *jīvas* — who are similarly endowed.

Therefore it is held that the *jīva* is intrinsically endowed with senses. If, however, as sometimes happens, a *jīva* should become envious of the Lord and no longer desire to serve him, then the senses of the *jīva* develop materially. He is thrown into the external energy, where it is possible to forget God, and is covered by the illusion of separation. Because he now directs his senses to secure his own enjoyment (instead of God's), his senses are "material," and because he lays claim to the object of the senses, as actually or potentially his for possessing and enjoying, the sense-objects also appear as "matter," as alienated from their real proprietor, God. Owing to the systematic misuse of his senses, God disappears from his sight, and he now sees only matter.

I have already described the *jīva* in this state as being on the plane of *karma*. If after much suffering in many births, the *jīva* comes to realize that the cause of his suffering is his materialistic, sensual life, he may embark on a program to negate the senses and renounce their objects. This is the plane of the *jñānī*. He errs, from a devotee's point of view, in thinking that suffering is due to senses as such rather than to the misuse of them. But having experienced his body, mind, and senses as suffering, he wants to be rid of them altogether. But so long as the *jñānī* suppresses his mind and senses and does not purify them, he is no more capable than the *karmī* of perceiving the personal feature of God.

Neither enjoying nor renouncing the senses and their objects, the bhakta engages both in the service of the Lord. And both, being linked through service to God, become cleansed of illusion and are thus transformed into spirit. *Bhagavad Gītā* 4.24 states that what is offered to the supreme, the agent who offers, and the act of offering itself all become, in that act, spiritual (*brahman*). Prabhupāda explains this spiritualizing process in his comments on that text:

> The materially absorbed conditioned soul can be cured by Kṛṣṇa consciousness as set forth here in the *Gītā*. This process is generally known as *yajña*, or activities (sacrifices) simply meant for the satisfaction of Viṣṇu or Kṛṣṇa. The more the activities of the material world are performed in Kṛṣṇa consciousness, or for Viṣṇu alone, the more the atmosphere becomes spiritualized by complete absorption. Brahman means spiritual. The Lord is spiritual, and the rays of His transcendental body are called *brahmajyoti*, His spiritual effulgence. Everything that exists is situated in that *brahmajyoti*, but when the *jyoti* is covered by illusion (*māyā*) or sense gratification, it is called material. This material veil can be removed at once by Kṛṣṇa consciousness; thus the offering for the sake of Kṛṣṇa consciousness, the consuming agent of such an offering or contribution, the

process of consumption, the contributor, and the result are — all combined together — Brahman, or the Absolute Truth. The Absolute Truth covered by *māyā* is called matter. Matter dovetailed for the cause of the Absolute Truth regains its spiritual quality. Kṛṣṇa consciousness is the process of converting the illusory consciousness into Brahman, or the Supreme.[40]

The devotional practice of *arcanā* is a highly effective way of utilizing matter in the cause of the Absolute Truth. Through it the senses of the devotee become purified, and when they are completely restored the devotee is capable of again associating with God in full consciousness. By becoming wholly absorbed in the service of the Deity, the devotee enters into his eternal life. Although he remains on earth, he is already in the kingdom of God, and his devotional acts are karmaless. Just as the spiritual form the devotee serves is the form of One who has no form, so his service is action that is not action. And his liberation occurs automatically, as a sort of accidental by-product.

The abundance of concrete sensual detail that characterizes the descriptions of God in Vaiṣṇava literature and the images of God installed in Vaiṣṇava temples, of course, invites misunderstanding. That is why Rūpa Gōsvāmī warns us, quoting the *Padma Purāṇa*, that the transcendental nature of the name, form, qualities, and pastimes of Kṛṣṇa cannot be apprehended by our materially contaminated senses; only to the senses purified by devotional service does the transcendental nature of the Lord's name, etc., become manifest.[41] A person with unpurified senses will surely see the *arcā-mūrti* as a lifeless statue, just as he is sure to understand the *līlā* of Rādhā and Kṛṣṇa in the light of mundane sexual affairs. Yet it is this very explicit presentation of spiritual richness and variety, this transcendental sensuousness, that gives spiritual objects to the senses of the devotee and makes possible the purification of the senses.

According to this account, then, it is wrong, on the one hand, to take the descriptions of God or the image of God as symbol or metaphor. On the other hand, it is equally wrong to understand them materially. In that case, what do words like *form, blue, garland, flute*, and so on, really mean when referred to God? Either they are literal, or they are not.

One answer is to say that the *literal* meaning of these terms obtains when they apply to God. Our worldly experience does not reveal to us the literal meaning. God and the kingdom of God, after all, constitute the real and original world, while this world is its imitation and reflection. Yet God is able to manifest himself within this world in the

The great chariot procession (*ratha-yātrā*) organized by the Hare Krishna movement moving down the streets of New York City. Photo courtesy of ISKCON.

form of words and images, and by concentrating one's mind and senses on the words that describe God and on the images that depict God, the mind and senses gradually become purified, and then one can at last apprehend the literal meaning.

This revelation is said to take place specifically in the stage of devotional development called *bhāva*.[42] In the stage of *bhāva* the devotee realizes that God and his name, his image, or his description are nondifferent. In this experience, the gap between the name and the named, the representation and the represented object, is transcended. The identity between word and object constitutes an immediacy of apprehension for which the term *literal* hardly serves.

Thus, with respect to the worship of the image of God in the temple, *darśana* as theory and *darśana* as practice reinforce each other. The theology that establishes God as a person endowed with specific form, qualities, and attributes of a transcendental nature allows for the concrete representation of God's own image in the temple. By the service of this image, the server develops the purified, spiritual instruments — mind and senses — capable of apprehending the transcendental nature of God's form, qualities, and attributes, so that God is seen directly in his image, through God-saturated senses. This is *darśana* according to Diana Eck's apt description: "sacred perception," "the ability truly to see the divine image."

Dancing Vēlār *cāmiyāṭi* possessed by the gods Iruḷappacāmi and Karuppucāmi. Velar Street, Arappalaiyam, Madurai District, Tamilnadu. Photo by Stephen Inglis.

5

Possession and Pottery: Serving the Divine in a South Indian Community

Stephen Inglis

DURING AN EXTENDED stay in Tamilnadu a few years ago, I was joined for a time by friends from North America. Their first walk through a potter's neighborhood was accompanied not by the whir of the wheel or thump of the clay beater, but by feverish drumming. Instead of a few people working or chatting in the twilight, a large crowd was packed into a narrow street, with all eyes turned toward a group of wild-eyed men wearing flamboyant costumes and waving large rusty knives. The crowd parted as the men swayed unsteadily.

Being seasoned tourists, my friends enthusiastically pressed forward for a better camera angle, yet I couldn't help thinking about the adverse reactions of earlier foreign observers in south India. For many missionaries and administrators, to whom we owe much information about religion and social life in this region, the spectacle of people such as these, possessed by their local deities, represented a "barbarous debauch" or "orgy."[1] Rituals involving possession, often accompanied by blood sacrifice and spectacular forms of aceticism, became a trump card in efforts to distinguish so-called Dravidian from Aryan cultural characteristics as well as "devil worship" or "demonolatry" from Brahmanical Hinduism and its philosophical traditions.[2]

Since the middle of this century, much has been written about possession as a feature of south Indian religious and social life.[3] Recent accounts, compared with those of early observers, are based on closer observation of the phenomenon and develop perspectives less weighted with historical or theological polemics. Contemporary studies of possession within the context of a description of cultural life in a particular caste or community are of special interest. Much study to date has tended toward a psychological or sociological interpretation of possession experiences. For example, typically a researcher may interpret possession as illness or as the expression of a particular social category or structure but neglect the role of hereditary specialists and the wider cultural framework of possession rituals.[4]

The Vēḷār potters of Madurai District in Tamilnadu are a community with an active tradition of possession rituals and are acknowledged possession "specialists" in their region.[5] The Vēḷār also create clay images for installation at local temples and conduct worship to the deities represented by those images. This chapter offers a brief description of these community responsibilities. It probes the nature of the affinity between becoming possessed by a deity and creating its image in clay, and suggests a basis for the generally perceived fitness of the Vēḷār to perform these tasks. The chapter concludes with comments on the special relationship between the Vēḷār and the deities to whom they give form through both images and their own bodies.

Some turn-of-the-century writers assumed that incidents of possession they had observed were spontaneous and could be performed by anyone attending a festival.[6] This was only one aspect of the characterization of Hinduism beyond the strict domain of the Brahmin priesthood as a religion with little specialization and few coherent traditions.[7] The dynamics of possession rituals have proved more complex and structured than was suggested by these accounts. Possession rituals among various Tamil communities show an extraordinary variety of forms and meanings. It will therefore be useful to locate Vēḷār rituals of possession among those general types which have been described for south India.

First, in the case of the Vēḷār we are dealing with examples of spirit possession rather than with shamanism; that is, the human is a receptacle for the spirits rather than the master of them. In terms of the dichotomy drawn by I. M. Lewis, all varieties of possession are viewed by a large majority of south Indians as the divine flowing downward rather than as the specialist reaching upward.[8]

Second, the possession we are here referring to involves spirit mediumship (in the sense used by Peter Claus),[9] the legitimate, solicited, and controlled possession of a specialist by a deity within the context of a specific ritual. It contrasts with the many forms of possession in south India which involve unexpected and unwanted intrusions by ghosts or demons, situations which create trouble and require exorcism.

Third, this form of possession is a ritual institution which is meaningful within the context of traditional caste or community obligations and privileges. The name for this institution and its officers in the Madurai area is *cāmiyāṭi* ("god dancer").[10] These must be distinguished from both individuals who become possessed in the course of carrying out personal vow fulfillment (*nērttikaṭaṉ*) and professional possession specialists usually called *kōṭaṅki* who ply the trade of soothsaying in a market or other public place for a fee.[11]

The Cāmiyāṭi

The institution of *cāmiyāṭi* is found in various forms throughout Tamilnadu, but is particularly well known to students of south Indian religion through descriptions of its occurrence in the southern districts.[12] It has been said that the possessed dance is the "central focus"[13] of a festival or "necessary for any festival"[14] and most observers agree that it gives testimony to the vitality of village cults by demonstrating the presence of the deity. The best known function of the *cāmiyāṭi* is to become possessed and to serve as a temporary mouthpiece for a deity during festivals. On these occasions devotees may lay their problems before the deity and receive advice and reassurance (*kuṟi collutal*). The *cāmiyāṭi* may also contribute to the festival by transporting materials to be used in the *pūjās* and by generally assisting during the proceedings. The ascetic feats performed by the Vēḷār *cāmiyāṭi*, such as walking on hot coals (*pūkkuḻi iṟuṅkutal*), attest to the power of the deity to protect the *cāmiyāṭi* from pain or injury.[15]

With the date fixed for a festival, the *cāmiyāṭi* prepares for participation by performing austerities for days or weeks preceding the event.[16] Among the Vēḷār, the duration and rigor of these observances vary according to the piety of the individual and the importance of the festival; but they invariably involve the restriction of social interaction, including avoidance of life cycle ceremonies and especially the pollution of birth, menstruation, and death. Sexual activity is avoided and diet restricted to vegetarian foods. For weeks before a festival a *cāmiyāṭi* may wear only a single cloth and must sleep on the floor rather than on a cot. All these measures are thought to increase the purity of the individual, making him a suitable vessel for the divine and enabling him to withstand the mental rigors of possession.[17]

Shortly before the phase of a festival in which possession is to take place, the *cāmiyāṭi* bathes, prepares his body, and dresses. The outfit includes a body cloth (*vēṣṭi*) and the cooling application of sandalwood paste and ash to the upper body and arms. "Cooling" substances counteract the effects of contact with local deities, which are almost invariably feverishly "heating."[18] A flower garland is worn as an ornament and a silver bangle (*kāppu*) is placed on the upper arm or wrist to bind the participant symbolically within the ritual sequence until its completion.

Wearing this basic outfit the *cāmiyāṭi* may serve as a vessel for any one of a number of local deities; however, more elaborate costumes are often assembled, and these are inherited by succeeding generations along with the right to become possessed by a particular deity. Such costumes include clothing, ornaments, and accoutrements which are considered appropriate to the deity being hosted. The deity is thought to feel pleased by this; and, for the devotees, the costume adds visual impact to the apprehension of the divine presence. A costume may include a sash (*kaccai*), shorts (*caṭṭi*) and leggings (*callaṭum*), an elaborate turban (*irupāl*), and an appliqué hat (*kullā*). The fearsome weapon of a local deity is a crucial part of the dress of a *cāmiyāṭi* whether a staff, iron bar, or billhook (*aruvāḷ*). It is unusual today for more than three of four deities to possess *cāmiyāṭis* during a single festival, but photos taken during the 1920s and 1930s and treasured in Vēḷār homes show groups of twenty-one *cāmiyāṭis* at important temples, stiff in their costumes and bristling with weapons. These twenty-one represent the full complement of deities traditionally worshiped at local temples in the southern region of Tamilnadu.

Once prepared and dressed at a community lineage shrine, the Vēḷār *cāmiyāṭis* are brought by festival priests and officials into the crowded streets. It is from there, in the heart of their own community's place of residence, that they will accompany a procession to the temple of the deity being honored. As they merge with the crowd they begin to grimace and breathe in short deep gasps. The playing of the hired musicians reaches a crescendo. With arms clasped and outstretched, the muscles of the *cāmiyāṭis* tense and stiffen as they become possessed. People fall back to avoid their often erratic movements. As it is described in Tamil, "the god descends" (*cāmi iraṅkutal*). Now the box containing the *pūjā* materials is hoisted on to the head of one of the *cāmiyāṭis* and the procession moves off, the *cāmiyāṭis* in the lead, "dancing" with short hopping steps. In some cases they carry pots of holy water or milk (*karakam, pālkuṭam*) to be used in the *pūjās*. Balanced on their heads, these may spill but are never known to empty. In other cases large new clay pots (*tāḻi*) may be carried in a smiliar manner and are used for cooking the festival food (*poṅkal*) which is distributed to devotees.

The procession halts at each house in the Vēḷār street, where mature married women (*cumaṅkali*) make an offering of fruit or some coins and, in many cases, bathe the feet of the *cāmiyāṭis* with water drawn from the river. The *cāmiyāṭis* adorn the foreheads of the devotees with holy ash (*vipūti*), often showering the worshipers from some distance. It is at this point that family members may ask for counsel concerning problems such as illness, community conflict, or the family budget.

The deity, speaking through the *cāmiyāṭis*, offers explanations, proposes solutions, and demands penances, sometimes scolding and at other times reassuring.

The procession leaves the Vēḷār street and continues until it reaches the temple of the deity. Here the *cāmiyāṭis* may interact with a larger group of local people from various communities. Once the images are bathed and adorned, the *cāmiyāṭis* may give up their state of possession to relax, undress, and become involved in other priestly duties. During the festival, which usually lasts several days, the *cāmiyāṭis* may again be required to host the deities for special events, but often with somewhat less fanfare than is characteristic of the initial procession. At the conclusion of the festival, the *cāmiyāṭis* accompany the *pūjā* materials back to the Vēḷār street.

For the Vēḷār, the participation of the *cāmiyāṭis* in a festival is a communal experience, and throughout the possession the involvement of the devotees is intense. The initial descent of the deity is accompanied by general cheering and cries of "*kōvinta*" and "*arō hara*" while women salute the procession with high-pitched trilling from lanes and rooftops.[19] Along the route of the procession and later at the temple, devotees occasionally become caught up in the experience of the deity's presence to the extent that they fall momentarily into a possessed state themselves, stiffening or reeling backwards into the arms of friends or relatives.[20] The period of possession, that is, of the manifestation of the deity, is one of extreme tension and rare excitement.

The institution of *cāmiyāṭi* is significant for numerous social groups who participate in a festival. A brief review of these groups will help to outline the social dynamics of this form of possession and help us to link possession with other community privileges and responsibilities.

The group that must be discussed in some detail is the lineage. Among the Vēḷār, the rights to serve a deity as *cāmiyāṭi* are rigorously controlled by patrilineal descent groups, as are indeed the rights to supply images and even pottery. Moreover the rituals of possession in which members of a lineage participate as *cāmiyāṭis* are directed exclusively toward the deities of their particular lineage temple and most importantly toward their lineage deity (*kula teyvam*). The major deities of the potter lineages, as well as of many other communities in the region, are powerful local protectors like Karuppucāmi, Muttaiyācāmi, and Cōṇaicāmi.[21]

Vēḷār not only act as *cāmiyāṭis* at the annual festivals of these deities, but also serve as priests (*pūcāri*), often on a more regular basis.

As major ritual specialists for local-level worship in the Madurai region, virtually all male Vēḷār perform priestly functions at one or more temples. Most Vēḷār men who live close to Madurai city are mill workers, laborers, or pot makers, and for these, priestly duties are a part-time responsibility undertaken during particular festivals or in certain years according to the hereditary allocation of rights in their lineages. The roles of *cāmiyāṭi* and *pūcāri* in local temples are integrated. In some cases a *pūcāri* also acts as *cāmiyāṭi* while in others, two sections of a lineage share the rights permanently or exchange them on an annual basis. The identification by Dumont of possession as "an institutionalized function complementing priesthood"[22] is fully applicable to the Vēḷār situation. The *pūcāri* makes the offerings to the deity on behalf of the devotees, and the *cāmiyāṭi* relays the advice and commands of the deity to those devotees.

The rights to act as *cāmiyāṭi* are passed down within the Vēḷār lineages, usually from father to son, grandson, or nephew, or are exchanged between brothers. Some of the elaborate "succession" procedures described by Dumont,[23] by which the deity is thought to accept his *cāmiyāṭi*, are known to the Vēḷār; but where these have been followed, it is clear that the purpose is to confirm the suitability of the hereditary designate rather than to select a replacement. It seems apparent that the Vēḷār *cāmiyāṭi* holds his position by virtue of an inherited right and the capabilities of his community as a whole rather than because of personal qualities of "devotion" or a particular mental disposition, as is often described.[24]

The ritual of the *cāmiyāṭi* is significant to the lineage because it dramatizes its claim to rights at a particular lineage temple and confirms the deity's acceptance of those rights. These rights involve access to temple lands (*māṉiyam*), harvest shares and gifts - assets which together constitute a major part of the annual income of many Vēḷār families. The rights often include control of rituals at other temples in the vicinity of the core temple.

The importance of the *cāmiyāṭi* as an expression of the vital and ongoing nature of a local cult and group rights to certain resources became aparent when members of a Vēḷār lineage recently staged an elaborate temple festival, reviving the role of *cāmiyāṭi* after a forty year lapse. The celebration of this festival then became part of the evidence presented during a court case in which Vēḷār fought with another community for control of the temple property.

The institution of *cāmiyāṭi* is significant for the Vēḷār community as a whole because it promotes a sense of solidarity in an atmosphere of devotion. Positions of authority and responsibility are reiterated and confirmed before the deity and the entire community. It is an occasion when marriage allies are called to contribute, one in which people not only worship the deity but acknowledge the right of their community to carry forward this special service to the divine and to all those who worship the deity. The *cāmiyāṭi*, by visiting each Vēḷār community house in turn during the initial part of the procession, not only provides each family with the opportunity to consult the deity, but also symbolically traces a divine path through the community residence area.

The significance of the Vēḷār rituals of possession to a wider group of south Indian communities lies in the fact that the deities which Vēḷār lineages identify as their *kula teyvam* may also be lineage deities for other communities. Members of a wide range of landlord, farmer, and service communities participate in the deity's festival. Just as Vēḷār priests serve these communities in many local temples, so the Vēḷār *cāmiyāṭis* demonstrate the vitality of the deity's presence to a wide group of devotees. The possession of specialists, such as the Vēḷār, during major festivals at local temples in the Madurai is one means by which a cult involving a cross-section of local communities lays claim to legitimacy, by which patrons of these temples, often Tēvar or Veḷḷāḷar land owners, exercise their authority, and by which communities other than the Vēḷār also claim privileges. Local communities recognize the skills of the Vēḷār *cāmiyāṭis* in manifesting deities as part of an overall set of rights and privileges.

Although *cāmiyāṭi* is an institution found among many communities in Tamilnadu, it is perhaps nowhere as well developed and specialized as among the Vēḷār in the southern districts. When studying such a community of specialists, it is important to look at other aspects of the life of that community which complement that role. We will thus turn to the making of clay images, another specialty of the Vēḷār.

Image Maker

In contrast to possession rituals, which attracted a great deal of interest, the use of clay images in local level worship in south India received little notice from early foreign observers. Because rural temples often appear to be abandoned, with their images exposed and deteriorating, some concluded that local deities are "seldom represented in Indian art"[25] and are "never worshipped in our sense of the word."[26] Even when clay images were unavoidably imposing, as in the central and southern districts of Tamilnadu where they may be over twenty feet tall,[27] a foreign observer, such as George Birdwood, could only regard the "monstrous swami forms of the Dravidian races"[28] as crude and misguided deviations from the classical image-making tradition.[29] Despite the fact that clay images remain one of the crucial elements in local ritual throughout much of south India, very little has yet been written about their use and meaning.

As part of their traditional service to local temples in the Madurai area, the Vēḷār are required to provide images of the local deities. These are hollow images modeled by hand, dried, fired, and then painted. Clay images are always festival images made for specific occasions and under arrangement with the patrons of particular temples. Although the Vēḷār know the approximate dates on which they will begin work on images for various temples under their care during an annual cycle, the announcement of the date of a festival is made by a messenger from the temple's patrons. He brings a detailed request and small gifts to the Vēḷār's yard as well as a handful of earth (*piṭiman̲*) from the temple floor to mix with the modeling clay.

The images are made over a three- or four-week period. Among the major deities, those which are worshiped at the temple are often modeled in life-size, while others are made smaller. An entourage of votive offerings, each specifically commissioned by individual devotees from the village at which the temple is located, are made to accompany the main images to their temple. These include figures of children, body parts, or animals, each representing a personal plea or bargain with the deity to overcome infertility or illness, or to recover something lost or stolen. Field workers commission small images of snakes, scorpions, or stinging ants from which they request the deity's protection. Most common in the Madurai region are figures of horses and bulls (and occasionally elephants, lions, or camels) which are offered as mounts to the equestrian deities which are invariably the main focus of the local cults.

As the appointed hour of the festival procession approaches, the Vēḷār complete the final preparation of the images, dressing them in appropriate clothing and expertly tying the larger figures onto palanquins or fitting them with carrying poles. Just before the arrival of the patrons and devotees, the Vēḷār modelers and their relatives offer a personal *pūjā* to the images in their lineage shrine, acknowledging the assistance of their family deity in enabling them to complete the work. This accomplished, all the images are moved to an open space on the potter's street.

Soon the patrons and devotees from other communities in the host village (where the temple is located) arrive amid a fanfare of music and the explosion of fireworks. From this point events move quickly. With all assembled, the Vēḷār *pūcāris* offer the initial full *pūjā* to the images. It is at this stage that the ceremony of "opening the eyes," well-known in image consecration throughout South Asia, often takes place.[30] The Vēḷār touch the bloodied toe of a cock to the eyes of the image in their version of a ritual of eye opening (*kaṇtiṟattal*).[31] At this moment of great intensity the deity "descends." People in the crowd chant rhythmically, often emitting a special cry associated with the deity being worshiped. The images are hoisted on to the shoulders and heads of male devotees, and a grand procession sets out through the Vēḷār street and away to the host village, sometimes as far off as ten or twelve kilometers. All along the way people worship and pay their respect. Upon completion of the journey, the images are worshiped on the village square (*mantai*) and are then moved to the temple or temples at which they are installed. At each point, Vēḷār priests supervise the worship. For the duration of the festival the stone images which are permanently installed in the local temples take a second place to the brightly painted and flower bedecked clay images. Soon after the festival, however, the prominently placed clay forms begin to fall apart.

Some clay images are destroyed at the conclusion of the festival, while others crumble long before they are replaced by a new image the following year. Some survive for years and are simply moved to the back of the temple as new ones take their places. Whatever the material life of an image, after the conclusion of the festival it is never again the exclusive locus of divinity. Any subsequent worship directed toward the image honors only the place where the deity resides, with the hope that it might be encouraged to take notice of a plea.

The rights to provide images, like those to be a *cāmiyāṭi*, are exclusive and hereditary functions of a Vēḷār lineage.[32] The ritual of clay image procession and installation during a festival provides much the same benefits to the Vēḷār lineage, to the Vēḷār community as a whole, and to the patrons and devotees of other castes as the ritual of the *cāmiyāṭi* described above. The image, for the few days that it becomes the focus of a cult, calls attention to the complex social arrangements by which diverse groups cooperate in order to receive protection by a powerful deity. The successful processing of the image is a public testament that each group has played its part according to traditional rights and that the deity approves.

Divine Vessels

By focusing on correspondences between the functions of the possessed dancer and the maker of clay images in the Vēḷār community, one can identify symbolic associations between the two ritual specialties. Both the hereditarily sanctioned body of the *cāmiyāṭi* and the clay image are viewed as indispensable vessels which are inhabited by the deity during his festival. In each case an otherwise ephemeral being is given a temporary locus in which to manifest itself.

Both the *cāmiyāṭi* and the image are carefully prepared for their role by purification rituals, are adorned, and are dressed in the clothing of the deity. Each vessel is subject to a climatic "descent" of the deity. Both are offered worship as they are processed from the highly exclusive shrine of a Vēḷār lineage to a comparatively public place in a local temple. Each is, in its own way, an *utsava mūrti*[33] of a cult, a highly charged mobile carrier of the deity's presence. In some cases, limited now to the more isolated areas of Vēḷār service, the functions of the *cāmiyāṭi* and image actually merge as a Vēḷār carries the image from his workplace to the temple. The devotees worship at the feet of the Vēḷār who becomes possessed by the deity whose image he carries.

However, at the temple both the *cāmiyāṭi* and the clay image gradually lose the force of their divine contents, the *cāmiyāṭi* reverting to mortal consciousness and mundane duties (such as cooking or cleaning up) and the clay image beginning the inevitable process of deterioration. As the festival concludes, worship is directed back toward the permanent stone images, which then receive whatever worship may be offered until the next festival. The stone image marks the place of residence of the deity, while the clay image signals its *presence*.

The *cāmiyāṭi* and the clay image are essentially identical. Both are impermanent, and this is an integral part of their nature as well as a crucial aspect of their meaning. By virtue of its being made of clay, the image is bound to disintegrate and to be reconstituted. By virtue of being a human being, with human needs and social responsibilities, the *cāmiyāṭi* (unlike the permanently god-possessed saint or god-conscious Brahmin) is also a temporary vessel of the divine, destined to be reactivated only periodically throughout a lifetime of service. The potency of the religious role of the Vēḷār lies in impermanence and in the potential for the deterioration, replacement and reactivation of their services to the deities. An apparent discontinuity, break, and lull are crucial to a reconstitution. The widely noted "abandoned look" of south Indian local shrines can thus be understood as a feature of design rather than simply as a result of neglect.

The impermanence of these embodiments becomes more meaningful when projected against more general beliefs current in Tamilnadu about the nature of life and creation.[34] Since ancient times life has been apprehended as a "closed circuit" with new life growing only from the destruction or transformation of the old. Creation, according to this first concept, is an ongoing, ever-renewing process, matter being continuously remoulded out of the remains of a former creation. There could hardly be a more dramatic illustration of this conception than in the work of the Vēḷār which exemplifies the sacred re-creation of form from the remains of what has been broken and discarded.

Those deities which are worshiped in the forms of the *cāmiyāṭi* and clay images are directly responsible for the creative process and the immediate problems of life and death. These deities determine fertility both in humans and in crops. They are called upon for protection, but their vigil can be assured only by constant renewal. The cyclical and often intermittent nature of the worship offered to them is integrally related to notions about the role they play.

Because of their specialized responsibilities in serving the local deities by serving as *cāmiyāṭis* and image makers, the Vēḷār are deeply involved in the process of creativity, and this in turn exposes them to extreme ritual pollution. This leads to a second important concept. In Tamilnadu the creative act is always one of pain, vulnerability, and danger, and any creation exposes those involved to the deterioration that preceded it and that will inevitably follow. The Vēḷār often speak of being involved in both birth and death through their work. This conception lies at the root of the social stigma which afflicts all craftspeople in south India and especially potters, for whom the creative cycle is collapsed into a relatively short temporal sequence. The new clay pot, purest of all ritual objects, quickly becomes the used pot, the archetypal symbol of impurity. When the deity departs from either the human (*cāmiyāṭi*) or earthen (image) vessel, this vessel is drained and at least symbolically destroyed so that the renewed vessel can be re-created. The Vēḷār are knowledgeable about the ambivalent process of creativity and are recognized as having an unusual ability to absorb the pollution generated. The specialized skills of a community like the Vēḷār derive not only from their ability to create but also from their ability to survive the dual nature of the creative process.

The introduction of a third concept will help us to appreciate the special nature of the relationship between the Vēḷār and the local deities. In all sacred matters the line between control and chaos is very fine. The local deities are thought to ride throughout their territory each night, and any contact with them while they are making their nocturnal rounds would be extremely dangerous and probably fatal. It is only under correct ritual conditions and through the agency of an appropriate vessel that the deity may safely appear and be approached. Such conditions can be arranged only periodically and require great care.

The local deities are most active on the boundary of the village. They repel intruders, fight evil forces, and live in constant contact with darkness and pain. They also straddle the boundary between life and death; they are masters of the ambivalent power over the creative cycle.

The Vēḷār believe that their work involves a similar dilemma. It has been suggested that south Indian craftspeople derive their sacred power from their medial position between nature and society.[35] The Vēḷār themselves express the idea that they turn natural materials into useful cultural products which then return to an unformed state. The pursuit of this work necessitates a constant passage across a boundary, one with many parallels to that between chaos and control.

A special affinity between the Vēḷār and local deities is acknowledged by the other communities among whom the Vēḷār live. This is evident since a Vēḷār may be called to assist when another community finds a deity too powerful for its own priest to handle.[36] The Vēḷār of the Madurai area have always used this affinity to their advantage during disputes with patrons of more numerous and powerful communities. Although the Vēḷār own no land and can be replaced by other potters (as happens in some cases), a careful patron will hesitate to unleash the potentially terrifying consequences of a situation where a local deity finds no appropriate vessel in which to receive honor and is unsatisfied with the medium, priest or craftsman who offers service.

The Vēḷār through their specialized community traditions, are masters of impermanence. Their own skills of creativity allow them to deal directly with the deities who control creativity in a way which few other humans could. They know how to prepare not only a vessel that can be filled but also one that can be emptied. Their special skills prepare the way for the reconstitution of new life, a new crop, the birth of a child, and prosperity.

In the opinion of the Vēḷār, the Brahmanical gods, who are responsible for the cosmos, may well be content with worship directed toward images made of permanent materials — worship mediated by men whose skills lie in exclusive knowledge of ancient phrases and whose ritual purity divides them from other humans. On the other hand,

Vēlār priests preparing an image of Coṇaicāmi for procession. Velar Street, Arappalaiyam, Madurai District, Tamilnadu. Photo by Stephen Inglis.

those deities who direct daily matters, the bloody and painful business of birth, the necessity of growth and the danger of evil, demand a vessel whose fragile nature reminds all of the immediacy of their problems and responsibilities. This vessel must be a living, breathing body which can convey the message in the streets.

This chapter has suggested some parallels in the logic of possession and image making as elements in a cultural pattern. This type of description and analysis adds another dimension to investigations limited to the sociological and psychological conditions of possession. Those who study rituals of possession in south India must attempt to understand the cultural context in which possession has meaning. The ways in which a community of possession specialists integrates this responsibility with their other traditional skills in the service of the divine have provided a useful focus for exploring that context.

Devotees of Murukaṉ carrying *kāvaṭi* (pole yoked to the shoulders for bearing offerings) to the Paḻaṉi Temple from Madurai, Tamilnadu.

6

God's Forceful Call: Possession as a Divine Strategy

Manuel Moreno[1]

AMONG THE VARIOUS schools of sociological thought which have been invoked in studies of the nature of Hindu gods, two appear to be widely influential in the contemporary scene. One is structural and is based on the writings of Dumont,[2] the other is "processual" and derives from the ethnosociological approach of Marriott and Inden.[3] From the structuralist point of view, gods are symbols of social realities, metaphors for human relationships. The divine attributes and the relationships of gods vis-à-vis other gods are treated as sources of information about the social order, and religion is viewed as the privileged domain wherein men gain insights into this order by homological inferences. Gods reflect the structure of society, and for this reason they are useful to the sociologist. Stripped of their bodily personalities, gods become disembodied residents of the Hindu universe, fixed homologies of structural positions of humans vis-à-vis other humans. The world of gods and the world of men are construed as separate domains, one abstract, the other concrete; and they come in contact only through a kind of intellectualized mediation. In the processual view, gods are understood to be persons, corporeal residents of the Hindu world, who are related among themselves and with humans by shared and exchanged bodily substances. Gods have personal biographies, particularized embodiments, bodily functions, and specialized relations to men. As persons, the gods' identities are not permanently fixed; to the contrary, they are fluid and transformable by their active involvement in transactions with other gods and with humans.

My research in the Koṅku region of Tamilnadu shows that the attitude of the Koṅku Tamils toward their gods is largely compatible with the view of Marriott and Inden — gods are considered to be divine persons. As divine beings, gods are thought to be higher, more powerful and generous than humans, and endowed with more refined substances. However, as persons, gods are also deemed to have bodies permeated with vital fluids (*rasa*) and humors (*dōṣa*),[4] to possess rights of residence over particular places,[5] and to be subject to the disturbing effects of "time" (*kāla*).

This personalistic view is crucial to an understanding of established patterns of worship, both at the individual and at the collective level. At both levels we can observe the dynamics of a mutually rewarding reciprocity between divine and human persons, carried out by exchanges of substances which are thought to be restorative and life-enhancing. I have analyzed reciprocal exchanges at the collective level elsewhere;[6] thus, I shall concentrate here on the individual dimension of worship.

Why do humans worship divine persons? During my research I received three types of explanations from my informants, which I shall briefly summarize. (1) Any human resident of the Hindu world may often find himself in an undesirable state caused by imbalances, deficiencies, or excesses of bodily substances, or by the influence of astral bodies, among other prominent causes. Various strategies are then available to him to ameliorate this situation. The worship of a god is a common procedure whereby Tamil Hindus may request a god to grant "that which is needed" (*vēṇṭutal*) to remove the unwanted condition. (2) Once the affliction is removed, the devotee may again worshipfully approach the god to "repay the debt" (*nērttikkaṭan̲*) contracted with the deity, thus restoring to the god part of his depleted power. (3) Sometimes a devotee may worship a "chosen god" (*iṣṭa teyvam*) merely for "love" (*an̲pu*) and "devotion" (*bhakti*), and this personal bondage then becomes the channel for exchanges of very subtle substances between the devotee, who becomes a "slave" (*aṭimai*), and the god, who also becomes dependent on the devotee's services.

Just as humans need gods as sources of relief and salubrious gifts, gods also require humans to relieve their deficient states, for they too must maintain or refurnish their well-being. This sort of complementarity between gods and humans is well-attested by devotees' statements, as well as by devotional literary sources. The needs of the gods are often disguised in poetic idioms of "hunger," "thirst," "need for play," for "shelter" and "love," among others.[7] Devotees also often say that a particular god is "overheated" or "sleepy" or "anxious." Furthermore, the needs of the gods are often experienced *by* devotees, and their behavior not infrequently manifests this experience.

Sometimes gods seem to depend entirely on the actions of devotees. For instance, a stone of unusual features may be "casually" found in the landscape of a town, village, fields, or forest. It may be anointed with special oils, marked with various colored substances, nurtured with offerings of various kinds of food, protected with burning lamps, and decorated with garlands of flowers. As the "stone" changes its visible appearance, it begins to accumulate power, which the devotee may use for his own benefit. This power is usually active for as long as the worship of the "stone" persists. In such cases a god is brought out, nurtured, and kept alive by the devotee's actions.

Gods have, however, other forceful ways to demand "that which [they] need" (*vēṇṭutal*) and which is rightfully their due (*nērttikkaṭaṉ*). In such contexts, the complementary exchanges solicited by the gods are not usually sought by devotees; gods take the initiative. When the gods thus call,[8] the immediate consequences are always unsettling for humans and at times dangerous, even lethal, if the call is not promptly recognized and acted upon. Even when the gods seek "love" and affective "devotion," their call may be accompanied by extraordinary trials of endurance.

I present here two accounts of forceful calls by gods upon human devotees. The events related here took place in localities of the Koṅku region of Tamilnadu. The first account relates how the goddess Kāḷi (locally known as Kāḷiyattā) visited a family and demanded to be worshiped in a temple dedicated to her. The family complied with the goddess's request, but did not at first recognize her demand. A young daughter of this family, an only child, was taken by the goddess as soon as the temple was completed. The second account relates the case of a girl who was possessed by the god Murukaṉ at a tender age; the god requested that she become his "slave" (*aṭimai*). In exchange for her services, Murukaṉ gave the girl extraordinary powers to heal (*cavukkiyam koṭuttal*) and to predict the future (*kaṇṇakku colvatu*). This pact was initially sealed with a request by the god that the girl engage in a long fast. The pact has remained in effect ever since, with the god frequently demanding that the girl fast and perform difficult tasks.

Case 1: The Call of Kāḷi

Kantacāmi (a pseudonym), a rich Kavuṇṭar landowner (the leading caste of Koṅku),[9] migrated to a southern Koṅku town from his neighboring village some twenty years ago. He built a substantial house at the outskirts of the town, in an area where other rich Kavuṇṭar farmers seeking the comforts of the urban center were settling in increasing numbers. Previously, that area had been a coconut grove and served as a dwelling for the goddess Kāḷi, who likes to reside in such places. After a number of years, the place came to be known as *Kavuṇṭaṉ tōppu*, "the grove of the Kavuṇṭars," taking its name from the caste appellation of the newcomers. A Siddha hospital[10] was built soon after; the police headquarters moved there; banks, mills and their personnel also settled in that place, extending the boundaries of the town to the distant railway station. There was no temple in that area, only a half forgotten *triśula* (Kāḷi's visible form) and a stone for offerings, which received only very infrequent worship. The dwellers of the *Kavuṇṭaṉ tōppu* went to the numerous temples of the town to worship, and nobody ever thought of building a temple in the area. Nobody but the displaced goddess, that is. She chose Kantacāmi's family as the recipient of her forceful request. This is the context in which the following events took place sixteen years ago. They were narrated to me by Kantacāmi himself during Kāḷi's annual festival.[11]

The Narrative

"One day during the month of Māci, I was talking to my neighbor Paḻaṉicāmi inside my house. My nine-year-old daughter was reading nearby. Suddenly, her tongue stuck out and her legs began to quiver. I became very worried, thinking that she might be afflicted by a 'demon' (*pēy*).[12] Paḻaṉicāmi went quickly and brought a *pūcāri* to recite mantras. The *pūcāri* placed sacred ashes (*vipūti*) on the winnowing basket outside in the courtyard and began to perform the rites of exorcism (*ācāram*), muttering mantras and making designs in the ashes. But after performing the preliminary rites, he could not continue. 'I have no powers against this demon' he said, and left the house.

"While the *pūcāri* was performing his rites in the courtyard, an old woman was dancing 'god's dance' (*cāmiyāṭṭam*) and reciting incantations in front of our house. I noticed her and called her to the courtyard. She invoked the god, and suddenly wanted to leave. 'This is the first time such a thing has happened to me. Just now I got my menses (*vīṭṭukkuttūram*)![13] I cannot enter your house.' The old lady disappeared. Paḻanicāmi and other friends who had come said that probably my daughter had gone mad (*paittiyam*) and advised me to take her to Madras. I hired a taxi and prepared for the long journey (over 300 miles). On the road, not far from our town, we again saw the old woman dancing in the middle of the road. My friends then said that she was an Ācāri lady (a woman of the Carpenter caste). We tried to move her aside, to one side of the road, but we couldn't. The lady was gesturing for margosa leaves (*vēppantaḻai*). A bunch of margosa leaves from a nearby tree was placed in front of her, and she ate them. Then she asked for turmeric water (*mañcaḷnīr*), and drank a full pot of it.[14] We thought then that she was possessed by a demon and made comments to this effect. The old lady said: 'I am Kāḷiyattā.' I looked at her and said: 'If you are Kāḷiyattā, look at the state my daughter is in!' She replied: 'Go back to your house, pour a pot full of water on the girl and apply sacred ashes on her forehead. Then the child can go to school.' We followed her instructions and returned to my house. The women of the house poured many pots of water on the child. I brought sacred ashes and smeared her forehead with them.

"That old Ācāri lady said one thing which I forgot to mention. She said that a temple should be built for her. Three days after this incident, my daughter again was affected by the demon while she was at school. I rushed to the school and brought her home in a horsecart. I told my friend Paḻaṉicāmi that that demon was greatly troubling my daughter and that I feared for her life. 'What shall I do?' I asked. Immediately my daughter woke and sat up in the horsecart. 'You said I am a demon. I am not a demon. I am Kāḷiyattā. You must build a temple for me.' I then recalled what the old Ācāri woman had said in the road. I went immediately to the timber shop and bought timbers and tiles. I took them to my house without knowing where the temple was to be constructed. The old Ācāri woman came in front of the horsecart and told me where to build the temple. 'Where the *triśula* is,' she said. She also said that the temple had to be finished before going for the pilgrimage of *Paṅkuṉi Uttiram* in the coming month.[15] So I had only twenty days to build the temple. The old lady also scribbled on the ground a blueprint of the temple and said, 'The architect (*sthāpati*) will meet you tomorrow. You should build according to the plan he will give you.' The architect received similar instructions in a dream.

"The architect met me the next day and told me about his dream. So we constructed the inner chamber (*garbhagṛha*) and tower (*kōpuram*) following his guidance. Thereafter, I was in the dark as to where the idol should come from. That old Ācāri woman came again to the construction site and danced 'god's dance' (*cāmiyāṭṭam*). Then, she told me where I should purchase the idol. Go to the stonemaker, pay the balance, and he will give you the idol.' Accordingly, I went to the stonemaker and asked for the idol. He said, 'Someone gave me a fifteen-rupee advance for this idol. If the man comes and asks for it, what shall I say?' I explained everything to the stonemaker in detail, and he gave me the idol.

"I took the idol to the chamber of the temple. A Brahmin priest performed the rite of installation (*piratiṣṭai*) and soon after we completed the temple. We finished it on time. I appointed some priests (*kurukkaḷ*) to charge the idol with power (*kumbhābhiṣēka*) with water from our sacred river. Five hundred people came to the riverside to bring sacred water (*tirttam*) for the ritual, almost everyone living in the *Kavuṇṭaṉ tōppu*. My daughter came with us and poured sacred water from the Kāḷiyattā copper pot into the river. While she was doing this, all the five hundred people were possessed by Kāḷi's gracious power (*aruḷcakti*). My daughter died there, instantly. From that day on, every year we celebrate the Kāḷiyattā festival and bring pots of water and pots of fire to Kāḷi.

"Once the idol was charged with power, we began worship in the temple twice a day. Prior to finishing the temple, I asked the old Ācāri lady: 'Whom must I appoint as a priest (*pūcāri*)?' She instructed me to give sacred ashes and bless the people, and said, 'A saint (*cāmiyār*) will come. You need not worry.' Accordingly, a saint came and performed *pūjā* for many days. Then he left suddenly and nobody could find him. So I appointed a *paṇṭāram*[16] as a regular priest, with two hundred rupees as his annual salary. He also receives the alms (*kāṇikkai*) collected during the worship.

"This happened sixteen years ago. I paid all the expenses of construction, and I also covered deficits of the yearly festival in the beginning. Now we have a surplus, one hundred and twenty-six rupees this year."

The Kāli Festival

I witnessed the Kāli festival that year (1980), a three-day celebration following the pattern common to many neighborhood and lineage celebrations in the area. The following is a summary description of it:

In the morning of the first Tuesday prior to the festival, a resident barber (Nāvitaṉ) went to all the streets of the *Kavuṇṭaṉ tōppu* to announce the festival to its residents. The organizing committee, that is the temple priest, the secretary-treasurer, and the president Kantacāmi, sent printed programs with details of the festival activities to the prominent residents of the neighborhood. [A printed program is nowadays the usual way to request contributions to help defray festival expenses. People may donate cash, or silver and copper pots to be used in the worship, but there is no "festival tax" (*vari paṇam*)[17] collected from the residents of the neighborhood, since the temple belongs to Kantacāmi's family, which derives the major benefits from the festival.]

Two or three days before the festival, a group of Kantacāmi's laborers built a structure of bamboo poles decorated with festoons, mango leaves and other greenery, in front of the temple. This structure, which is called *tōraṇam*, is a common sight in all celebrations of well-being and fertility such as festivals and marriages.

In the evening of the first day (the first Tuesday of the month of Cittirai), a long bamboo pole painted with white and red stripes was inserted in the northeast corner of the temple entrance. This ritual literally means "[marking of the] auspicious time" (*mūkurttakkāl*) and was followed by another ritual called "the pacification of the settlement" (*kirāmacānti*), in which a huge pumpkin was cut open in the temple hall in front of the *triśula*, its pieces smeared with vermillion (here a substitute for blood) and then flung to the four corners of the temple by the priest.

On the second day, men and women of the neighborhood carried black earthen pots full of burning sticks to the temple. This ritual, called *akkini caṭṭi* ("fire pot") or more often *pūvōṭu vaittal* ("placing [pots] with flowers"), is a domestic celebration, in which all the members of a household participate. Commonly, people take fire pots to the temple to "repay a debt" (*nērttikkaṭaṉ*) contracted with the goddess for past boons (*varam*). At times, they are taken to press the goddess for some specific need (*vēṇṭutal*), such as removal of some undesirable state. Devotees claim that the fire pots, which they carry in their bare hands from a nearby pond, do not burn, because they are devoted to and trust in the goddess. In the temple, Kantacāmi and the priest receive these pots, which, devotees say, contain the fiery heat of the goddess. The priest burns camphor (*cūṭam*) in the pots, and they are then thrown outside the temple or immersed in the pond.

On the third day, residents of the neighborhood go to the river with copper pots (*kalaśa*) to collect water (*tīrttam*) which is later to be used to wash (*abhiṣēka*) and cool (*kuḷircci*) the temple icon of the goddess. Going to a river is an important sequence of this and other festivals. As Tamils say, "worship always starts in the river and ends in the mountain." During the procession to and back from the river, those who serve as the goddess's mouthpiece sing, dance in procession, and predict the future. In theory, anyone can be possessed by the goddess, but in many festivals certain persons regularly experience possession.

On this occasion, when the devotees returned to the temple, the goddess entered a young married woman of Kantacāmi's lineage and spoke through her. The woman fell on the ground, paralyzed. The priest poured sacred water on her, but with no positive results. Kantacāmi approached her. He threw a great quantity of sacred ashes on her body, then placed a lemon in her hand. The woman began to move and gasp. Kantacāmi placed her head on his lap and questioned her, addressing her as Kāḷiyattā. "What is the matter, Kaḷiyattā? What do you wish?" The possessed woman replied in a voice quite different from her normal speaking voice, "I don't like this festival, people are not coming!" Kanticāmi replied, "What can I do? It is in your hands for people to attend." The dialogue went on for about ten minutes. The goddess seemed to blame Kantacāmi for the lack of attendance on the part of some people of the lineage (whose names were mentioned), but Kantacāmi repeatedly turned the argument against the goddess. He had been made the goddess's trustee at her request, but he derived his competence from her power. Their mutual dependency was clearly and publicly demonstrated in this interesting dialogue.

In the evening of the third day, the central sequence of the festival took place, which went well until the early hours of the next morning. Once the permanent idol (*mūlamūrti*) of the goddess had been washed, dressed, and offered various kinds of food, especially sweetened boiled rice (*carkkarai poṅkal*), attention was focused on the movable icons of the goddess, one of metal (*utsavamūrti*) and the other a clay pot (*kumpam*). The trunk containing the jewels and festive vestments of the goddess was brought in a solemn procession from Kantacāmi's house to the temple. Then, this trunk and the two movable icons of the goddess were taken to a nearby well. The procession passed through all the streets of the *Kavuṇṭaṉ tōppu*. Prominent in the procession were a young man dressed up as Kāḷi, carrying a bunch of margosa leaves, and two other men, one dressed as Karuppaṉacāmi, the goddess's attendant, the other as a legendary demon. Both men were carrying a sickle (*aruvāḷ*).

The copper icon and the clay pot were washed in the well and decorated, the former with the vestments and jewels from the goddess's trunk, the latter with special designs (*kōlam*), a coconut, mango leaves, and floral garlands. Women were seated some distance away from the well and were not allowed to observe the dressing of the two icons. While these operations were going on, the men dressed up as Kāḷi, Karuppaṉacāmi, and the demon performed various battle dances, in which the demon attacked Kāḷi, Karuppanacāmi protected her, and she eventually killed the demon. When the two icons were fully dressed and decorated, a young black kid was sacrificed (*kaṭā veṭṭutal*) in front of the clay icon. (A curtain had been drawn in front of the copper icon to obstruct the sight of the sacrifice.)[18] At this moment especially, women were forcefully pushed away to a place where they could not see the goddess or the clay pot. The beheaded kid's blood ran on the ground (which is thought to be an embodiment of the goddess too), and the dead carcass, I was told, was shared by the temple priest (who killed the animal), the barber who announced the festival, and the washerman who carried the processional torch. After the sacrifice, a *pūjā* with vegetarian offerings was performed in front of the copper icon, and women were allowed to participate. The power-filled leavings (*piracātam*) were consumed by all the participants. During the rest of the night devotees engaged in battle dances to entertain the goddess. Many were possessed and forecast the future, and many secretly drank country liquor. Before dawn, the clay pot was taken to the well and immersed there, and many people jumped into the well to bathe. The copper icon was undressed and was taken to the temple without ceremony. Next, a pot filled with turmeric water (*mañcalnīr*) was placed at the temple's entrance. During the entire morning, men and women of the neighborhood came to the temple, dipped their hands in the pot and sprinkled one another with the yellow water. This ritual of termination, a way of wishing prosperity for one's fellow devotees, ended the three-day festival to the goddess Kāḷi.

These festival events, as well as the account related by Kantacāmi, illustrate well a Hindu attitude of viewing and treating gods as divine persons. Various plausible interpretations could be given to these events. Some sociologists would be inclined to read these events as statements on the expansion of caste boundaries to an unsettled territory, accompanied by a forceful claim on Kantacāmi's part to an elevated social status. The goddess would then be viewed as a "symbol" of solidarity, or just the opposite, as a "symbol" of the tensions which arise in connection with new settlement. These interpretations would be partially accurate, for indeed, in other contexts, Kantacāmi's social behavior clearly conveys such a claim to superior status, and the festival is both a source of solidarity for the residents of the *Kavuṇṭaṉ tōppu*, as well as a potential source of innumerable conflicts. But it would fail to account for the dynamics of the process. Kantacāmi's superiority, the solidarity of his neighborhood residents, and the potential conflicts all derive from Kantacāmi's contract with the goddess and, most importantly, both Kantacāmi and other residents of *Kavuṇṭaṉ tōppu* would offer such an explanation.

Kāḷi is a goddess traditionally known to be very difficult to please. Her demands are always extreme and very costly, but she is also known to be very generous to those who comply with her requests.[19] The most prosperous families are usually those which have dared to recognize the call of the goddess and have complied with her extraordinary demands.

A more dynamic reading of these events would have to be based on the undesirable state of the goddess's person when she sought out Kantacāmi's services. When Kantacāmi's town was smaller, Kāḷi had her own place in the coconut grove. She dwelled there, and the *triśula* was her visible embodiment. With the expansion of the town, new houses built by Kavuṇṭars encroached upon and eventually completely displaced the coconut grove. The goddess was left without a residence. The *triśula* was almost forgotten; people went to other places to worship other gods.

Divine persons such as Kāḷi are always immanent in places, always rooted in a particular territory which is considered to be rightfully owned by them. Territoriality is their characteristic trait and their right,[20] and thus the god of one place is always different from the god of another place, although they may bear identical names.

The Kāḷi of the vanished coconut grove lacked a dwelling place, just as humans often do. She was in a state of "need" (*vēṇṭutal*); she sought relief from a state of wandering. A place where she could be worshiped was rightfully hers. She therefore called upon Kantacāmi to rectify this undesirable situation. This state of deprivation and constant flux altered the bodily constitution of the goddess, making her extremely "hot." The sudden menses of the old Ācāri lady (who was also wandering and could not enter the house), her request for margosa and turmeric water (both considered "cooling" substances), and the cooling of Kantacāmi's daughter with water and sacred ashes should be seen as indications of the goddess's "heat."

The wandering Kāḷi was also anxious. Her repeated urging, the rigid deadline, and the minute details for the construction of her temple are indications of her anxiety. So anxious was her call that Kantacāmi mistook her urging for the nuisance of a demon, also a wandering and anxious being. Only the evidence brought by his own daughter — a corporeal part of himself and thus a kind of self-evidence — made him realize his error. Kantacāmi complied with the goddess's request, and in exchange he was made her trustee and custodian, with the priestly authority to receive her "heat" (contained in the fire pots), to give sacred ashes,[21] and to bestow blessings on devotees. His household became prosperous, his lands fertile, and his granary has been the envy of his neighbors ever since. Kantacāmi's daughter, a manifestation of the wandering goddess in human form, left this life as soon as the goddess was settled in her temple. In a way, Kantacāmi's loss was the goddess's gain. He lost a daughter, she gained a temple. But Kantacāmi now enjoys the superior blessings of the contented goddess.

Case 2: Murukaṉ's Call

Murukaṉ, an offspring of Śiva, is the most beloved god of the Tamils. He is a child, a warrior, a householder, a teacher, and an ascetic, and he resides in these various forms in his six hill temples (*aṟupaṭai vīṭu*) that once marked the boundaries of the Tamil country. His hill temple at Paḻani, a town located in southern Koṅku in the border area between the ancient territories of Koṅkunāṭu, Cēranātu, Pāṇṭiyanāṭu and Cōḻanāṭu, is the most popular and most often visited in Tamilnadu. He resides there as an ascetic (*aṇṭi*), without the company of his two spouses, Teyvayāṉai and Vaḷḷi. The idol of the god is said to have been built by an ancient alchemist (*siddha*), Pōkar, at the beginning of the *Kali yuga*, the present age of moral deterioration and precariousness. Pōkar made the idol from a combination of nine metaloid poisonous substances (*navapaśaṉam*), medicinal herbs and roots, all found in the hill that houses the temple. The special proportion of these substances is said to be unique and to have extraordinary healing powers upon the devotee who comes in contact with the idol. Thus, the god of Paḻani is also known as the "Healer" (Vaidyanātaṉ). It is said, however, that the god's balance can be upset by seasonal and astral influences, and by an excessive depletion of the god's vital fluids which may occur as a result of attending to the innumerable requests of his devotees. Should this happen, it is thought that the god's healing power would be transformed into a source of illness and death. Both the everyday and the "extraordinary" procedures of worship in the temple of this god appear to focus on protecting the god's healing power by regulating the proportions of his component substances. Twice a year, in the cold and hot seasons, the idol of the god is said to contract and swell, respectively, due to an "excess of cold" (*kuḷir tōṣam*) or an "excess of heat" (*cūṭu tōṣam*),[22] and special procedures are adopted to prevent the god from falling into a state of imbalance. Thus, these two seasons are the occasions for the two most important festivals in this temple, which are always accompanied by well attended pilgrimages.[23] *Tai Pūcam* is the winter festival when pilgrims of a "cold" caste[24] bring the god an offering of unrefined sugar (*carkkarai*), which is thought to be a "heating" substance. *Paṅkuṉi Uttiram* is the festival of the hot season, and pilgrims of a "hot" caste bring the god pots of water from the Kāvēri river for his festive bath, and this water is said to be as "cooling" as water from the Ganges. In this manner, by "warming up" the god when he is "cold" and "cooling" him when he is "hot," the healing proportions of his embodiment are maintained. This thermically vulnerable divine person is the god that sought the loving and devoted services of Valliyammā some ten years ago.

Vaḷḷiyammā, presently known as *Cāmiyāṭi*, "the dancer of god's dance," was born twenty-three years ago, the first and only child of a Kavuṇṭar family of modest means. She was born without a right ear, a sign (*sakuṉam*) of great significance, for ears are corporeal expressions of the sacred syllable OM (ௐ), Murukaṉ's mantra and the primordial sound.

The village where Vaḷḷiyammā's family has resided for generations presents most of the characteristics of traditional Koṅku village organization. A cluster of Kavuṇṭar and Tēvāṅka Ceṭṭiyār houses, each in separate streets, constitutes the core of the village. These are castes traditionally known to be of the "Right-hand" and "Left-hand," respectively,[25] or relatively "hot" and "cold."[26] At a distance from this cluster, untouchable laborers reside in separate settlements, and at the periphery of the central cluster, a few artisan, two barber and three washerman families provide services to Kavuṇṭars and Tēvāṅkas. On the western dirt road, which connects the village with the main regional arteries, there is a well-kept temple to the goddess Vañciyammā, the ***kula teyvam*** of the larger Kavuṇṭar clan in the village. A non-Brahmin priest (*paṇṭāram*) resides with his family in a house near the temple in which he performs weekly services.

Like many villages in the Koṅku region, this was an enclave of Kavuṇṭar dominance in the past. Tēvāṅka Ceṭṭiyārs originally came from the Kannada country, fleeing Muslim persecution, and settled in the village. Although weavers by tradition, presently only two of the forty-two resident Tēvāṇka families in the village are engaged in their original craft. Most of them are small farmers and either cultivate lands of their own or work as tenants for Kavuṇṭar landowners.

Unlike other Koṅku villages, in Vaḷḷiyammā's village there is no recorded history of animosity between the Right-hand Kavuṇṭars and the Left-hand Tēvāṅkas. Although intercaste commensality is rare in these villages, each group invites the other to its annual communal feast. Tēvāṅkas provide a new sacred thread for the Kavuṇṭar's goddess in her annual festival, and Kavuṇṭars offer them a feast. Kavuṇṭars are, in turn, invited by Tēvāṅkas to the annual changing of the sacred thread ceremony during *Āvaṇi Avittal*, their most important celebration, and serve Kavuṇṭars a solemn feast.

It is in such a seemingly peaceful village that Vaḷḷiyammā grew up, a weak and often sickly child, according to some villagers. Her family was very devoted to the god Murukaṉ, and fasted every Monday, New Moon day, and on the day of the Kārttikai constellation,[27] all days which are considered to be special to Murukaṉ. Beginning in the first year of her life, Vaḷḷiyammā was taken to the Murukaṉ temple of Paḻaṉi in the annual pilgrimage of *Paṅkuṉi Uttiram*, the occasion in which Kavuṇṭars bring Kāvēri water to the overheated god.

When she was twelve years old, Vaḷḷiyammā was possessed by Murukaṉ during the pilgrimage. At that time the god requested that she become his slave (*aṭimai*) and ordered her to "fast and keep silent"[28] for six continuous months. As soon as the pilgrims returned to the village, she began this long period of fasting and silent seclusion. As time went by, her parents and neighbors became increasingly worried, for Vaḷḷiyammā was growing thinner and weaker by the day. Warned by dreams, her parents did not interfere with her devotion and set aside a room for her.

News of her fasting soon spread to neighboring villages, and people came to Vaḷḷiyammā's place out of curiosity or to seek relief from ailments. But she would not see or speak to anyone. After six months, she emerged from her fasting with a "radiant face" (*mukavacīkaram*), or so neighbors recall.[29]

On the first Kārttikai constellation-day following the conclusion of her fast, Vaḷḷiyammā had a dream in which Murukaṉ requested that she walk for seven days around the neighboring villages with a needle (*aḻaku*)[30] pierced through her tongue; then, she was again to go to the god's temple at Paḻaṉi. Vaḷḷiyammā complied dutifully with Murukaṉ's request and set out on the tour. In each village she would dance along the streets, possessed by Murukaṉ. Hence, people began to call her *Cāmiyāṭi*, "the dancer of god's dance." Many people followed her from village to village and finally to Paḻaṉi. There, in the temple, she was again possessed by Murukaṉ, who gave her a secret mantra which enabled her to cure diseases and to predict the future.

Vaḷḷiyammā returned to the village with this powerful mantra in her mind and purchased and had framed a picture of Murukaṉ, in accord with the god's instructions. The picture was installed in her room, which henceforth became a "temple-house" (*vīṭṭukkōyil*), and she began to conduct *pūjā* twice daily. Devotees from the surrounding areas came to the *cāmiyāṭi*, seeking relief from their ailments, and now she attended to them all.

Since then, during the last ten years, the *cāmiyāṭi* has been called by Murukaṉ many times and he has ordered similar trials. His calls seem to have a special "timing," and usually coincide with the times when Murukaṉ is more vulnerable to thermic imbalances and to depletions from the innumerable boons that he grants to his devotees. Days of the New Moon, the Karttikai constellation, and the period around *Paṅkuṉi Uttiram* seem to be the special times when the god's calls are more forceful and demanding. At times he orders her to fast for one *maṇṭala*,[31] with only lime juice as nutrient, or for two *maṇṭalas* with only milk. Her daily diet, imposed by the god, consists only of "raw" rice (*paccarici*), a more "cooling" (*sattvik*) nutrient than the usual Kavuṇṭar diet of parboiled rice (*puḻuṅkalarici*). The god calls her in dreams or in trances. Every day, when the bell of the Paḻaṉi temple tolls for the midday worship (*uccikkālam pūcai*) — the hottest portion of the day — she is said to become possessed and to dance in her "temple-house." In 1980, while I was visiting Vaḷḷiyammā's village a few weeks before the *Paṅkuṉi Uttiram* pilgrimage, she received a command from the god to walk the pilgrimage path with twenty-one needles pierced in her body, one in her tongue and ten in each arm. She is to continue this trial for another six years. Then she will become a *sannyāsi*, the god said.

After every *pūjā*, the *cāmiyāṭi* comes out of her "temple-house" and distributes sacred ashes and sacred water to the waiting devotees. Then she attends to the various requests of devotees. They approach her, touch her feet, and wait. The *cāmiyāṭi* asks, "Why have you come?" The devotee stands and usually indicates his or her trouble with a wordless gesture, a swollen leg, headache, stomach pain, or arthritic hands being the most common ailments. With her right hand on the devotee's forehead, the *cāmiyāṭi* silently recites her secret mantra. Then she gives sacred ashes and sacred water and, depending on the devotee's ailment, herbs (*mūlikai*) and roots (*vēr*), with instructions for their use. She may also give dietary instructions, especially in cases of ailments caused by "excess of heat" (*cūṭu tōṣam*). Devotees place some coins in a platter and leave.

The requests devotees submit to the *cāmiyāṭi* vary, but generally concern deliverance from some undesirable state of being. Sickness caused by an excess of heat and many types of anxiety seemed to me to be the most common complaints. Deliverance from them is very often characterized by villagers as *vīṭu* (the Tamil equivalence of the Sanskrit *mōkṣa*), which is usually described as a healthy, thermically balanced and peaceful present and future life. Unhealthy, excessively "hot" or "cold" and anxious states of being are believed to be the result of improper diet, improper actions, and not infrequently, the direct consequence of malevolent influences of various kinds. These malevolent influences are generally known as *cāpam* ("curse," "effect of malevolent power"), the removal of which is one of the particular blessings of the Murukaṉ of the Paḻaṉi hill temple.[32]

Every Sunday the *cāmiyāṭi* goes to a small Murukaṉ shrine in a nearby village and dances the god's dance. After the dance, in a state of calm possession, she sits on the ground with a lemon in her hand and with a platter of sacred ashes placed in front of her. Devotees then approach her with questions that trouble their hearts and cause them anxiety. Family economic or health problems, court cases, crops and cattle, jobs, examinations, pregnancies, and marriages are the most common subjects of these questions. The *cāmiyāṭi* asks the name of the village and of the petitioner, listens to the complaint, and makes a short statement concerning what the petitioner may expect in the future. Then she dismisses the petitioner with some recommendations and a pinch of sacred ashes. Her replies are not always reassuring. I have seen petitioners (mostly women) crying their hearts out upon hearing the *cāmiyāṭi* forecast the death of a husband or a child, the failure of crops, or the postponement of a long awaited marriage.

During her ten years of servitude to Murukaṉ, the *cāmiyāṭi* has become very popular in this area (and her family quite wealthy), since she has been recognized as *aṭimai*, a devoted servant who can bestow the blessings of the god. "She was born without an ear" (that is, the corporeal OM), villagers say, "but due to her devotion, Murukaṉ gave her his powerful OM."

Vaḷḷiyammā's transformation into a *cāmiyāṭi* illustrates a god's strategy of seeking relief from humans when he finds himself in a state of need. This, however, differs from the strategy employed by Kāli in the case discussed above. The god Murukaṉ does not lack a temple of tiles and timber like the Kāḷi of the vanished coconut grove. He has his six abodes (*aṟupaṭai vīṭu*) which are daily visited by thousands of his devotees. His need (*vēṇṭutal*) is of a different nature. He was in want of a heart to dwell in. Murukaṉ is a god of the heart and, although he has claims to particular territories,[33] his foremost claim is to the hearts of his devotees. One of his popular epithets is *Guka*, "the one who dwells in the cave of the heart." Devotees often invoke him as *Guru-Guka*, "the Teacher who dwells in the heart."

Murukaṉ's forceful claim to Vaḷḷiyammā's services could be symbolically understood in various ways. One may plausibly argue that

Vaḷḷiyammā's family turned to a code of sainthood as a way of dealing with an abnormal child. When the sickly child was dedicated to the service of the god, her inborn abnormalities were symbolically transformed into signs of divine calling, and thus Vaḷḷiyammā's family gained social recognition and potential wealth. Murukaṉ's call could also be symbolically understood as a statement of the peaceful relations of two traditionally antagonistic groups of castes, the Right-hand and the Left-hand. Through Vaḷḷiyammā's adoption of a code of conduct more typical of the Left-hand, whose members consider themselves and are often considered by others as being more "cool," the differences between these two groups were somewhat bridged. Valliyammā would thus be viewed as a symbol of mediation between social opposites, a status enforced by the calling of the god. However, these and other plausible interpretations fail to account for the dynamics of the process which is based on the conceptualization of a divine power as a person. By bringing into the analysis the needs of the god, these events recover the personalistic dimension lost in a mere symbolic analysis.

Bothered by the continuous demands of devotees and by the changing cyclical alignments of the planets and stars, Murukaṉ often becomes inordinately depleted of fluids, and this imbalance makes him excessively cold or excessively hot. The timing of his forceful calls to Vaḷḷiyammā indicate that Murukaṉ seeks relief from a state of excessive heat. Being loved burns the god; it is a positively heated emotion, which dries out the god's vital fluids. Murukaṉ chose Vaḷḷiyammā's heart (or liver, according to Ayurvedic physiology) to become a receptacle for the excess heat which is harmful to him. With her fasts and trials of endurance, she has become the permanent cooler of the god.

Being a recipient of overheat is a task that Tamil society seems to entrust primarily to wives. Through the wife's fasting and other religious observances, such as *viratam* and *nōṉpu*,[34] her husband and children are spared or relieved from unwanted states, which are "burnt" by the wife's ascetic observances. The Murukaṉ of the Paḻaṉi hill temple has no wives to relieve him of such intimate dangerous states. Vaḷḷiyammā, by her intimate and regenerative relationship with the god, is engaged in the process of becoming his ascetic wife, and her present trials of endurance may also be understood as the necessary "polishing" (*samskāra*) to ready her for this difficult wifely task.[35] It is then not inappropriate that Vaḷḷiyammā describes herself as a "bonded laborer" (*aṭimai*) of the god.

Love of the god is also kinetic; it sets things in motion and keeps them moving. According to most devotional interpretations, the love of god is the force that sets the "flow of life" (*saṃsāra*) in perpetual motion.[36] Thus, Vaḷḷiyammā became a *cāmiyāṭi*, a dancer of this divine movement. In exchange for the god's claim to Vaḷḷiyammā's heart, the girl has received the god's powerful mantra. With it, she can cure diseases, cool the heat which oppresses other people, and relieve the anxiety of broken hearts. Her sickly body has become a blessing to all.

Conclusion

The events that transformed the lives of Kantacāmi and Vaḷḷiyammā are useful illustrations of Tamil Hindus' view of their gods as divine persons. The analysis of these events, taking into account this personalistic view, is offered here as an alternative to other types of analysis in which gods are treated as "disembodied symbols" of social realities and human relationships. This latter form of analysis may uncover hidden aspects, not readily observable in social behavior, which is the primary domain of the social scientist. These aspects often enrich our understanding of the structure of human relations, but they also often fail to account for the dynamics of the process. They become increasingly distant from the understanding that Hindus have of their own society, in which gods and humans coexist as persons.

The events described here seem to emphasize the Hindu belief that gods and humans exist in spatio-temporal contiguity, and that they are related by complementary, mutually rewarding bodily exchanges. Possession is a dynamic context in which this type of complementary exchange is initiated by divine persons as a strategy to refurbish their depleted powers. These events also underscore a basic quality that humans must possess to become recipients of the gods' forceful calls, namely a sort of "matching" or "compatibility" (*sātmya*)[37] of their natures with the gods' needs. Kantacāmi and Vaḷḷiyammā both were well-matched to Kāḷi's and Murukaṉ's respective needs, the former as a well-established householder who could afford the construction of a temple, the latter as a divinely "marked" child of a devoted family. After the fulfillment of the gods' forceful call, this initial compatibility was transformed into "competent authority" (*adhikāra*) to remove afflictions from other humans and to bestow divine blessings upon them. This was their personal gain, a boon to the society of humans.

Finally, there is an additional aspect of the events that I have presented here which needs some elaboration. Why is the call of such generous divine persons so extremely unsettling for human recipients? Is there any new dimension to be learned from such forceful calls? Gods are essential actors in a Hindu world characterized by reciprocity. More powerful and generous than humans, they can alleviate problems that are beyond human capacity. Endowed with such powers, the function of gods is to subsume human deficiencies — human states of *vēṇṭutal* — and to bestow blessings. In this reciprocal order, the relationships of humans and gods are asymmetrical. Gods give things different in nature and more valuable than what they receive, but in these exchanges humans and gods are both transformed. Through repeated asymmetrical receipts and expenditures, gods may find themselves unbalanced, in deficient states. They seek relief from humans, thereby inverting and completing a reciprocal relationship; gods give away their negative qualities and receive something positive in return. The forcefulness of the gods' call to humans and its many unsettling consequences for some humans are the result of this inversion. At a later stage, when their demands have been fulfilled, gods more than repay their debts to humans, for as far as humankind as a whole is concerned, what the gods give is of greater value than what they take.

Garlanded portraits of Mahatma Gandhi and Jawaharlal Nehru among the deities in a pots and pans shop in Mylapore, Madras City. Photo by Dick Waghorne.

7

Founders, Swamis, and Devotees: Becoming Divine in North Karnataka

Lise F. Vail

For I of all acts of worship
Am both the recipient and the Lord;
But they do not recognize me.
Bhagavad Gīta IX.24

ASCETIC RENOUNCERS AND ecstatic devotees of God have long been held in high regard in Indian religion. Yet their role with regard both to disciples and ordinary people in the world remains somewhat clouded in mystery – precisely because they seem otherworldly, yet are visibly living in this world and often interacting with others. In this study we will be taking a brief look at popular beliefs about renouncing swamis and their relationships in north Karnataka state. This entire region appears to share a common understanding of the position of the renouncer within a widely accepted popular theological system – a system that is not bound by the walls of the monastery but which permeates the life of the surrounding community. Here the swami sits at the center and not on the periphery of religious life.

This study has emerged from fieldwork conducted in Gadag town, Karnataka (100,000 pop.) during 1977-79. It centers around a Virakta renouncer-swami who resides in Tōṇṭadārya Jagadguru Maṭh, a Liṅgāyat or Vīraśaiva sectarian monastery. The monastery houses the Jagadguru (literlly, "world-guru") swami named Siddhaliṅga, a small group of employees, and about fifty boarding college students. The data and quotations I utilized come from sixty-seven lengthy interviews on sectarian history and the meaning of religious concepts and relationships. They are taken primarily from Liṅgāyats (fifty of the sixty-seven) of varying socio-economic and personal backgrounds, many of whom claim to be bhaktas (devotees) of the Tōṇṭadārya swamis and their lineage. Significantly, however, the content of the non-Liṅgāyat interviews, which ranged over a broad selection of castes, hardly varies from that of the Liṅgāyats. Although the area has been undoubtedly influenced by Liṅgāyat religious tradition, I would claim that the popular religious system found here is *regional* rather than, strictly speaking, sectarian.

The broadest theology of popular religion in north Karnataka centers around the concept of formless, pure *śakti* or spiritual power. It deals with the awakening and embodiment of that power within renouncing holy persons, and also devotees and holy objects. The body of the Virakta renouncer or swami is a focal point for the unfolding and concentration of spiritual power and purity and for its distribution to others. Thus a swami's relationships with others form a dynamic experiential core, and this idea is expressed in religious conceptions concerning the mutual exchange of *śakti*, devotion (bhakti), knowledge, and grace. It is crucial therefore to recognize that these beliefs are transformational rather than static and therefore can be related to other ideas concerning the nature of "exchange" in India which have recently been espoused by scholars.[1]

I will explore here two relationships — founder-swami and swami-devotee — in order to consider how the Indian renouncer might be seen with regard to the world. Is he always separate and aloof — a resident of another more spiritual realm? Should he properly be called an "individual" in a social or personal sense as Dumont suggests?[2] Or is he somehow a part of mainstream Hindu religion and society, involved in exchanging gifts and dealing with others in terms of hierarchy, purity, and impurity? Perhaps he is part of the world in some respects and separate in others. Some of McKim Marriott's suggestions concerning the "mutable" nature of the Hindu personality[3] can be fruitfully considered in light of our findings.

The Maṭh and Its Link with Divinity

Tōṇṭadārya Maṭh itself is a Virakta Jagadguru monastery, which indicates both that it is of the top order of Liṅgāyat *maṭhs* and also that it is associated with the Virakta group of swamis, most of whom trace the origin of the Virakta lineage back to a fifteenth century saint, Eḍiyūr Siddhaliṅgēśvara. There is another line of Liṅgāyat Jagadguru swamis which usually traces its origins to the Pañcācāryas or "Five Great Teachers," whose dates are not recorded historically and who are said to be manifestations of the five "faces" of Śiva (Sadāśiva).[4] Western scholars have suggested that the twelfth century figure, Basava, was the founder or reviver of Vīraśaivism. Viraktas and Pañcācāryas (also called Guruvargas or Gurusthalins) for some time have not seen eye to eye on the question of Vīraśaiva origins, the Viraktas tending to revere Basava, and the Pañcācāryas referring back to the Five Great Teachers.[5] Either way, it is evident that both are concerned with establishing the divine origin of Vīraśaiva religion.

The Viraktas establish this link with divinity through both Basava and especially Siddhaliṅgēśvara (1425-1456),[6] who is said to have become completely spiritually realized and whose powerful tomb may be found in south Karnataka today in Eḍiyūr Village. I shall be speaking of him again shortly. Informants say that Tōṇṭadārya Maṭh was built by devotees during the time of Kaṭagihaḷḷi Rācōṭi Swami who occupied the *pīṭha* or seat from 1557-1607,[7] and who was seventh in the spiritual lineage (in Kannada: *parampare*, Sanskrit: *paramparā*) which can be traced back to Siddhaliṅgēśvara. It was constructed on the site where one Karibasava Swami once dwelled. Most informants agree that he was not originally part of the Tōṇṭadārya line, but was "adopted" (somewhat like a cousin) by receiving the grace (*anugraha*) of Rācōṭi Swami during the latter's sojourn in Gadag. The Jagadgurus of the Tōṇṭadārya line resided in Tōṇṭadārya Maṭh only intermittently until about 100 years ago when the Gadag *maṭh* in effect became the permanent "home" of the lineage. It is considered to be a spiritual center which is also the locus of control over affiliated Tōṇṭadārya *śāka* (branch)*maṭhs*. Groups of traditional devotees, especially Banajigas (traders) and Baṇṇagārs (color-dyers and shroff), were thus able to form residential communities near Tōṇṭadārya Maṭh and its swamis.

The World and the Awakening of Power

Religion in north Karnataka is based on a distinction between two "realms" of existence, and the distinction between the two is especially important in reference to humans. The first is simply called *saṃsāra*, "worldly realm," by informants, the second may be called the "spiritually powerful realm" — variously designated *jāgṛta* "alive, awake" (in reference to places and objects), or *sannyāsa* (in reference to powerful people). Here *saṃsāra* does not denote the wheel of rebirth and transmigration in a strict sense, although such a link probably exists. *Saṃsāra* represents those places, objects, and especially people where dirtiness, dullness, and/or darkness predominate. They contain some tangible impurity, and their spiritual power (*śakti*) is weak since it is "covered up" and scattered by the above qualities. This can be likened to dirt and oil impeding the proper flow of electric energy in a sensitive piece of machinery. Worldly people, called *saṃsārikarus* or *prapañcikarus*, may also be characterized by the above qualities and are generally said, in addition, to have dull eyes and scattered thoughts, feelings, and energies (*śakti*). They also gravitate toward selfish but yet unfocused attachments to particular objects, money, and people — especially family members. The paradigmatic *saṃsārikaru* is a married person living a family life, since it is generally believed that "saṃsāric characteristics" are part and parcel of such a lifestyle.

By contrast, the realm of *sannyāsa* persons or *jāgṛta* objects and places refers to those same persons and objects that inhabit the saṃsāric realm *after* they have been "cleansed." As one informant aptly stated: "Wipe your face of the dust of *saṃsāra* and you'll know that it is clean." Included in this realm are persons such as ascetics (swamis, Viraktas, or *sannyāsis*), temple idols (*mūrtis*), and the tombs of saints — all being places or persons whose *śakti* (spiritual power) has become, or is, awakened (*jāgṛta*). They are thus awake, alive, and animated by concentrated holy power, which is found in conjunction with purity, brightness or light (for example, an aura around a swami), and heat. Such holy power is also likened to a current, such as electricity, and the "magnetic" attraction associated with the presence of divine power. In persons, notably Virakta ascetic swamis, (who can also in general be called *sannyāsis*) this pure *śakti* is said to underlie their charisma and holiness. It is described as *divya* ("divine") and *pavitra* ("pure"). Because it is concentrated, it naturally radiates outward to others, thereby attracting people to the monastery or causing them to bow to the swami. It can also be utilized by the swami as he wills. Lastly, although informants generally believe that the *jāgṛta* realm and the saṃsāric realm are intracontrovertible (e.g., dirty mirror-clean mirror), they also tend to characterize particular objects, places and people as belonging to one realm or the other. Thus ascetics are usually contrasted with householders.[8] They do believe, however, that all things and people have their origin in God (Paramātmā, Dēvaru or Śakti) and so possess an underlying identity grounded in *śakti* (power of God). For this reason both realms are defined in terms of the type or quality of *śakti* they manifest.

A number of scholars have also noted the prominence of *śakti* and other names and forms of spiritual power in all types of Hindu literature, as well as in various popular traditions found in India.[9] The tendency among north Kannadigas to define holiness as the presence of *śakti*, and also to use it to define realms and types of people, is thus not unique or peculiar to this region of India. There are a great number of parallels for instance between the *kuṇḍalinī* traditions of yoga and tantra, the Śaiva (Vīraśaiva, Kashmiri Śaiva, and Tamil Śaiva) doctrines of the grace-bestowing power (*śakti*) of God, and this popular tradition.[10]

In order to further facilitate the discussion, I have diagrammed the relationship between *saṃsāra* and *sannyāsa/jāgṛta* as described by my informants.

Diagram 1: Śakti in the World

SANNYĀSA/JĀGṚTA REALM — Founder/Gurus/Realized Swamis

Swamis

Devotees

Ordinary people

SAṂSĀRA REALM — Evil people/beings

pure power, concentrated, pure divinity

impurity, dirt, ego, etc., powerful evil, when concentrated; saṃsāric influence.

This diagram represents an unbroken continuum, which ranges up from strong, concentrated impurity or evil, through scattered and weak *śakti* (ordinary *saṃsāra*) and finally up to the realm of pure and concentrated power, thus expressing a popular belief about the nature of all reality. Full power is correlated with full divinity, yet the range of existence displayed in the diagram is also informed by this same divine power (represented in light grey) which underlies the whole of existence. Power is noticeably concentrated at the top and bottom of the spectrum due to its strength in these locations. At the top (pure divinity) it is completely unadulterated,[11] whereas at the bottom the same pure power still underlies saṃsāric qualities even though the latter are concentrated in force. Thus only divine power can ever be totally "pure" — here in the sense of totally unadulterated as well as in the sense of "good." Thus, informants believe, it always prevails over evil.

In this view, swamis are situated at or near the top of the diagram; they are purely powerful and so fully divine. People believe that swamis must become spiritually realized in order to actually *be* at the apex, but generically they *should* be there. Model swamis *are* there. The founder of a lineage or a particularly eminent guru within the lineage would be considered model swamis. In the Tōṇṭadārya *parampare*, for example, Siddhaliṅgēśvara is believed to have become fully realized and thus assimilated to all other beings who are fully divine (Śiva, *avatāra* figures, Paramātmā, and so on). One informant noted, "A swami is in the position and own form of God. Guru is the same as God is the same as swami. God is one. God is formless and dwells in the soul (*ātman*)." The swami's physical form thus is seen as an important example of the "formed" aspect of God. In Hinduism it is generally believed that the formless God can take on a form to help others. This idea is expressed in explanations of the temple idol and of the *avatāras* of God. According to my informants, since the formless God dwells in (or is) the soul, the uncovering of its power results in a fully divine being, and thus the formless God dwells fully within a "form" (the swami's body).

The present Siddhaliṅga Swami, who is nineteenth in the lineage which originates with Siddhaliṅgēśvara, is in effect the latter's disciple (although he is also the disciple of the guru who immediately precedes him in the lineage). Most informants consider that since he is young (about thirty-three years old) his full divinity and spiritual realization are as yet unrealized. He has, however, exhibited many powerful qualities, they believe, and so has great potential. "Śakti is visible in Siddhaliṅga Swami's deeds and preaching and possibly in his face." Siddhaliṅga Swami would then be placed in the swami (but upwardly mobile) category on the diagram.

Bhaktas (devotees) may be placed somewhere in the upper reaches of the middle of the diagram, indicating that they are still influenced by *saṃsāra* to a certain extent. Most of them are involved in family life, around which saṃsāric traits cluster. Ordinary people and, finally, evil beings or persons are placed even lower on the diagram. Ordinary people, as one would expect, possess a normal quantity of saṃsāric traits, while evil beings *cultivate* such traits (ego, desires, evil, impurity) to such a degree that they attain an extraordinary power which is sometimes also called *śakti*, or more often, impure *siddhis*).[12]

Informants believe that such evil tendencies (those represented here in dark grey) are not ultimately real. Thus this appears to be a monistic religious system. Instead what they represent are human or demonic distortions of pure *śakti*. Demons too are often associated with human beings — as, for example, an evil person who died and became a demon or ghost. It is most important to consider the relationship between energy and matter here. We are not dealing with a simple material conception — "dirt" as earth or dust covering the soul. Instead we are dealing with the results of a type of basic "energy" distortion and the condensation and manifestation of energy into subtle and gross matter. Saints and evil people alike have perfect *śakti* at their core. It is for this reason that all beings are ontologically *equal*; they are of equal value in an ultimate sense. The manifest differences in people's goodness (we might say in their "spiritual or moral inequities") come about through distortions of what is essentially perfect.

Such a diagramatic representation would seem to offer a convenient hierarchical rank ordering for various types of beings in terms of both power and purity. It can thereby prove useful in determining the exact relationship between the two (power and purity) in Hindu thought.[13] One might of course also suggest that the relatively stable hierarchical rank-ordering in the Hindu caste system is a possible parallel.[14] But like the religious model of the caste system which suggests that modification of caste, role, and personal identity are possible over the course of several births, this popular model has dynamic change inherently built into it. Such changes in character are believed possible within one lifetime (although not necessarily attained within one) and can result in immediate transformations. One element that makes this possible is the malleable character of each "role" and the fact that the roles are not solely based on birth, but also on "achievement." Another element which allows for flexibility in roles is the concept of *śakti*, a dynamic spiritual power which also may be transmitted between persons or between persons and objects. It combines with other qualities such as inner purity, grace, and blessings, and can be placed in material objects or transmitted directly from person to person. It can elevate human beings to higher spiritual levels, levels at which a greater quantity of *śakti* would manifest within them. Thus the potential exists for "ascending" the scale of being represented in the diagram all the way up to pure and totally powerful divinity.

In this system, divinization occurs primarily through the inner dynamics of human relationships or through the relationship between a human and the *iṣṭaliṅga*.[15] Leaving aside the latter, divinization occurs particularly through the two dyadic relationships mentioned previously — founder-swami relationship (for instance Siddhaliṅgēśvara and Siddhaliṅga Swami), and the swami-devotee relationship (for instance Siddhaliṅga Swami and one of his Banajiga devotees). These crucial relationships depend on a gift-giving process through which subtle power flows from the higher to the lower member of the dyad. At first glance such gift-giving might appear to be yet another means of establishing those hierarchical relationships which are so often supposed to be the foundation of all Hindu social relationships. However, when *divinization* is the goal of such human relationships, the gift-giving process does not reinforce hierarchy; it creates equality.

As this diagram indicates, completely pure power/divinity is the most powerful; only this kind of power is unadulterated. Impurity or evil — the saṃsāric tendency represented in dark grey — also is powerful but is nonetheless undergirded by the pure power of God and is thus weaker. Equality-creating relationships utilize this superiority of the spiritually realized founder, guru, or swami. Such a person can in effect *purify* those in lower positions by removing their saṃsāric tendencies (ego, impurity, lust, sickness, wrong attachment, fickleness, lack of cleanliness, evil, and so on). He utilizes the pure power he possesses to raise another person from a lower position to a higher one by means of certain actions, by the exercise of his will alone, or by the natural radiation of his *śakti* out into the environment. This is indicated in the diagram by the marks radiating from the top of the scale. The founder or guru is not endangered by the radiation of impurity (see the bottom of the scale), because his power is stronger; thus he can be a purifier — a destroyer of impurity.[16]

Such equality-creating relationships are not, I am claiming, unique to monastic relationships in north Karnataka. In fact they are found especially in bhakti and yoga[17] traditions. A bhakta is said to be able to *become* God through devotion; the yogi becomes assimilated with God through meditation. C. J. Fuller[18] has likewise noted, in a recent article, that Harper and others were not correct in saying that the high gods in Hinduism can become impure. He finds, as I have, that there is an invincible level of purity and power at the top of the spiritual ladder. This data also suggests that the model of "the untouchable-fearing Brahmin," or of any person who must remain isolated from contact with impure people and things in order to remain pure,[19] is only part of the story. Such a person's purity and power is weaker than that of the Karnataka founders, gurus, and realized swamis. Only by increasing his purity and power through spiritual advancement can he become an equality-creator in a complete sense. This would explain why established monastic ascetics are usually attributed with more power, purity, and spiritual advancement than Brahmins or Jaṅgamas (Liṅgāyat priestly caste members).

The equality-creating relationships can be shown to extend beyond the yoga or bhakti tradition.[20] But what is important for this study is that the process of divinization in north Karnataka is interlinked with a process of power transfer and power development which ideally should end in the full realization of divine power within all members of this religious fellowship. The details of this process of divinization must be traced within the two key dyadic relationships referred to above.

Subtle Gift-Giving in the Founder-Swami Relationship

The intent of the founder-swami relationship is to allow for the divinization of the swami, or rather the recovery of his pure divine *śakti*. In the case of the Tōṇṭadārya lineage, each swami in the line is believed to have been directly connected with Siddhaliṅgēśvara. Since the latter is assimilated with pure divinity (informants say he reached *nirvikalpa samādhi* or *liṅgaikya*),[21] he is capable of effecting an equivalent state of being for each of the *parampare* swamis through his relationship with them. Siddhaliṅgēśvara is thus said to be still alive, both in his Eḍiyūr tomb (which is very *jāgṛta* — "awake" with power) and within the Tōṇṭadārya lineage. He also helps devotees who maintain a direct relationshp with him, but the scope of this study does not permit dealing with this different kind of dyad. This saint has therefore, in effect, transcended historical circumstances, yet (rather like an *avatāra* or a *bōdhisattva*) he frequently reenters history to help each member of the lineage. In fact, he is always present in the person of each Tōṇṭadārya swami. For instance, "Anādi Siddhaliṅgēśvara or Śiva gives *śakti* to the swamis of the Tōṇṭadārya Math lineage seat (*pīṭha*)."

The creation of such lineage relationships is a subtle and complex matter, and occurs primarily through what I shall call mutual *subtle gift-giving*.[22] One could also characterize such relationships in terms of the transmission of subtle qualities, including the swami's offering love or devotion and meditational worship to the founder/guru. Similar worship is also offered in the Liṅgāyat monastic and lay traditions to the *iṣṭaliṅga* — the small *liṅga* which the devotee holds in the left palm and gazes upon steadily (*istalinga pūje*). The relationship with Siddhaliṅgēśvara need not involve visible worship such as *pūje*, although a living guru will most likely receive *pādapūje* ("worship of the feet"). The founder in return offers his grace (*anugraha*), blessings (*āśīrvād*), knowledge, assistance and power (*śakti*).[23]

One example of such a relationship within the lineage is found in an oral historical account about one of the Tōṇṭadārya swamis — the ninth Jagadguru, Ardhanarīśvara Swami (1672-1722). It is said that Ardhanarīśvara was installed as Jagadguru when a young boy and that the elder disciples were not at all happy with being passed over in this way. Their jealousy led them to chase him through the Karnataka countryside until they reached Ḍambaḷ village, today the site of a Tōṇṭadārya branch *maṭh*. Along the way they were delayed by a river which flooded just as they arrived at its banks!

> After three days the flood subsided and the hundreds of disciples crossed the river. When they reached Ḍambaḷ they went to a temple where the new Jagadguru Ardhanarīśvara was in *dhyāna yōga* (the yoga of meditation) — floating up in midair as light as a feather. They were flabbergasted and spontaneously began chanting *Jay Ghōṣ* (like "Jaya Siddhaliṅga" or "Jaya Hara Hara Mahādēv"). Seeing such a sight, they repented of their folly and said, "Now we know you are Abhinava Siddhaliṅga (the new or recent manifestation of Siddhaliṅgēśvara). They then became his *caramūrtis* (disciple-swamis) and were sent out to various villages such as Sondūra, Hospēṭ, Kuruvathi, Mysore, Uravakoṇḍe, and others.

In another part of the narrative, Ardhanarīśvara Swami tells a royal devotee, the Keḷadi Queen Mallamambe, that her wish to bear a child will be fulfilled. "Ardhanarīśvara had been told by Siddhaliṅgēśvara that this was true." Here is another story:

> Once at the time of an Ardhanarīśvara Purāṇa Maṅgala (final day of telling of a *purāṇa* about this swami) the king's family wanted to arrange for *dāsōha* (free food distribution) at the Ḍambaḷ Maṭh. (Since they lived in Keḷadi) everyone in the family prepared for the journey to Ḍambaḷ. Ardhanarīśvara (who was in Ḍambaḷ) knew through Siddhaliṅgēśvara's *antarada jñāna* (inner knowledge) and his *ātma śakti* (the power of his soul) that the Keḷadis wanted to come. He also knew how much inconvenience that would mean for them. So he caused himself to be transported telepathically to Keḷadi.

These stories reveal that a great deal of subtle gift-giving and communication is believed to take place between the founder and the lineage swamis. The swami receives a stream of such subtle gifts beginning at the time when he is given *paṭṭābhiṣēka* (installation as Jagadguru), which initiates the subtle communication process.[24] The swami must give up worldly thoughts and focus on Siddhaliṅgēśvara for the process effectively to be actualized; the installation ceremony alone does not ensure the desired effect.

The founder-swami relationship is viewed as a spiritual family (*adhyātmika kuṭumba*) relationship, and resembles other sorts of familial relationships in India in a number of interesting ways, such as in the emphasis upon male linear relationships and the belief in transmission/sharing of subtle qualities such as love, knowledge, blessings, authority, and *śakti*.[25] The family members are, as Davis[26] and others have pointed out, like "one unit." They are made one by this subtle sharing.

Likewise, the intent of the founder-swami relationship is a sharing of inner qualities or subtle gifts which will result in both equality of status and "Oneness" in a very intimate sense . People clearly believe that each swami in the Tōṇṭadārya lineage not only receives qualities such as *śakti* from Siddhaliṅgēśvara, but that this results in his *becoming* Siddhaliṅgēśvara. One example may be seen in the first story related above (about Siddhaliṅgēśvara manifesting himself as Ardhanarīśvara). Another is represented by the present Siddhaliṅga Swami (who was named after the founder): "Siddhaliṅga Swami is Siddhaliṅgēśvara so we bow and seek his protection." The actualization of this Oneness is described as merging with God: "Paramātmā (God) will give *śakti* to a person but he must take up God's work. He merges with the person's soul (*ātman*) to give the latter *śakti*." Interestingly, informants attest that the current swami is *potentially* a full manifestation of Siddhaliṅgēśvara, and also that he *is* the founder. This accords with their belief that though generically swamis are realized beings, they still have to attain that realization in most cases. Importantly, Siddhaliṅgēśvara is said to offer his qualities and his assistance, in effect *himself*, to each swami of the lineage.

What is curious about this conception of Oneness or mutual identity which is formed between founder and swami is that each lineage swami also is said to retain his own distinct personality. Stories about lineage swamis always begin with a word or two about the unique attributes of each member. There is thus an interesting "identity-cum-difference" situation portrayed here which bears resemblance to Hindu philosophical *bhēdābhēda* and *viśiṣṭādvaita* positions.[27] Sometimes this seeming paradox is explained by the idea of the founder/guru being in the heart of the swami.

"Siddhaliṅgēśvara is in the heart of all swamis who occupy the seat (*pīṭha*) of this lineage. They naturally receive some of his *śakti*." Informants also say that the swami becomes a vessel (*pātre*) for Siddhaliṅgēśvara, who then in effect can "shine out" through the swami's personality. The attainment of such Oneness is the culmination of each lineage swami's spiritual practice (*sādhane*); if he acquires the

the subtle qualities and guidance of the founder he thereby attains the identity of the founder (complete assimilation with divinity). The relationship, however, can and should continue. This is made possible by the "difference" part of the "identity-cum-difference," which, in a fashion similar to certain theological traditions such as Rāmānuja's Śrī Vaiṣṇavism, preserves the distinction between the *two* (God and human being, founder and swami) who love each other. Whatever the swami accomplishes henceforth is appropriately seen as the work or inspiration (*prēraṇe*) of the inner Siddhaliṅgēśvara; he should not claim his inner power as his own.

The Meaning of Gross Gift-Giving in The Swami-Devotee Relationship

With the *śakti* and grace of a realized being at his command, the swami is expected to enter voluntarily into relationships with householder devotees (bhaktas) — people such as the Baṇṇagārs and Banajigas who have traditionally visited Tōṇṭadārya Maṭh. In addition, people of other Liṅgāyat and non-Liṅgāyat castes and subcastes visit the *maṭh*, either because it is a family or community tradition, or because they are attracted by a particular swami occupying the monastic seat (*pīṭha*). Again, initially the relationship is hierarchical; the swami is treated as a loved superior and devotees visit the *maṭh* and offer fruit and other cooked and uncooked food, flowers, money, and grain to the swami. Sometimes lands and service in the form of manual or administrative labor are also given. Such offerings should be made within a model framework of ritual action: the bhakta enters the swami's chamber, places his gift before the swami, and bows or fully prostrates before him. The swami then may offer advice to the bhakta, help him to solve a particular problem (*mārga darśana*), or make general inquiries about the bhakta's welfare. The swami then returns some of the offered food or any other material gift which he has blessed to the devotee. These gifts are variously called *āśīrvād* (blessed gift), *prasād* (blessed food — either raw fruit or an entire cooked meal), and *bhasma/vibhūti* (sacred ash), to name but a few of the most common gifts. The devotee will at some point eat, drink, smear on his body, or otherwise utilize the gift.

Similar interactions take place if the swami should visit a devotee's home. For instance, the bhakta will perform a *pādapūje* worship of the swami's feet from which blessed water (*pādōdaka*) is obtained. This water is then drunk or sprinkled in the house. This type of holy gift-giving has been documented extensively throughout India at *maṭhs* and temples as well as in homes.[28]

Although on the surface there appear to be many differences between the gross workings of the swami-bhakta relationship and the subtle ones of the founder-swami relationship, the disparity is less than it may seem. For instance, in both cases mutual gift-exchange takes place. In the founder-swami relationship most of the gifts are subtle gifts – love, concentration, *śakti*, grace and blessings, and knowledge. In the swami-bhakta relationship material gift-giving is predominant. However, the crucial link lies in the similar subtle contents of these visible material gifts. These are elements like love which an external observer may tend to miss, but they form the core of informants' beliefs about the true meaning of each interaction and each gift.

It seems people are suggesting that there is a substance-energy continuum in the world which links gross matter with subtle qualities such as energy, love, intentions, and thoughts or feelings. Indian yoga systems have similarly clearly connected the three (or four) bodies and realms – causal, subtle, and gross (and perhaps supra-causal – the Self). The *sūkṣma* (subtle) realm includes thought, feeling, and intent, as it does in the Karnataka system.

Secondly, yoga consistently attributes greater importance and sanctity to the subtler levels of existence. This would make feeling and thought, for instance, more important than the gross human body or material gifts. They would also be more "real" in the sense that they are closer in the cosmic creation process to the subtlest of subtle – the inner self (*ātman*) or God. Finally, while feelings and intentions are important, their significance lies in their ability to express (e.g., through love) or mask (e.g., through hatred, greed, ego) the inner divinity.

Subtle qualities are transmitted between swami and bhakta and appear to interpenetrate all lives of both. Gross material gifts such as money, bananas, or cloth can contain and be penetrated by subtle qualities. In the swami-bhakta relationship these elements are in fact nearly the same as those passed between founder and swami: love and devotion (*prēma* and bhakti), humility, a spirit of service, and trust (*viśvāsa*) offered by the bhakta; and purifying *śakti*, grace, blessings, knowledge, and the impulse to devotion (*prēraṇe*) given by the swami. The blessed gifts which the swami gives thus are especially important for the bhaktas in affecting their spiritual progress because the swami's qualities and so he himself are contained within the material gifts. Here are a few samples of the numerous statements which informants made concerning this process:

> Every particle of dust from the swami's feet contains power. This gets mixed in with the *dhūlpādōdaka* (foot-wash water), which is then sprinkled in the house, purifying (*śuddha māḍuvadu*) it.
>
> Bad qualities will go when the swami gives *āśīrvād* (blessing, blessed gift); *śakti* will flow from his hand into our heads. There is a current in the feet of the swami. It will flow through our bodies.
>
> Persons with great spiritual power have a merciful attitude toward living organisms, wanting to remove their problems — thus miracles (*pavādas*) are performed. Love directed downward toward the poor is called *karuṇā* (compassion). When a person with bhakti (devotion) seeks the *darśan* of a swami, the swami will fill his sight full of grace, and then the bhakta's sins are removed.

The gross material aspect of these gifts — to which external observers have at times given undue emphasis in their attempts to extrapolate religious (or economic) principles — is in fact only the external casing for an inner dynamic exchange of qualities involving holy power and grace. One might simply suggest that the inner traits have been "embodied" (as holy power gets embodied in a temple idol) for the benefit of the less spiritually advanced devotee. And, in fact, the swami-bhakta relationship is also characterized by the giving of subtle gifts apart from the medium of material objects. For instance, the swami gives *darśan* (his holy sight) and the subtle form of *āśīrvād* (blessing rather than blessed gift). These too, however, are usually transmitted through the medium of eye-to-eye contact (*darśan*) or hand-to-head, feet-to-head contact (*āśīrvād*). They are thus still actively utilizing contact on a gross physical level to accomplish subtle tasks.

> *Āśīrvād* is a blessing, a physical manifestation of a spiritual blessing. Humans need something to touch and feel rather than something abstract. People go away more contented; they have *proof* of the blessing.

For the devotee the visible form of the gift can serve — as Geertz has noted concerning religious cultural systems and rituals[29] — both as an externally expressed *model of* those subtle gifts (e.g., giving a gift to the swami expresses love), and as a *model for* the cultivation of these inner feelings (giving a gift should help to cultivate love in the giver). The material form of the gifts also allows the swami to transmit *śakti* or grace to or into the bhakta (e.g., through simple ingestion or skin contact) even though the devotee may not be able to receive it easily in subtle form. A person who has not advanced far spiritually could thus obtain some benefit from a swami's power.

The effects of a swami's power on the bhakta are believed to vary widely; they range from very little observable effect to full spiritual realization. The range of answers given by my informants suggested that each person's views of what he or she wanted in a particular instance represented what he or she believes is attainable. Although initially confusing, such findings do not indicate that a random logic is at work here. The system, with regard to both the founder-swami relationship and the swami-bhakta relationship, is so constructed that it gives great importance to the *intentions* of the lower status member in each dyad. Intensions — for example, what the bhakta wants and expects from the swami, or how he feels about the swami — will determine, in large part, the effect of any gift which the swami gives. The swami's power and blessings are not thereby devalued; they are in effect put at the disposal of the needs and desires of the bhakta. They "effect" the attainment of those needs and thus contribute to the devotee's spiritual advancement. The following statements demonstrate how this process works:

> *Āśīrvād* has the power to fulfill our desires if we have a strong determination and faith — our faith (*nambike*) draws on the spiritual power [which the swami possesses]. The swami touches his chest [in *namaskāra* or greeting] after the person does *namaskāra* [by bowing].
>
> When we bow before a swami he wishes that our desires be fulfilled. We bow with desire and then it is fulfilled by his desire; it's reciprocal.
>
> The swami-bhakta relationshp is the same as the guru-disciple (*śiṣya*) relationship. The guru has the lamp. We have the oil and the wick. The guru has both bhakti and good conduct. The *śiṣya*) comes to the guru and develops devotion toward him; then the guru can light the *śiṣya's* lamp. Good actions are also necessary. The guru is like a philosopher's stone (*maṇi paruṣa*) changing iron into gold.

The evidence suggests that the swami-bhakta relationship, like the founder-swami relationship, has spiritual liberation as its final goal. This is made clear by the fact that so many factors run parallel in the two types of relationships. In addition, a number of statements by informants indicate potential equality between swami and bhakta, thus identifying this relationship as an equality-creating one much in the manner of the founder-swami relationship:

> Through *āśīrvād* (blessing) we can become like swamis. A bhakta can become a swami if his will is strong enough.
>
> A bhakta has a strong mental conviction that the guru [swami] is superior to him. He offers him all respect. So the guru helps the bhakta to get *mukti* (spiritual liberation).
>
> A bhakta may become a swami through education.[30]

Conclusion

It is hardly surprising that the swami-devotee relationship should parallel that of founder-swami in its overall pattern, equality-creating intent, and exchange of subtle qualities and personal identity. In both cases the lower member is aided by being "infused" with superior knowledge and qualities which combine with his own traits to raise him to the level of the superior member of the dyad. This can occur slowly or rapidly, depending on the karmic state and intentions of the lower member and the actual achievement of the superior member. The final goal, however, is human divinization — the attainment of the person's own true identity which is characterized by purity and power (see Diagram I). Purity, power, goodness, and wisdom are natural concomitants to one another in this system; all express the state of divinity. "Power" (*śakti*) however seems to be informants' favorite mode of expression, with "purity" running a close second.

This concept of "pure power" or "powerful purity" differs from the sense in which either Louis Dumont or Mary Douglas, for instance, speak about purity. For Dumont purity is more a religio-social concept than one which explains a powerful divine or even physical reality. For him it is to be contrasted with (political) "power," not connected with it, and is a distinguishing feature only of a hierarchical religious/social system.[31] Purity without power is, according to the equality-creating model, not powerful enough to resist impurity, and under these conditions, a hierarchical caste system predicated upon avoidance of impurity might result. Douglas' model of purity is similarly a social one. She says concern with purity has to do with protecting weak points in the social or religious order. Here, too, the explanation reduces purity to a useful man-made concept rather than allowing for the view of informants that it reflects *actual* purity or power.[32] It also tends to present purity as a relatively "weak" religious idea. This limits the idea of its active transmissible and transformational potential. In Karnataka these capabilities are crucial to the entire religious world view, and purity can further be connected with both spiritual unity and a move toward religio-social equality.

Secondly, we must question the nature of the Hindu renouncer himself. Dumont has suggested that he is an "individual" both in a social and in a personal sense.[33] This data from north Karnataka suggest that such is not strictly speaking the case. Throughout his life, both as a disciple-swami and as a teacher of his own devotees, the swami in this system is interacting on both gross and subtle levels with others. Although he is to remain physically separate during his meditation and mentally detached, he is also exchanging subtle qualities with others and thus modifying his identity or that of his devotees in the direction of spiritual perfection. The generally accepted Hindu conception of a renouncer similarly insists that he or she become "One" with God or guru, or at least cultivate free-flowing inner communication with the divine. The result, seen for instance in the concept of seeing the whole world as the play of divine Consciousness (*cit*), or experiencing nothing but God, would not in fact be the consciousness of one who is an "individual."

In the external observable sense, renouncers are also frequently not totally separate "individuals," as Dumont himself has noted.[34] Indian holy persons and renouncer-gurus have always been expected to receive and give gifts to devoted persons who approach them. This is true even for those elusive sages who live in caves in the Himalayas. In general, Hindu holy persons avoid interacting with people and giving and receiving gifts only for fear of being polluted or absorbing undesirable qualities from others. These include impure thoughts, intentions, ritual impurities, and various forms of karma or undesirable influences. They have also been obliged to avoid family and caste obligations which were often seen to result from gift exchange. For instance, the *jajmānī* system involves required exchange of goods and services between castes and individuals. But in the Karnataka system there is a strong sense that a true swami has absolutely nothing to fear from the receipt of any gift or from interaction with any type of person. This is so since his "inner fire" is completely pure and powerful. He is fully divine. For this reason informants say that he not only can, but *should* interact with devotees and accept gifts from those who give them. He should do so because he has the ability to purify others of their saṃsāric tendencies. Gift-giving and interaction still create a "sharing" of qualities. But this sharing brings *up* the status of the bhakta or disciple-swami rather than bringing *down* the status and purity of the superior giver. Historically, monastic renouncers have been involved in the ordinary social world in a great many ways — providing educational facilities, acting as judges in disputes, running resthouses, trading, and so forth. Thus, many types of acceptable interaction between renouncers and "the world" have occurred in addition to the giving of blessed gifts and spiritual knowledge.

My view of the renouncer, the devotee and other figures discussed in this chapter is compatible with McKim Marriott's view that the South Asian person is "composite and capable of transmission."[35]

Such a perspective is far less static than the fixed view of the renouncer as an "individual," and it is more representative of the fact that people are believed to be able to achieve change in their internal personal states and in their ritual and social statuses as well.

But in an important sense a realized swami or renouncer *is* properly regarded as an individual. His essential connection with Siddhaliṅgēśvara, guru, *liṅga*, or God means that he has gained complete mastery over himself and over any fears he may have had of being polluted. He thus need not remain in a cave, isolated from social contact, if he does not wish to. As my informants attest, he has a responsibility to help people (as God does, and of course God is also an equality-creator!), since he is able to do so. Supremely powerful, with a corresponding compassionate interest in gracing others with power, he is naturally "moral" (as God is "moral") and so does not need to abide by a paltry set of ordinary social rules. To facilitate his task, which requires that he not be bound by such rules and obligations, his *sannyāsa* or Virakta status allows him officially to separate himself from family and caste.

Although the Karnataka religious system seems to support Marriott's position more than it does Dumont's, I have found it possible to draw from both Dumont's and Marriott's data and conclusions in expressing the model of the renouncer-swami and his relationships in north Karnataka. The key to the renouncer's religious centrality in this system is that he has become a vehicle for the dissemination of purifying power and grace to the other members of the monastic and lay communities. In a sense, therefore, he stands at the *top* of Hindu society as he also stands *apart* from it in certain regards. Like a judge in a courtroom, he participates in the proceedings of life's drama but remains aloof from whatever case is at hand due to his meditative detachment and inner unity with God. Only thus is he fit to render judgment and offer assistance to the people who come to him. In most cases, however, courtroom judges cannot award the defendant spiritual power, grace, and self-realization! The renouncer's aim here is to lead others (within the context of dyadic relationships[36]) toward spiritual unity with God and by extension to promote greater ritual and social equality in the world.

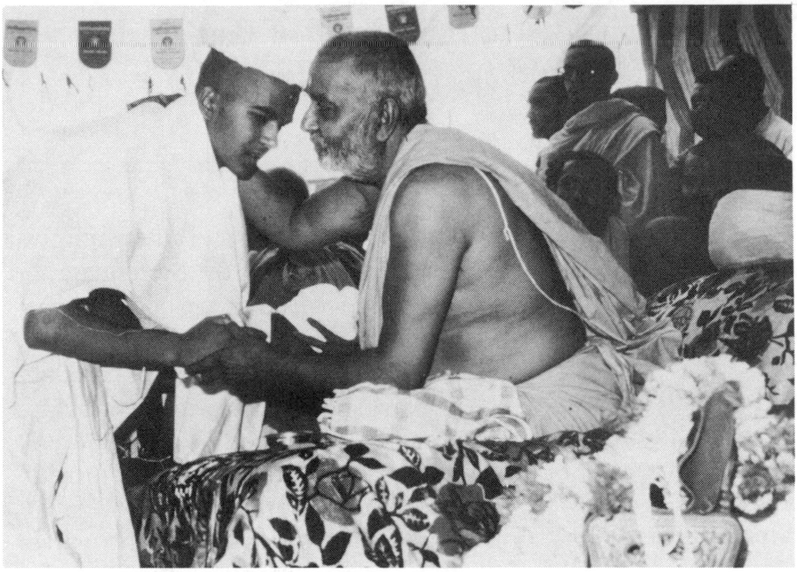

Narayanswarupdas Swami (Pramukh Swami) giving the new name during the ceremony for an initiate into the first stage of ascetic life. Photo by Raymond B. Williams.

8
The Holy Man as the Abode of God in the Swaminarayanan Religion

Raymond B. Williams

SHASTRI NARAYANSWARUPDAS SWAMI, the spiritual and administrative leader of the Akshar Purushottam Sanstha of the Swaminarayan religion, always keeps before him a small metal image of Swaminarayan. The literature of the group and the conduct of his followers make it clear that both the person and the image are believed to be the abode of god. The practice of regarding a holy man or woman as divine, a manifestation of god, or as a deity, is common in India. Several schemata or general concepts formulated within Hinduism provide the contexts for understanding the relation of the holy person to the deity or divine principle. Those who claim divine status for themselves or for others have a common store of texts, images and concepts for teaching and apologetic purposes. The Upaniṣadic verse is often quoted: "The one who knows Brahman is Brahman." The Vaiṣṇava doctrine of *avatāra* provides the theoretic framework for many manifestations of god. The *purāṇic* literature describes the activities of divine persons and provides the charter for contemporary devotional activities. The teaching that the consort of the deity is the perfect devotee is transposed to the idea that the primary devotee in the devotional sect is the eternal companion of the deity. These are only illustrations from the great store of concepts and images present in what we have come to call Hinduism, which are available to validate and explain the position of the holy man or woman.

Hinduism is an amalgam of many traditions, and the individual is not a "Hindu in general" but a "Hindu in particular." He or she participates in a particular tradition (*sampradāya*) handed down from a founder through successive religious teachers which forms the followers into a distinct fellowship with institutional forms. Particularity is an essential feature of religious and group affiliation. Holy or divine persons are such only within the confines of a set of doctrines, practices, and rituals, the constellation of which is unique to the *sampradāya*. The form and function of instruction through various media regarding the holy person's relation to god or to a divine principle is specific if not exclusive to the group.

This chapter examines one such tradition: the form and function of the doctrines, practices, and rituals which validate and explain the position of Shastri Narayanswarupdas Swami (1921-) in the Akshar Purushottam Sanstha of the Swarminarayan religion in Gujarat. Followers honor him with the title, "His Divine Holiness Pramukh Swami Mahārāj," and revere him as the abode of god. The Akshar Purushottam Sanstha, of which he is the undisputed leader, is one of the two major divisions of the Swaminarayan religion. The doctrines and practices which ascribe to him and to his predecessors status as the abode of god are the primary causes of the separation of the Akshar Purushottam Sanstha from the larger, older institutions of the Swaminarayan religion.

This modern form of Vaiṣṇava religion is based upon the life and teaching of Sahajanand Swami (1781-1830), a *sādhu*, who taught in Gujarat and who instituted a number of religious reforms in the chaotic first part of the nineteenth century, when British control of Gujarat catalyzed significant social change.[1] He has been called the last of the medieval saints and an early representative of neo-Hinduism. His followers gave him the name "Swaminarayan" and worshiped him as an *avatāra* of god. He placed images of Kṛṣṇa, as well as images of himself, in temples he built, and it seems that some followers worshiped him as a new manifestation of Kṛṣṇa according to the traditional Vaiṣṇava teaching that a new *avatāra* of Viṣṇu appears on earth to save devotees from chaotic situations. Soon, even during his lifetime, they came to believe that Swaminarayan was the highest manifestation of god in human form, superior to Kṛṣṇa and Rāma and all other divine figures. The religious community which he founded now has hundreds of men who have become *sādhus*, many temples and shrines, and several million followers among Gujaratis, primarily in India, but also in East Africa, Great Britain, and the United States.

Two significant aspects of the theology of the group provide elaboration and transformation of the traditional *avatāra* doctrine: (1) Sahajanand Swami, now worshiped as Swaminarayan, is the human manifestation of *puruṣōttama*, but his corporeal form is not simply a vehicle for god's presence on earth. The bodily manifestation is not viewed as analogous to the manifestation of divinity in metal or stone images (*arcā*); rather, his body is conceived to be in some way non-material and outside or beyond the level of being manifested in the *avatāras* or in the temple images. (2) The human manifestation of *puruṣōttama* is coupled with a second kind of manifestation of divinity in the person of the supreme devotee, who both serves god and embodies the very god he serves. This doctrine is called *akṣara*, and in some ways the personal *akṣara* is a human equivalent of the material image (*arcā*). This relation is clearly demonstrated when Narayanswarupdas is outside a temple, for a small metal image of Swaminarayan is always prominently kept in his presence. Devotees take *darśana* of both together. The theology has not been accepted without dispute and even factional division in the *sampradāya*, but it provides insight into this modern form of Hinduism.

Sahajanand Swami taught that five eternal entities exist: *parabrahman, akṣarabrahman, māyā, jīva*, and *īśvara*. The last two, including deities and previous *avatāras*, are affected by *māyā*. The first two are eternally free from the effects of *māyā*. All are dependent upon *parabrahman* which is eternally independent. In the literature of the group, the terms "*brahman*," "*akṣarabrahman*," and "*akṣara*" refer to the same entity. Followers accept Swaminarayan as the full, perfect human manifestation of *parabrahman*, the supreme person. No distinction is made between the human form of Swaminarayan on earth and the eternal form of *puruṣōttama* in the eternal abode. "*Puruṣōttama*" is interpreted as supreme [*para*], reality [*sat*], self [*ātman*]. It is often translated as "the supreme person" and is considered to be the highest divine reality. This eternal abode is identified with *akṣarabrahman* as *akṣardhām*. Thus, Swaminarayan is the focus of the theology and ritual of this *sampradāya*. He is the human face of god.

Swaminarayan is thought to be the single, complete manifestation of the supreme person, and, as such, is superior in power and efficacy to all other manifestations of god. A reordering of divine beings is suggested. The deities as forms of *īśvara* are involved in the flux of the world (*māyā*) through their activities of creation, sustenance, and destruction of the universe. Each *avatāra* was sent into the world by the supreme person and was manifested at his will. Not every form of *īśvara* manifests the same level of perfection according to this interpretation, and preference is given to those in human form. Superior to all, then, is Swaminarayan, thought to be the perfect and complete manifestation of *puruṣōttama* in his human form on earth. Human form and light are recurrent themes in the descriptions of the form of *puruṣōttama*. An important passage of the *Vacanāmṛtam*, a collection of philosophical sermons delivered by Swaminarayan between 1819 and 1829 and compiled by four of his disciples, contains this description:

> Within this shining light I see the image of God as extremely lustrous. Even though the complexion of God is dark, with the extreme luminosity

> emanating from Him, He appears fair. He is almost human in shape with two hands, two legs, and has a fascinating charm. He does not possess four hands or eight or a thousand hands. He is perfectly like a human being and a young person.[2]

Sahajanand agreed with Rāmānuja, against Śaṅkara, that *puruṣōttama* is not formless.

The second eternal principle eternally free from the effects of *māyā* is *akṣarabrahman*. The modified non-dualism of Rāmānuja allowed for some degree of distinction within ultimate reality, and Sahajanand elaborated this duality by indicating that two entities, *puruṣōttama* and *akṣara*, are eternal and free from the effects of *māyā*. *Akṣara* is the eternal abode of *puruṣōttama* and has an impersonal form and, according to the Akshar Purushottam Sanstha, also a personal form. Although mythic references to *akṣara* as a location exist in the literature, the philosophers of the sect explain that it is an immaterial state. Van Buitenen's conclusion, based upon the history of the *akṣara* concept in Indian philosophy, that the term suggests "the first and fundamental principle of the cosmic order"[3] is applicable in Swaminarayan theology. Thus, *akṣara* has the character of a state or abode of *puruṣōttama* and functions as the intermediary of the activities of the supreme person.

The state of *akṣara* is such that when *puruṣōttama* manifested himself on earth as Swaminarayan, *akṣara* was not vacant; indeed, *akṣara* was present on earth as the abode of god. This theology is centered in the nature of divine form. *Akṣara* is both space and form much like a vessel that at once can be the body for god as well as the place of his dwelling. Sahajanand is quoted in the *Vacanāmṛtam*:

> Lord Purushottam can manifest simultaneously in His divine form in each and every universe whenever He desires and in whatever form He desires. . . . But at no time has He to leave His divine Abode, Akshar, for various such incarnations. He is always seated in His Akshardham inseparably attached to Akshar. Therefore, it is said that whenever He manifests, Akshar is said to be in the centre around Him.[4]

According to Sahajanand, *akṣarabrahman* and *parabrahman* are two distinct realities related to each other through the *śarīra-śarīrī* relation. That is, *akṣarabrahman* is the *śarīra* of *parabrahman* who is its *śarīrī*. This means that *akṣarabrahman* is pervaded by *puruṣōttama* and depends upon him for existence and activities.[5] In Rāmānuja's philosophy the entire universe is seen as the body of god, and it is only rarely that the terms are used of the god-devotee in Śrīvaiṣṇava theology. Here the specialized relationship is between *puruṣōttama* and *akṣara*. *Akṣara* is the eternal abode of god and ultimately the abode of all released souls. All followers of the Swaminarayan religion share these teachings regarding *puruṣōttama* and the impersonal form of *akṣara*.

The Akshar Purushottama Sanstha, a twentieth-century movement, developed an elaborate theology of *akṣara*. The formal split from the parent group took place when Swami Yagnapurushdas (1865-1951) left the Swaminarayan temple at Vadtal in Gujarat in 1906 with six *sādhus* and a few lay followers to form a new institution. From that modest beginning the group has grown to approach the older group in numbers of temples, men of *sādhu* standing, and total membership. The central and unique teaching of the new group is that the *akṣara* is an eternally existing spiritual reality having two forms, the impersonal and the personal. The impersonal form is essentially that described above. It is everywhere; yet it is formless.

His teaching concerning the personal form of *akṣara* (presently manifested in the person of Shastri Narayanaswarupdas) caused Swami Yagnapurushdas to be expelled from the Vadtal temple. Swami Yagnapurushdas taught that *puruṣōttama* appeared in the world in the form of Swaminaryan along with the personal form of the *akṣara*, who is his eternal abode. The personal *akṣara* was always present with Swaminarayan, but not all persons were able to perceive the presence of the *akṣara*. Thus, the two eternal entities appeared together. According to the literature and iconography of the group, other *muktas*, or eternally-released souls, appeared with *puruṣōttama* from *akṣardhām*. The essential difference is that whereas the other entities had achieved a state of release through a process of ethical and spiritual discipline, *akṣarabrahman* is the eternally existing ideal for devotees. Yājñavalkya's discourse was accepted as a sacred text by Swaminarayan, and it contains the proof-text regarding *akṣara*: "if one does not know this *akṣara*, then one's oblations, sacrifices and austerities for many thousands of years in this world will come to an end; and when one departs from this world without knowing the *akṣara*, one is miserable."[6]

Swami Yajnapurushdas identified the *akṣara* with Gunatitanand Swami (1785-1864), who was a close companion of Sahajanand Swami. He was from a Brahmin family of the small village of Bhadra near Jamnagar in Saurashtra. He became a *sādhu* in the order of Swaminarayan and for forty years was the *mahant* of the large Swaminarayan temple at Junagadh. The Akshar Purushottam Sanstha teaches that he was the perfect devotee of Swaminarayan and, as the abode of god, was the manifestation of *akṣara*. Hence, he is worthy of worship. Followers quote the instruction of Swaminarayan:

> As one offers worship to God by performing rituals, similarly the choicest devotee of God also should be equally offered worship by performing the same rituals and offering him the same sanctified offerings which are graced by God."[7]

Swami Yagnapurushdas was forced out of the Vadtal temple because the officials feared he would attempt to place an image of Gunatitanand Swami in the central shrine building of the temple. Indeed, images of Gunatitanand Swami are now found beside those of Swaminarayan in the central shrines of the temples of the Akshar Purushottam Sanstha.

The concept that god is accompanied by his perfect devotee or abode is illustrated by *purāṇic* and iconographic examples. Viṣṇu is accompanied by Śrī, who is thought to be the mediatrix through whom the devotees approach god. Rādhā is always in the presence of Kṛṣṇa as the perfect example of devotion. Rāma incarnates with Lakṣmaṇa and Kṛṣṇa with Balarāma. Lakṣmaṇa and Balarāma are devotees, servants, and constant companions of the deity and are represented as *avatāras* of Ādiśēṣa (the bed, if not the abode of Viṣṇu). These are only illustrations of the relation between *puruṣōttama* and *akṣara*, between Swaminarayan and Gunatitanand. Identity of the images is not affirmed. The conceptual links between "abode of god," "perfect devotee," and "consort of god" relate the logic of this sect to that of other Hindu theologies. However scholars of the group perceive a difference; whereas Śrī and Rādhā do not have impersonal forms, *akṣara* has both personal and impersonal forms.

A further development of the doctrine came with the teaching that *akṣara* continually manifests on earth in the form of the perfect devotee. This implies a succession of persons who are earthly manifestations of the divine principle. Gunatitanand was the first in this spiritual lineage, a *sādhu* from a Brahmin caste. The second is an unlikely figure because he was a householder from a *sat-śūdra* caste. Pragji Bhakta (1829-1897) was a loyal disciple of Gunatitanand at Junagadh, and his place in the teaching and iconography of the group indicates that theoretically householders, even those from very low castes, can attain the highest spiritual status. Yagnapurushdas, the third in line, was the first to form a separate religious institution. He was a *sādhu* from a Vaiṣya caste and was the spiritual and administrative leader of the new institution until his death. He was accepted as the perfect devotee and abode of god. Swami Jnanjivandas (1891-1971), also a *sādhu* from a Vaiṣya caste, was his successor and was particularly effective in stimulating strong devotion and in greatly augmenting the ranks of *sādhus* and of householders associated with the institution. Swami Narayanswarupdas, also a *sādhu* from a Vaiṣya caste, was appointed president and administrator under Jnanjivandas. He was given the popular name "Pramukh Swami" or "President Swami." He is now the spiritual leader as well as administrator, and he is accepted as the current manifestation of *akṣarabrahman*. The last half of the century has thus far been marked by rapid growth, which is attributed to the attractiveness of these men, who as perfect devotees and as the abode of god, lead followers to god and ultimately to release in *akṣardhām*.

Devotees believe that a succession of divine manifestations of *akṣara* will continue until the end of time, thus providing examples for followers and appropriate leaders for the Swaminarayan religion. The manifestation of *puruṣōttama*, and, one supposes, of *avatāras*, have ceased with Sahajanand Swami, while the historical visibility of god now depends on a succession of perfect devotees. The *akṣara* doctrine makes more accessible and further humanizes an already human god. Followers maintain that *akṣarabrahman* is one and not many, so each of the manifestations possesses all the characteristics of *akṣarabrahman*. The figures merge, and differences of perception of characteristics are in the eyes of the beholders. Only one personal manifestation of *akṣara* is thought to exist at a time, and although each shows different personal characteristics depending upon the requirements of the times, in terms of the spiritual hierarchy they share the same divine attributes. Current devotees have three gurus in living memory — Yagnapurushdas, Jnanjivandas, and Narayanswarupdas — but they see in the present guru the remanifestation of those who preceded him. The individuals are accepted as manifestations of *akṣara* and are believed to be the same as the eternal reality which is always present with and serving *puruṣōttama*. Images of Gunatitanand Swami in the central shrines of the Akshar Purushottam Sanstha represent the other manifestations of *akṣara* as well, but their images, usually in pictorial form, are placed in subsidiary shrines and are the objects of worship and devotion.

Swami Narayanswarupdas maintains a paradoxical position: he is the perfect, humble devotee and also the supreme spiritual leader of the institution and current manifestation of *akṣarabrahman*. The special character of his acts of worship displays the paradox. He is at the same time the primary worshiper and himself the object of worship. Like all *sādhus* and many householders of the sect, Narayanswarupdas performs the ritual of morning worship with the image of

Swaminarayan before him. His ritual performance is the same as that of the others, except that male devotees sit before him in a reverent attitude as he worships. It is clear that they direct their worship to him, and he directs his worship to the image of Swaminarayan that is always kept in his presence. All garlands and gifts presented to him are first presented before the image. When the assembled devotees chant the list of the spiritual hierarchy, he stops with the name of his predecessor or chants "Narayana" while the other devotees shout "Pramukh Swami Mahārāj."

He does not claim for himself divinity or demand such honors. His role forbids such claims because pride, self-praise, and ostentation break the rules of conduct for a *sādhu*. When I asked him if his physical body is divine, he said that it is not his place to say. He maintained that his goal is not to encourage people to worship him, but to point them to correct worship of Swaminarayan. Followers view his response as a demonstration of the humility and self-denial that is appropriate to a devotee, a covering of the true radiance of *akṣarabrahman*, and this inspires them to shower him with even greater honor and worship. They follow the injunction of one prominent devotee that "he should be worshiped with the same idolatry which one offers to God."[8] Such bhakta worship is a theme of widespread currency in both Vaiṣṇava and Śaiva bhakti sects. In earlier times, the person of the sacral king was also venerated in festivals as the living icon and the king was thought to be the perfect devotee of god who manifested the *śakti* in human form. Narayanswarupdas is called "Mahārāj." It may be that in the future the character of Swaminarayan will become more remote and cosmic while the humanity of god will rest in the living icons of Narayanswarupdas' successors. It is, however, too early to chart the course of such a development.

During a private interview on 2 March 1980 Narayanswarupdas spoke about his understanding of his identification with *akṣara*. He indicated that at every moment he is aware of being the *akṣara* of *puruṣōttama*, the manifestation of the abode of god. He came to this awareness when he met his spiritual guru and predecessor in the spiritual hierarchy, Swami Yagnapurushdas. He said that without the constant knowledge of his identity as the abode of god, he would not be able to do all the work that is required of him. He feels a constant union with Swaminarayan and attempts to observe all the requirements prescribed for a devotee.

The eternal cosmic form is enshrouded in human form. Observers see Narayanswarpudas as a man with all the limitations of human existence. His disciples insist that he behaves as a man because most people would not be able to stand the full revelation of *akṣara*. The idea that a human manifestation of divinity behaves as a "mere mortal" out of regard for people who are unable to bear a full divine revelation has famous mythological parallels in Kṛṣṇa stories. Even though his disciples believe that he has complete knowledge of everything that is going to happen and seek his advice and counsel, he nonetheless asks, as one devotee observed with some amusement, for their assistance. Followers believe that he is so filled with divinity that he attains the greater state even beyond knowing of his divinity.

The next manifestation of *akṣara* is already present in the institution, but only Narayanswarupdas knows who that person is. He has not yet been designated even though Narayanswarupdas said he knew him as soon as he entered the institution because "one soul knows another." The theory is that Narayanswarupdas is indicating in various ways who will succeed him, and that the choice will be clear when the time comes. In fact, the legally constituted trustees of the Akshar Purushottam Sanstha will make a determination based on their judgment of Narayanswarupdas's intention. The exact status of the soon-to-be *akṣara* is not carefully worked out even though it has significant theological and administrative implications. Clearly the period of transition of administrative power and devotional loyalty is a critical time for the institution. Both laymen and *sādhus* indicate that they are not supposed to concern themselves with the succession in advance, but it seems that some followers scrutinize Narayanswarupdas's actions in an attempt to determine the identity of the chosen one. The recent illness of Narayanswarupdas (a heart attack in February 1983) makes this a pressing issue. All agree, however, that a personal manifestation of the *akṣara* will always be present in the form of the perfect devotee who will be the mediator between man and god.

Members believe that in 1781 and in 1785 the two primary eternal entities appeared in Gujarat in the persons of Sahajanand Swami and Gunatitanand Swami. Both are prominent in the teaching and iconography of the group as is shown by the name Akshar Purushottam Sanstha. The name "Swaminarayan," which is the sacred mantra, is said to contain both; "Swami" refers to Gunatitanand as *akṣara* and "Narayan" refers to Sahajanand as *puruṣōttama*. Images of both receive worship in the central temple shrines and at home shrines. Those who receive initiation into the sect wear a necklace (*kānthi*) of wooden beads in two strands, one for *akṣara* and the other for *puruṣōttama*. The sect mark on the forehead is a U of yellow sandalpaste with a red dot of *kumkum* powder in the middle. The sandalpaste represents *puruṣōttama* and the kumkum represents *akṣara*. The bicentenary of the birth of Sahajanand was celebrated by all followers of the Swaminarayan religion in 1981; the Akshar Purushottam Sanstha plans a large celebration in 1985 for the bicentenary of the birth of Gunatitanand. It will serve as an affirmation of the theological and administrative position of the person believed to be the abode of god and to differentiate the Akshar Purushottam Sanstha from other groups of the Swaminarayan religion.

Thus, the doctrine of the *akṣara* has been elaborated within this Hindu tradition to provide the theoretic foundation for its institutional practices and for its identity as a distinct religious institution. The doctrine provides coherence and unity within the group and provides points of contact with the doctrine and practices of other devotees of Swaminarayan and with the larger Hindu community. The form of the doctrine provides the schema by which devotees of this modern form of Hinduism, now primarily Gujarati, describe their religious faith.

Next to be discussed is the function of the *akṣara* doctrine within the Akshar Purushottam Sanstha. Devotees refer to two functions which could be called the manifest functions of the doctrine. The presence of the *akṣara* is essential (1) for individual salvation and (2) for the survival of the *sampradāya*.

The Swaminarayan religion emphasizes the bhakti path, and the elaboration of the concept of the *avatāra* by the addition of the *akṣara* as the companion of god provides the devotees with a visible object of devotion, a living icon. Only after the devotee has reached Swami, which is *akṣara*, can he reach Narayan, who is *puruṣōttama*. The *akṣara*, as one of the succession of "god-realized" saints, is the representative of god on earth; he provides the perfect example, speaks with the authority of god, and receives the reverence and worship of the devotees. He is accepted as the perfect ideal for emulation by all spiritual aspirants. Members of the old school believe that Swaminarayan is present in the images, when properly installed by the *ācārya*, and in the sacred scriptures which he left. Members of the new school believe he is primarily present in the person of the guru and also in the images and sacred scriptures. The guru is spoken of as "the sacred texts personified" because he lives in harmony with all the precepts of the scriptures given by Swaminarayan. Without such a guru, it is said, there can be no *satsang*. It is only through association with the *akṣara* who has come to earth in a personal form that one can get rid of his vices, baser instincts, and the clutches of *māyā* and thereby gain release.[9]

Narayanswarupdas is revered by members of the Akshar Purushottam Sanstha as the first disciple, most strict in his observance of the commandments, most active in propagation of the religion, the best interpreter of the meaning of the scriptures, and most effective in eradicating the ignorance that separates man from god. In short, he is the devotee who exemplifies all the ideals of the religion. He has totally renounced the world so that he can be completely devoted to god. Viewed from one perspective, he holds his position because of his devotion and attainments. No other person is thought to be as worthy as a devotee. Thus, the guru/disciple relationship is heightened because it is placed in a new context in which the guru is thought to be the body of *parabrahman* through whom he reveals all his powers for the salvation of individuals. One follower said that the whole theology of the Akshar Purushottam Sanstha and its distinction from the older Swaminarayan group can be summarized in the statement of Jesus: "He who has seen me has seen the father." He said, "He who has come into fellowship with *akṣara* has come to know *puruṣōttama*." Followers believe that at death, Narayanswarupdas or one of his successors will appear and take them to *akṣardhām* where they will have "astral bodies of light."

The doctrine provides the structure for positioning the Swaminarayan *sampradāya* in relation to other religious traditions. God has manifested in many forms, some of which are only partial manifestations, as, for example, deities in non-human form. Various deities are identified as divine forms which are bound in *māyā*. The highest reality and the supreme person is *puruṣottama*, whose present abode in the world is the *akṣara*. Therefore, according to this tradition, the one supreme god is *puruṣōttama*, and the best way to approach him is through his most perfect devotee and abode. A hierarchy of divine beings exists. Followers do not criticize other deities, nor do they attack other religious teachers, but when persons from other traditions transfer allegiance to Narayanswarupdas as their spiritual guide, it is taken as a natural advance in spiritual understanding. The presence of a visible object of devotion in the person of a guru, who is believed to be the abode of god in the form of *akṣara*, has greatly intensified the devotional fervor within the group.

The continuation of the line of manifestations of the *akṣara* contributes to the survival and strength of the institution. The cosmology validates the religious and administrative position of Narayanswarupdas. Indian government regulations stipulate that the Charities

Commissioner is the custodian of all trust property and that a Charitable Trust and a Religious Trust with elected trustees oversee the affairs of the institution. The institution is incorporated in other countries according to the local laws. Nevertheless, it is clear that Narayanswardupdas, as president of every trust, has absolute authority. His word regarding the assignment of *sādhus* and the allocation of financial resources is taken as the direct will of god. Devotees take to him matters of personal, family, and business affairs and submit to his decisions. He is the focus of the personal loyalty of devotees, and weekly accounts of his activities are sent to all the followers. Since the group has grown rapidly over the past two decades, attempts have been made to reduce the burden of travel, home visits, and administrative activity through the delegation of responsibilities to the *sādhus*, but Narayanswarupdas remains the symbol of the unity of the sect. The doctrine of *akṣara* is significant in this regard because the authority does not rest ultimately on personal charisma or showmanship, as seems to be the case in some modern Hindu movements, but has been routinized within a doctrinal construct.

The theoretic framework for validating the succession maintains the unity of the *sampradāya*, but the exact mechanism is not clearly defined. The belief is that one manifestation is present at a time and the succession will continue for all time. Each leader chooses his successor, but until now the decision has not been announced publicly. Veiled indications of the selection, only partly understood until the time of the succession, create a kind of "*akṣara* secret." Only two changes of leadership have taken place since the Akshar Purushottam Sanstha was founded, and these did not cause major division. It seems likely, however, that a more formal process of succession will evolve. "*Sampradāya*" means tradition, and some orderly mechanism for transfer of power is essential.

The doctrine validates numerous rituals, additions to the sacred calendar, and the iconography unique to the group which mark it as distinct from other Hindu sects and from other branches of the Swaminarayan religion. It may be more accurate to say that the rituals and sacred calendar validate the distinctive doctrine of the group. Indeed, it may not be possible to isolate the doctrine from these means of transmitting the tradition. Without exploring the merits of that argument, it is sufficient to say that all elements of transmission cohere to announce the central message of the *sampradāya*.

The *akṣara* doctrine serves other functions not so obvious to participants, and I designate these as latent functions. The concept and accompanying rituals function to elevate the *sādhu*, now given honors appropriate to the deity, as undisputed leader over householders. The emphasis on the direct line of spiritual descent of perfect devotees, even though it does not rule out the elevation of a householder, as the example of Pragji Bhakta shows, does strengthen the role of the *sādhu* in leadership of the group. The *sādhu* is president and sole guru in the Akshar Purushottam Sanstha, while the leadership of the older Swaminarayan institution is vested in two Brahmin householders. Sahajanand Swami adopted two nephews and placed them and their descendants over the two dioceses of Ahmedabad and Vadtal.[10] The leadership of a *sādhu* in the new wing of the Swaminarayan religion is an example of what has been called the "sadhuization" of modern Hinduism.[11]

A concomitant factor is the removal of religious leadership from the hands of Brahmins. Sahajanand was a Brahmin as are the *ācāryas* of the Ahmedabad and Vadtal dioceses. Gunatitanand Swami was a Brahmin, but his successors have been from lower castes. The presence in the line of the anomalous Pragji Bhakta, who seems not to have been recognized as *akṣara* during his lifetime, indicates that even a *sat-śūdra* may rise to the position of leadership in the Akshar Purushottam Sanstha. This reduction of the authority and influence of Brahmins may explain in part the fact that caste restrictions have been greatly reduced in this group. *Sādhus* from Brahmin castes in the older group wear clothing that distinguishes them from other *sādhu* groups and have special prerogatives regarding care of the deities and the preparation of food. Young men from *sat-śūdra* castes receive only preliminary initiation and do not wear saffron-colored clothing. Now all men of *sādhu* rank in the Akshar Purushottam Sanstha, from castes of *sat-śūdra* and from castes of higher rank, are initiated together, wear the same clothing and are assigned the same tasks. M. N. Srinivas indicated that a characteristic of such devotional sects in Gujarat has been a reduction in Brahmin prerogatives and caste distinctions.[12] The association of the *akṣara* doctrine with spiritual and administrative leadership in the Akshar Purushottam Sanstha functions to accelerate that process.

The *akṣara* doctrine validates a powerful mechanism for social and religious adaptation and change. Two levels of authority exist within the Hindu scriptures. The *śruti* are the most authoritative texts and cannot be changed. The *smṛti* are sacred texts which are thought to be revealed for a *sampradāya* within a specified age and are subject to change. The category of *smṛti* can be extended to include new religious texts and even the customary religious and social behavior (*dharma*) expected of followers. Traditionally within Hinduism, the guru has had the authority to interpret sacred texts and to apply them to new situations. This is the common, but slow, means of adaptation and change. The authority of *akṣara*, the divine abode of *puruṣōttama*, stands above the sacred texts themselves. *Akṣara* embodies all the wisdom and requirements of the sacred texts. Therefore, he has absolute authority to interpret and even to change the requirements. Within the *sampradāya* his word is accepted as absolute. The result is a powerful and efficient mechanism for changing the practices of the institution. For instance, during the bicentenary of the birth of Swaminarayan, Narayanswarupdas virtually abolished all caste distinctions from the activities of the Akshar Purushottam Sanstha. He elevated men from low castes to the status of *sādhu* and removed all caste distinctions from among those of *sādhu* rank. He later proclaimed that Harijans and members of scheduled tribes are to be accepted without discrimination in Sanstha activities, including even festival meals in the temples. This was not just a moot decree; these changes were made at the time of caste tension and riots in Gujarat in 1981. His word was accepted even by Brahmin followers as the word of god. Few institutions have a centralized authority with accompanying validating doctrine similar to that of the Akshar Purushottam Sanstha. The centralized authority and the resulting ability to bring about rapid but orderly change in the institutions have facilitated growth and the success of the group among Gujaratis in the diverse cultural contexts of East Africa, Great Britain, and the United States.

The Vaiṣṇava doctrine of *avatāra* implies the corollary of specificity. Manifestations of god appear sporadically according to the demands of society and the needs of devotees. Thus, each manifestation is specific to a particular time and place, even if in the dim mythical past. According to the teaching of the Swaminarayan religion, the supreme person appeared only once in his full form in Swaminarayan, even though partial manifestations of his qualities have appeared in other divine beings. The manifestation of the abode of god is not so sporadic or occasional; it is always present in human form. Each successive manifestation is thought to demonstrate the qualities most needed by the institution and by devotees in a given generation. He constitutes the *sampradāya* and is specific to it. The entire body of doctrines, practices, and rituals of the group conform to the implication of this central doctrine of a bhakti sect. The form and the function of the concept of the manifestation of the ***akṣara*** in the Akshar Purushottam Sanstha demonstrate the institutional particularity of the doctrine.

Musicians play in a pavilion dedicated to Sarasvatī, the goddess of all arts. Mylapore, Madras City. Photo by Dick Waghorne.

Conclusion

Norman Cutler

IN HIS RECENT study of the history of Kṛṣṇa bhakti in south India, Friedhelm Hardy writes, "The religious history of India is marked by the conflict and the interaction of two major trends: to conceive of the absolute either in terms of a (mystical) state of being or as a personal God."[1] He speaks of the former as a "normative ideology" which in Hindu tradition became known as Vēdānta but which also found expression in different garb in Buddhism. Although Vēdāntic Hinduism and Buddhism differed in their respective postures *vis-à-vis* the authority of the Vedas, ritual, and societal norms, both valued an abstract, impersonal conception of a plane of being that is completely free of the limitations inherent in "man's empirical situation." In contrast to the trend represented by the *brahman* of the Upaniṣads (as well as the later philosophical expression of this principle in Śaṅkara's *advaita-vēdānta*) and the *nirvāṇa* of the Buddhists, is a second trend in India's religious history. In the religious traditions which belong to this second trend, Hardy tells us, the absolute is conceived of as a personal God.

Hardy's analytic framework has much to recommend it, but as the essays in this volume make clear, it may be more useful to define this second trend in terms of the "embodiment" of divinity. Of course even Śankara allowed a place for embodied (*saguṇa*) divinity in his system, but only as a sort of a halfway house enroute to a more perfect conception of an abstract, formless (*nirguṇa*) absolute. Over and against this sort of orientation are the many theologies and ritual complexes for which an embodied image of divinity is central. This "second trend" encompasses within its boundaries an extensive and varied range of religious traditions, each with its own particular place in history and geography and its own favored idioms of religious expression. This volume brings together work on a number of Indian religious traditions that share at least one thing in common — an emphasis on the embodiment of divinity. The volume is offered as a map, albeit a partial one, of this varied landscape.

Looking over the eight preceding essays, one question insistently calls for attention: are we dealing with a unified or with a fragmented landscape? Should the accent be on the unity or on the diversity in Indian (and here we are primarily concerned with Hindu) culture? It is hardly necessary to point out that in terms of surface features the traditions treated in these essays exhibit tremendous diversity. The question remains, to what degree are they undergirded by a unifying vision? What more can be said about this underlying unity (if it exists) beyond the self-evident fact that each, in one way or another, focuses attention upon divinity as an embodiment?

In Hardy's view, both major trends in India's religious history are rooted in the Vedas. He writes, "What at a later stage emerged as two different ideological positions appear in the *Vedas* as two aspects of one conception."[2] And quoting Gonda, "In the Veda, we notice the tendency not to distinguish strictly and precisely between personal and impersonal powers."[3] Subsequently, when under the rubrics of Vēdānta and Buddhism the impersonal facets of the Vedic conception were extracted and further developed, "other features were ignored and pushed down to the level of folk religion."[4] Hardy raises the possibility that when "a few centuries before the close of the pre-Christian era, conceptions of a personal absolute emerged . . . it may, but only may, be possible to see in these developments the re-emergence of those aspects of ancient Vedic *Weltanschauung* which involved personal cosmic powers. . . ."[5] While we cannot here verify whether or not and to what degree the religious ideas and practices discussed in this volume can ultimately be traced to origins in a Vedic *Weltenschauung*, we can get some sense of the extent to which their ideological foundations are mutually compatible. A high degree of mutual compatibility at least leaves open the possibility of a common origin.

To begin, religious traditions such as Śrīvaiṣṇavism and Gauḍīya Vaiṣṇavism, which are themselves highly evolved intellectual traditions, offer some assurance that the overview of Indian religious history as a (sometimes competitive) interplay between "abstract" and "embodied" apprehensions of divinity is not merely a superimposition from the outside. The formulators of Indian theologies often fashioned the systematic statements of their positions as refutations of competing theologies. Accordingly, both Gauḍīya Vaiṣṇava and Śrīvaiṣṇava thinkers often developed their ideas in opposition to the *advaitin's* conception of *nirguṇa brahman*. William Deadwyler's presentation of the Gauḍīya Vaiṣṇava view is a paradigm of the genre.

It comes as no surprise that both Bengali and southern Vaiṣṇavism should regard the *advaitin's* position as contrastive to their own, since the two traditions may be related in quite specific historical ways.[6]

But what about the other traditions represented here, traditions which may not necessarily define their theologies in opposition to Śaṅkara's *advaita-vēdānta*, or traditions, such as those discussed by Moreno and Inglis, which do not even offer self-consciously formulated theologies? Do these traditions form a unified field along with those which self-consciously take issue with an abstract conception of divinity? Do they possibly form a complex, interlocking network, with each of the traditions represented here connected to some (but perhaps not all) of the others by specific thematic bonds? In order to seek answers to these questions, let us consider some of the themes which weave in and out of these essays.

1. Impermanence

Preston, Courtright, and Inglis, in their analyses of their data, all emphasize the *impermanence* of the divine embodiment. Preston and Inglis both demonstrate that this understanding of the way in which divinity takes palpable form in the world ensures the livelihood of the image maker. But more essential to an understanding of the ideology of divine embodiment is their observation that the process by which the embodiment of god comes into and passes out of existence mirrors the cyclic alternation of creation and destruction, a movement that lies at the heart of Indian cosmologies. Further, just as time, as it is understood by Indian cosmologists, circulates in cycles of relatively short and long duration, so the divine embodiments cover a spectrum of forms, some *relatively* sustained, others *relatively* fleeting. Compare, for instance, the twelve-nineteen year "lifetime" of the wooden Jagannāth images with the short-lived clay images constructed for the *vinayakacaturthī* celebrations in Maharashtra. One might also contrast a relatively sustained human embodiment of divinity, such as the manifestation of *akṣara* in the person of Narayanswarupdas with the more ephemeral "descents" of deities into the bodies of Vēḷār *cāmiyāṭis* during festival times in Tamilnadu.

How does one account for this variety in the duration of a divine embodiment? As others have noted, when dealing with "material" images, the substance from which the image is constructed is a relevant variable. Worshipable images are usually constructed of stone, metal, wood or clay; the most enduring images are made from stone or metal and the most ephemeral from clay. Common sense would predict such a correlation of durable materials with long-lived images, and perishable materials with short-lived images, but the real question is why do certain ritual performances favor a more permanent and others a more ephemeral image? A temple which serves an extensive community of worshipers naturally favors a relatively permanent image as the focus of its continuing, day-to-day ritual activities. A periodic ritual, such as a festival celebration, tends to use an image that is constructed specially for and is destroyed or abandoned at the end of the special ritual occasion. Thus, the images, like the rituals with which they are associated, can be classed as *nitya* ("eternal") and *naimittika* ("occasional").

But unfortunately, such a simple and logical picture does not adequately account for the great range of data which a survey of religious practices throughout Hindu India reveals. In the south where large temples that follow Brahmanic ritual codes play a greater part in religious life than in other regions, we find metal festival images which lie dormant until the critical time in the calendar arrives, when they are "revived," only to return to a dormant state at the festival's conclusion. In non-Brahmanic "village" temples of the same region, however, festival images are made of clay and may simply be abandoned at the termination of the festival period. Yet, in Maharashtra and Orissa, where clay images are also commonly employed in festival rituals, the ritual context shifts from the temple to the family or other social institutions (some, such as neighborhood associations, are of relatively recent origin), and more explicit attention is given to the destruction of the image at the conclusion of the festival period.

Turning from material to human embodiments, the *nitya/naimittika* distinction once again carries us at least part way in an attempt to account for the variation in the duration of the divine embodiment. The *cāmiyāṭi*, in this respect, is like the festival image. His state of "possession" endures only as long as the special occasion with which it is associated endures. On the other hand, a sectarian leader who is viewed by his followers as an incarnation of divinity is comparable to the more permanent temple image which receives worship on an ongoing basis.

Probably no single dimension of analysis can do justice to the variety we find among the media and temporal frameworks which give specific form to embodiments of divinity. If we are to account for the full range of these embodiments in one comprehensive scheme, as the Indian cosmologists attempted to pull together and interrelate the several astronomical and organic cycles they observed in nature, we will have to account for a number of variables. The distinction between ongoing and occasional ritual performances is but one of these. Regional variation is a second, and a third may be called "cultural register," the difference, for example, between a Brahmanic and a non-Brahmanic frame of reference. Thus, even if we restrict our attention to a single theme like "impermanence," we are dealing with a complex map.

2. Divinity as a mode of perception.

The preceding discussion of differences between specific embodiments of divinity in terms of the materials from which they are constructed runs strongly against the grain of at least one of the traditions under discussion. The Śrīvaiṣṇava *ācāryas* emphasize that to speak of the divine image in terms of gross material substance is a heinous sin. The image of god is to be thought of *only* as being made of a perfectly pure, non-material substance. (See chapter 3.) This assertion, and others like it, shifts attention from the image itself to the devotee's perception of the image and to a metaphysics which does not, in the final analysis, recognize hard and fast distinctions between the realms of divinity and humanity and/or the material world. The difference between so-called empirical reality and the supra-real realm of the divine is largely a matter of perception and the perceiver's sensitivity. As William Deadwyler reminds us, the devotee perceives the image as God, because the image *really* is God. That which we naively think of as inert matter is, in actuality, an emanation of God's energy and thus God. Similarly, Lise Vail's Vīraśaiva informants are convinced that the *jāgṛta* ("awakened") and *saṃsāra* realms are introcontrovertible. The difference between divinity and humanity is simply a matter of one's situation within an all-encompassing economy of *śakti*. From this perspective the embodied image of God is simply a point at which the worshiper *perceives* the contінguity, indeed, the identity, of the empirical and divine realms.

3. The divine image as microcosm and hologram.

In his contribution to this volume James Preston speaks of the image of God as a "cosmic implosion," that is, a concentration of the entire cosmos into an image contained in space and time. The idea that the divine image is a concentrated embodiment of the entire cosmos frequently occurs in the religious ideologies discussed in this volume. Paul Courtright demonstrates in vivid detail the centrality of this principle in the "enlivening" ceremony for Gaṇēśa's image which is performed during *vinayakacaturthī*.

The divine image is a microcosm of a special kind. It is not only a concentrated representation of the entire cosmos; the material of which it is made is a part of the cosmos. The image is simultaneously part and whole. Like everything in the world, it is a part of God insofar as everything is an emanation of God's energy (or the energy which is God). At the same time, many of these theologies emphasize that the image is *fully* God.

Borrowing an image from optics, the relationship between God as universe and God as concentrated embodiment can be thought of as analogous to the relationship between a hologram and any part of it. Holography is a technique whereby a three-dimensional visual image of an object can be reconstructed from a photographic plate on which an "image" of the object has been recorded under special conditions. In holography, unlike conventional photography, waves of light that are reflected from all parts of an object being "photographed" are recorded on all parts of the photographic plate. For this reason, any part of this plate, called a hologram, no matter how small, can be used to reproduce a complete image of the object. In our terms, a small part of a hologram "embodies" the whole.

We find here several striking parallels with the divine image in relation to God/the universe. First, as mentioned previously, the embodied image of God is a full account of God's nature. At the same time, the image does not exhaust God's nature. Embodiments may come and go, but God remains. Further, many "full" embodiments of God can coexist. Thus a Śrīvaiṣṇava will worship both the *śālagrāma* in his home and the *arcā* in the temple and consider both to be fully Viṣṇu. Narayanaswarupdas, leader of the Akshar Purushottam Sanstha of the Swaminarayan religion and himself regarded by members of the Sanstha as the abode of god, attends a metal image of Swaminarayan which is also considered to be the abode of God. In like manner, the Vīraśaiva devotee offers worship both to his swami and to the *iṣṭaliṅga*. Each of these embodiments is a part of the whole which is God and the universe, and yet each is considered to be fully divine.

4. Divinity and divinization.

To conceive of the divine embodiment as a "cosmic implosion" implies another theme which runs very deep in Hindu religious traditions. Behind the word "implosion," and for that matter, behind the word "embodiment," lies a verb — "to implode," "to embody." This is important, for it suggests that Hindu conceptions of divinity are dynamic. For Hindus, divinity is essentially a process rather than a thing, a becoming rather than a static being. We have encountered the theme of impermanence in several of the chapters of this volume. Certainly impermanence is one of the broader themes which serve to unify the diverse material discussed in this volume. However, immanence is just one aspect of a theme which is even more deeply imbedded in many of these religious traditions. Perhaps we cannot precisely pin down this theme with a single, adequate label, but words like *process, flux,* and *becoming* will serve to steer us in the right direction. In this world view everything is considered to be an emanation of God's energy and, at certain times and places, a particular person or object in the world can take on an expanded significance so that it is perceived not as a part of the cosmos, but as the entire cosmos writ small. Under these circumstances it becomes appropriate to venerate this person or object as God. In such a world there is no insurmountable separation between the divine and the mundane. While, in the final analysis, everyone and everything is actually a part of the divine, in a more specific sense everyone and everything has the potential for becoming the locus of a "cosmic implosion." This being so, the goal of the religious life is seen as a quest to realize that potential — to *become* an embodiment of God.

This point is brought out with particular clarity in Lise Vail's essay. She puts the issue in an appropriate perspective when she speaks of "divinization" and "divinization potential." As she shows, the devotee strives to realize this potential by transacting with a realized embodiment in the person of a swami. Sometimes a material embodiment can also serve as catalyst for a devotee's realization of his "God potential." For instance, in the *prāṇapratiṣṭhā* ceremony which Paul Courtright has described, the patron, in the course of enlivening the clay image of Gaṇēśa, realizes his identity with the cosmic Puruṣa. Not only is manifested divinity impermanent, it is unbounded and its center of gravity is continually shifting.

5. Chains of divinity.

As the previously cited examples suggest, divinization is not a random process, and indeed one embodiment of divinity can, and often does trigger another kind of chain reaction. We find one instance of such a chain of divinity in Vīraśaivism as it is practiced in north Karnataka. The founder, an embodiment of God, "triggers" the "God potential" in the swami, who in turn helps the devotee to become divine. Raymond Williams's material on the Swaminarayan religion demonstrates that devotion can be the instrument through which a chain of divinity is formed. By definition, the leader of the Akshar Purushottam Sanstha is deemed to be the perfect devotee and hence divine. Devotion engenders an expansion of realized "God potential;" it is the medium of divinization. The *paramparā* or guru-disciple lineage which is the mainspring of a spiritual tradition (*sampradāya*) is a classical expression of this principle.

The "chain of divinity" theme can be viewed as just one aspect of a metaphysics of emanation. By way of illustration, let us consider Śrīvaiṣṇava metaphysics as outlined by Vasudha Narayanan. In this evolutionary scheme Viṣṇu is the point of origin, and all the basic elements of the universe evolve hierarchically from Viṣṇu. This scheme expresses the by now familiar idea that everything in the universe is essentially an emanation of God. Potential in this scheme is another in which the components of the universe which have evolved from God are themselves regarded as full representations of God's nature. In Vīraśaiva terminology, the first scheme represents the realm of *saṃsāra* while the second represents the *jāgṛta* realm. As we have come to expect, the two realms inhabit the same space. Latent in the evolution of the "empirical" world there lies a chain of divinity.

6. Multiple dimensions of the divine.

Divinity not only is manifested in a plurality of vessels, each of which is regarded as fully divine, but divinity is also apprehended in different dimensions or registers. The most explicit statement of this idea is found in the Śrīvaiṣṇava doctrine of the five forms of Viṣṇu. Taken as a whole, this scheme forcefully expresses the idea that divinity is infinite and its manifestations not only are unlimited in space and time, but can be apprehended from a variety of perspectives. The human mind can conceive of the infinite in a number of ways — in terms of spatial and temporal extension and also, though with more difficulty, in terms of a plurality of planes or dimensions of being. Taken together, the five forms of Viṣṇu in the Śrīvaiṣṇava scheme amount to a statement that no matter what lens one uses to refract one's perception of the world, the world so perceived is suffused with divinization potential. In the case of the *arcā*, for instance, the realm of physical matter is perceived as an arena for divinization; the *antaryāmin* matches a similar insight to the interior world of consciousness; the *vibhava* to the realm of animate creatures in historical time, culminating with the human being; the *vyūha* with a broader metaphysical vision of the world in evolution; and finally the *para* with heaven, the world beyond the empirical world.

The Śrīvaiṣṇava doctrine is probably the most detailed and self-reflective expression of the idea that divinity is multi-dimensional. But this principle provides an explanatory framework wherever we find juxtaposed embodiments of divinity in different media or modes. Most commonly, we find juxtapositions of human and material embodiments — the Swaminarayan devotee venerates both the human embodiment of *akṣara* and the temple icon; the Vīraśaiva devotee seeks divinization by transacting both with the living swami and with the *iṣṭaliṅga*; in Tamil villages, gods manifest their presence among men both in clay images and in the human *cāmiyāṭis*. The fact that divinization can be multiply focussed in many temple icons or in many human embodiments implies that the process of divinization is unrestricted in space or in time. Concomitantly, the fact that many Indian religious traditions juxtapose human and material embodiments in a common ritual context points to the multi-dimensionality of divinization.

Let us now take stock of our catalogue of themes to see whether or not they fit together to form an overarching religious worldview that is true to the beliefs and practices discussed in these essays:

1. impermanence
2. divinity as a mode of perception
3. the divine image as microcosm and hologram
4. divinity and divinization
5. chains of divinity
6. mutiple dimensions of the divine

What we have before us can hardly be described as a sequence in a Cartesian sense. These terms cannot be derived from another in logical progression through a step-by-step application of deductive logic. But the themes are interrelated, and any one of them could serve as a point of entry into the "system" as a whole. If each does not necessarily imply all the others, at least the implications and ramifications of each are tightly intertwined, so that one theme shades almost imperceptibly into another. Perhaps the themes can most profitably be viewed as shifting vantage points on a central religious insight. Each implies a dynamic vision of the divine. This vision will not be pinned down; it is always changing and evolving; it refuses to respect neat boundaries between the "sacred" and the "profane."

If we accept that the themes culled from these essays do coalesce as a coherent system of belief, we then will want to ask whether the data and analysis presented by each contributor really does belong to this system. Rather than trying to gauge the content of each essay against the yardstick of the six themes discussed above, let us try to compress these themes even further into a kind of *sine qua non* for a theology of embodiment and then see where we stand. For heuristic purposes, let us say that in order for a religious tradition to be deemed a full-fledged subscriber to a theology of embodiment in our terms it must (1) advocate a dynamic conception of divinity, (2) regard the embodiment(s) of divinity as inseparable from divinity in its most fundamental sense, and (3) regard the embodiment of divinity as a full manifestation of an infinite absolute. It is the second condition in particular that distinguishes this phase of Hindu religious thought from the *advaitin's* conception of an abstract, formless absolute. There is no room for a distinction between (a lower) *saguṇa brahman* and (a higher) *nirguṇa brahman* in this kind of theology. God and God's embodiment are indistinguishable, and no "elevation" in one's perceptions can cancel this truth. All the traditions discussed in this volume accept this premise *on an operative level*. In each case the worshiper apprehends divinity as an embodiment. However, based on the evidence at hand, only the Śrīvaiṣṇava, Gauḍīya Vaiṣṇava, and perhaps the Swaminarayan material offer us clearcut examples of religious ideologies that unequivocally insist that the embodiment of God is a comprehensive account of God's nature. Other traditions, such as Vīraśaivism, include a place for formless divinity in their theologies, and when this is the case, the formless aspect of God is usually seen as ontologically prior to the embodiment, even if religious practice emphasizes the latter.[7] Thus in Vīraśaivism the realized swami is said to be a vessel for formless, pure *śakti*. To take another example, Paul Courtright's material on the *prāṇapratiṣṭhā* ritual clearly demonstrates that the ritual patron and the enlivened clay image of Gaṇēśa are identified with the cosmic Puruṣa and thus are identified with the entirety of the universe. His material also suggests, but does not confirm beyond doubt, that a formless (*nirguṇa*) *brahman* lies behind each of these embodiments of divinity. (Even his informants are divided on this issue.)

The religious environment described by Manuel Moreno (and most likely, by Stephen Inglis also) suggests a different kind of mismatch with the "theology of embodiment" outlined above; here it is the second premise that does not apply. In this non-Brahmanic environment, gods, like humans, are viewed as embodied beings, but unlike Viṣṇu in Śrīvaiṣṇava theology, to offer just one example, these gods are not necessarily taken to be full accounts of the entirety of creation. Gods may "be higher, more powerful and generous, and endowed with more refined substances than humans" (see chapter 6), but finally gods, like humans, are inhabitants of the world, not microcosms of everything which makes up the world. As cohabitors of a common spatial and temporal plane of being, gods and humans are involved in mutual interactions. Sometimes their embodiments even coincide in the phenomenon we commonly call "possession." As Moreno points out, we are still concerned here with a "processural" view, but process in this case does not mean "cosmic implosion" but something else. In Moreno's words, "gods are understood to be persons, corporeal residents of the Hindu world, who are related among themselves and with humans by shared and exchanged bodily substances.... As persons, the gods' identities are not permanently fixed, but are fluid and transformable by their active involvement in transactions with other gods and with humans."

Returning now to the question of whether or not the religious traditions discussed in these essays coalesce as interconnected facets of a unified religious vision, we can only give an equivocally affirmative answer. Underlying these various idioms of religious expression is not a single, uniform theological "deep structure," but a spectrum of theologies, each shading almost imperceptibly into the next band on the spectrum. In all these traditions religious truths are understood in dynamic terms, and the worshiper, *at some level*, responds to and interacts with divinity as an embodiment. But the concomitants of these unifying threads sometimes differ radically. At one end of the spectrum we find a firm commitment to the embodied nature of divinity, but without an equally firm commitment to the idea that God is infinite and all-inclusive. Religious ideologies which fall on this end of the spectrum can be described as pluralistic and concrete. At the other end of the spectrum this ratio is inverted. Divinity is identified with a formless "first principle," and its embodiment is theoretically secondary, even if important in practice. Finally, in the middle distance, we find religious traditions which both regard embodiment as an essential and indispensible aspect of the divine nature and insist on the infinitude of the embodied god. God, while infinite, is always particular and cannot be conceived of otherwise.

This overview suggests that evaluations of Indian religious history as a dialectic between abstract and personal conceptions of divinity, while useful to an extent, do not really get at the root of the matter. While ultimately words cannot capture but can only suggest the deepest layers of religious awareness, a vocabulary that steers our attention to the "embodied" rather than to the "personal" nature of God promotes a more profound understanding of the Hindu mind. The idea of a personal God is, in this system, just one aspect or a consequence of a more basic religious attitude which may be termed *embodiment*.

In India a "personal" relationship between deity and devotee is possible as a consequence of the embodiment of both. Deprived of a body, neither human nor deity is capable of particularized, "personal" interactions. The tremendous variety found in Hindu tradition can be at least partly attributed to the different degrees of emphasis they give to God's embodiment in relation to other themes and to the varied ways in which God's embodied image is represented. But embodiment as such also contributes to the observer's sense that in Hinduism a unity lurks behind a complex and diverse surface. A Tamil villager who carries a fire pot as an emblem of his devotion to Māriyamman̠ and a Śrīvaiṣṇava Brahmin who performs an "eight-limbed" prostration before Viṣṇu are both worshiping an embodied God.

Notes and References

Complete bibliographical entries are cited in the Bibliography, beginning on page 201.

Introduction

1. Examples can be found in A. L. Basham's *The Wonder that was India*, in which three out of over 500 pages mention image-worship (pp. 335-338). J. N. Banjerjea allows image worship only three pages of his article on "The Hindu-Concept of God" in Kenneth Morgan's *The Religion of the Hindus*. Banerjea concludes that devotees accept "the usefulness of images for their religious uplift" (p. 33).

2. John B. Noss's *Man's Religions*, an old standard "world religions" textbook, classifies image worship as the worship of "the common man of India" led "through experience or family habit . . . to adopt one god or goddess . . . whose image or symbol he enshrines in his house" (pp. 204-205). Even David R. Kinsley's recent text *Hinduism* still adopts the term "common worship" to describe daily devotion to an embodied god (pp. 116-121). Thomas J. Hopkins's *The Hindu Religious Tradition*, calls the worship of deity in the form of an image, "a direct expression of popular theistic religion" (p. 111). Indian scholars themselves have long adopted this attitude and were bent on proving that the pure Vedic religion had no consonance for images whose origins then must have been "in lower or ignorant masses of Vedic India." See P. V. Kane, *History of Dharmaśastra*, Vol. 2, Part II, p. 707.

3. Richard Lannoy, *The Speaking Tree*, pp. 21-30.

4. See Diana L. Eck, *Darśan: Seeing the Divine Image in India.*

5. Edward B. Tylor, *Anthropology*, pp. 202-203.

6. James G. Frazer, *The New Golden Bough*, edited and abridged by Theodor M. Gaster, p. 35.

7. For example, see *Return to Order of the House of Commons, dated 21 June 1849 for a Copy "of any Communications in relationship to the Connection of the Government of British India with Idolatry or with Mahometanism."* Parliamentary Paper No. 664 of Session 1845. Printed by the House of Commons, 1 August 1849.

8. For a detailed account of the British involvement with temples in India see Arjun Appadurai, *Worship and Conflict under Colonial Rule: A South Indian Case.*

9. F. Max Müller, *Lectures on the Origin and Growth of Religion, as Illustrated by the Religions of India*, p. 51.

10. Here Max Müller had precedent for this approach in India's own *advaita-vēdānta* philosophy which argued that seeing God as an external person or object was only a stage in full spiritual development. See the essay by William Deadwyler (chapter 4) for the philosophical reaction to this position.

11. *Origin and Growth of Religion*, p. 32.

12. Ibid. See chapter 4.

13. This position was most forcibly developed by Ernst Cassirer as early as 1923.

14. Garrett Green, "Reconstructing Christian Theology: A Review of Gordon D. Kaufman's *The Theological Imagination: Constructing the Concept of God.*" *Religious Studies Review*, p. 221.

1. Creation of the Sacred Image

1. Lawrence Babb, *The Divine Hierarchy*, p. 184.

2. Arjun Appadurai and Carol Breckenridge, "The South Indian Temple," pp. 5 and 12.

3. Stella Kramrisch, "Traditions of the Indian Craftsman," p. 19.

4. Milton Singer, "Changing Craft Traditions in India," p. 265; Milton Singer, *When a Great Tradition Modernizes*, pp. 118-123; and Baidranath Saraswati, *Kashi*, p. 30.

5. The following information on the *navakalēvara* ceremony is gathered from several sources. I am particularly indebted,however, to G. N. Tripathi's elegant and detailed article describing this extraordinary aspect of the Jagannāth tradition ("Navakalevara," pp. 223-264).

6. An important question that can be raised is why the amalgamation in the Jagannāth triad was accomplished under a Vaiṣṇava rather than a Śaiva theology. Is there something in the Śaiva process of divinization which would have prevented the same kind of synthesis? Obviously the *avatāra* tradition in Vaiṣṇavism lends itself quite easily to the incorporation of various sects (i.e., Śaiva, Śākta, and Vaiṣṇava in this case) under one umbrella because of the concept of divinity descending into the world in an incarnation. But this cannot be the complete answer, since the Orissan variant of Hinduism universally, even in the case of Śaivism, amalgamates various sects rather freely whenever convenient. It is eclectic by nature. Thus, if it had been politically advantageous to subsume the three sects under an overarching Śaiva umbrella, it would have been neither impossible nor incongruous. There are numerous reports of unusual mixes of these various sects in the Orissan context.

7. Anncharlott Eschmann, "The Vaiṣṇava Typology," pp. 103-104.

8. Ibid., p. 111.

9. Ibid., p. 99.

10. Hermann Kulke, "Early Royal Patronage," p. 151.

11. H. von Stietencron traces the complex history of the Śaiva component in the Jagannāth triad, suggesting that Vaiṣṇava and Śaiva communities both worshiped the Wooden God at Purī (considered to be Bhairava by the Śaivas and Nṛsiṃha by the Vaiṣṇavas). Since the Śaiva sect could not be totally wiped out, it is likely that two gods of the same shape were juxtaposed, placing both deities on the same platform. Ultimately, when the Gaṅga dynasty took full power (with Anaṅgabhīma III about 1230 A.D.) the two deities became brothers. Thus, Balabhadra is Jagannāth's Śaiva brother and is considered to be Śiva in Purī even today ("The Śaiva Component," pp. 122 and 123).

12. James J. Preston, "Goddess Temples in Orissa."

13. Anncharlott Eschmann, "Hinduization of Tribal Deities," p. 97.

14. K. C. Mishra, *The Cult of Jagannātha*, p. 5.

15. A legend explaining the Śabara origins of Lord Jagannāth is found in the *Utkal Khaṇḍa* of the *Skanda Purāṇa*. A very brief synopsis follows: Lord Viṣṇu, in the form of a stone image under the shade of a tree, was worshiped by the chief of the Śabara tribe. But when a Brahmin emissary of King Indradyumna tried to view the stone image, it vanished. In a divine dream the king was told that Lord Viṣṇu would no longer appear in his usual form but would instead assume a new shape and would henceforth be worshiped as a deity made of wood carved by Viṣṇu himself through his Śabara devotees. (K. C. Mishra, *The Cult of Jagannātha*, pp. 76 and 77, and G. C. Tripathi, "Jagannātha," p. 478).

16. The *navakalēvara* ceremony is performed only in the year with two Āsāḍhas according to the Hindu lunar calendar.

17. G. C. Tripathi, "Navakalevara," p. 229.

18. Some thick branches are not buried. These are taken to the temple at Purī, kept in a storeroom, and used either as arms for the two male deities (the goddess Subhadrā has no arms) or distributed to Jagannāth temples throughout Orissa for constructing sacred images of the three deities (G. C. Tripathi, "Navakalevara," p. 250).

19. A similar pattern for the cutting of trees to be used in the construction of sacred images is noted by Stella Kramrisch ("Traditions of the Indian Craftsman," p. 20). The carpenter typically

asks for pardon from the spirits associated with the tree. The axes are anointed with honey and butter, and the carving takes place in a secluded place.

20. G. C. Tripathi, "Navakalevara," p. 229.

21. Buddhism took hold in Orissa in the first century A.D., reaching its peak under the Bhauma-Kara rulers in the 8th to 10th centuries (H. von Stietencron, "The Advent of Viṣṇuism," p. 4) and gradually declining. This tantric form of Buddhism was absorbed in later periods by Śaiva, then Vaiṣṇava sects which came to dominate Orissan religion. In the Orissan literary tradition (ranging back as far as Sāralā Dās's Oriya version of the *Mahābhārata*) Jagannāth has often been characterized as the ninth (or Buddha) incarnation of Viṣṇu. The idea that the "souls" of the deities, which are transferred from the old icons to the new ones, is a Buddha's tooth is probably linked to these early literary references to the "Buddha nature" of Jagannāth in Orissan literature. There appears, however, to be no substance to the speculation that the "soul" of the deity is a Buddha's tooth.

Some have also conjectured that the "life-substance" is the remains saved (possibly in the form of ash) from the original icons of the Jagannāth triad burnt by the Muslims in their raid of 1568 A.D., a custom that would establish a clear continuity with the original images. There is, however, no proof for this interesting idea. The "life-substance" transferred in the *brahmapadārtha* rites is most likely a sort of śālagrāma (a black stone with a fossil ammonite, which is a coiled shell of an extinct mollusk sacred to Vaiṣṇavas). This is the opinion of the Brahmin priests at Purī, and we find support for this view when we consider that śālagrāmas are placed in new Jagannāth icons established in temples outside of Purī by Purī priests who are invited to consecrate such new images (G. C. Tripathi, "Jagannātha," pp. 260 and 261).

22. G. C. Tripathi, "Navakalevara," p. 264.

23. Anncharlott Eschmann, "The Vaiṣṇava Typology," p. 270.

24. The data for Durgā Pūjā and the image makers of Cuttack City are derived from field work I conducted in Orissa during 1972-1973.

25. See James J. Preston and James Freeman, "Two Urbanizing Orissan Temples," pp. 97-117, and James J. Preston, *Cult of the Goddess*.

26. Bhabagrahi Misra, Personal Communication.

27. Stella Kramrisch, "Traditions of the Indian Craftsman," p. 21.

28. In the grand spectacle of popular street images festively displayed at Cuttack City during several major festivals (particularly Durgā Pūjā) government institutions sponsor floats with elaborated sacred images of various deities. These frequently consist of scenes from the *Mahābhārata* or the *purāṇas*. The name of the institution is usually part of the float. Typical patrons are the State Bank of India, universities, and the postal services, among others. I am not sure whether any public monies are used for such floats. Most likely individuals and groups who work for these government institutions sponsor the construction of the icons by pooling their money.

29. James Freeman, *Scarcity and Opportunity*, p. 56.

30. Rajendra Jindel, *Culture of a Sacred Town*, pp. 164-169.

31. Baidranath Saraswati, *Kashi*, pp. 29 and 30.

32. L. P. Vidyarthi, *The Sacred Complex of Kashi*, p. 75.

33. Lawrence Babb, *The Divine Hierarchy*, pp. 62, 63, 159-160.

34. Milton Singer, *When a Great Tradition*, p. 122.

35. James Freeman, *Scarcity and Opportunity*, p. 156.

36. Lawrence Babb, *The Divine Hierarchy*, p. 193.

37. Sheila Walker, *Ceremonial Spirit Possession*, p. 37.

38. Ibid., p. 42.

39. Octavio Paz, *The Bow and the Lyre*, p. 97.

40. Ibid., p. 117.

41. James J. Preston, "The Goddess Chandi," pp. 210-226.

2. On This Holy Day in My Humble Way.

I would like to express my appreciation to Professor D. K. Kharwandikar of Ahmednagar College, Ahmednagar; Professor S. G. Tulpule of Pune, and Dr. Gudrun Bühnemann of the Bhandarkar Oriental Research Institute, Pune, for their help in the preparation of this essay.

1. Ākos Östor, *The Play of the Gods*, p. 9.

2. Translation and commentary in Paul B. Courtright, "Gaṇeśa and the Gaṇeśa Festival in Maharashtra: A Study in Hindu Religious Celebration," pp. 48-51.

3. P. V. Kane, *History of Dharmaśāstra*, vol. 2, pt. 2, p. 717. See also: Veena Das, "On the Categorization of Space in Hindu Ritual."

4. Nārāyaṇaśāstri Jośī, *Śrī Gaṇeśa Aradhanā*, p. 108.

5. *Skanda Purāṇa* 1.1.11.1-25.

6. Ibid. See also: *Gaṇēśa Purāṇa* 2.148.47-52.

7. Arnold Van Gennep, *The Rites of Passage*; Victor Turner, *The Ritual Process*.

8. A. Y. Javadekar, trans., *Now Begins the Worship and Story of the Fourth Lunar Day of the Lord of Troops*, p. 1. See also: Jośī, p. 50.

9. Jośī, p. 53.

10. See Brenda E. F. Beck, "Heat and Colour in South Indian Ritual."

11. Javadekar, p. 2.

12. Jan Gonda, "Pratiṣṭhā," p. 1.

13. *Bṛhadaraṇyaka Upaniṣad* 4.1.12; *Chāndōgya Upaniṣad* 5.19-24; *Śatapatha Brāhmaṇa* 4.3.1.22.

14. *Chāndōgya Upaniṣad* 5.1.7.

15. Ibid. 5.1.12.

16. *Ṛg Vēda* 10.90.13.

17. *Chāndōgya Upaniṣad* 5.19.1.

18. Jan Gonda, "The Indian Mantra," p. 259.

19. Östor, p. 68.

20. See Lawrence A. Babb, *The Divine Hierarchy*, pp. 31-68.

21. Jośī, p. 69.

22. Ibid., p. 70-71.

23. Transcribed from tape recording of the *pūjā* made by the author.

3. Arcāvatāra.

1. On the Vīraśaivas, see A.K. Ramanujan, *Speaking of Śiva*.

2. The distinction between the "all pervasive form" and "auspicious divine nature" is made explicitly by the Tirukkurukai Pirāṉ Piḷḷāṉ, a cousin of the eleventh-century preceptor Rāmānuja. Tirukkurukai Pirāṉ Piḷḷāṉ, *Ārāyirappaṭi*, commentary on the *Tiruvāymoḻi*, 3.2.8, in S. Krishnamacary, ed., *Śrī Bhagavad Viṣayam*.

Vēdānta Dēśika (A.D. 1268-1368) emphasizes this distinction and discusses it in some detail. Vēdānta Dēśika, *Gadyatrayabhāṣyam (Śaranāgati gādyam), Catuḥślōkabhāṣyam, Stōtraratnabhāṣyam, Gadyatrayabhāṣyaṃs ca*, p. 143. Also in Vēdānta Dēśika, *Rahasyatrayasāram* henceforth, *RTS*, Vol. 1, pp. 42-43.

3. *RTS*, Vol. 1, pp. 42-43.

4. There may be a theoretical distinction between the doctrines of *antaryāmitvam* and *hārda*. In this connection, Carman says:

> The Pāñcarātra Āgamas also called this form of God Hārda, meaning "God dwelling in the heart," and this was conceived as a veritable incarnation of God in the hearts of those specially devoted to Him. The *antaryāmi*, on the other hand, may be understood as the general immanence of God in all His creatures. John Carman, *The Theology of Ramanuja*.

Vēdānta Deśika (13th cent.) uses the words *hārda* and *antaryāmin* interchangeably; thus in the

RTS, Dēśika says that the Lord's "non-natural" (*aprākṛta*) body appears in five forms (*para*) *vyūha, vibhava, hārda* and *arcāvatara*) (*RTS*, vol. 1, p. 43). However, in *Cillaṟai Rahasyaṅkaḷ* Dēśika substitutes the word *antaryāmin* for *hārda*. Vēdānta Dēśika, *Cillaṟai Rahasyaṅkaḷ* (henceforth, *CR*), pp. 35-36.

Piḷḷai Lōkācārya (born A.D. 1264), a senior contemporary of Dēśika, understands the word *antaryāmin* or Inner Controller to mean both the "inner self," i.e., the *ātman*, as well as the Lord's image (*vigraha*) within the heart. Both meanings, he says, are implicit in the words of the *āḻvārs*. Piḷḷai Lōkācārya, "Artapañcaka," in *Aṣṭādaśa Rahasyam*, p. 29.

5. Tirumaṅkaiyāḻvār, *Periya Tirumoḷi* 2.4.1.

6. Tirumaḻicaiyāḻvār, *Tiruccanta Viruttam*, verse 64.

7. *Periyāḻvar Tirumoḷi* 4.5.3.

8. M. R. Rajagopala Ayyangar, trans., *Rahasyatraya Sāra of Vēdānta Dēśika*, p. 39.

9. *Svayam Vyakta* shrines, where the Lord "self-manifests," are said to be just eight in number. Not all of these are *divya dēśas*. Some are called *abhimāna sthalams*, i.e., shrines held in great reverence. These are said to be Śrī Raṅgam, Śrīmuṣṇam, Tiruvēṅkaṭam, Śālagrāmam, Naimiśāraṇyam, Cīrivaramaṅkai (or Tirunīrmalai), Puṣkaram, and Badri. This classification is adapted from Dēśika, *CR.*, vol. 1, pp. 215-216.

10. Piṉpaḷakiya Perumāḷ Jīyar, *Ārāyirappaṭi Guruparamparā prabhāvam*, pp. 233-235.

11. "The Thousand names of Viṣṇu" (*Viṣṇu Sahasranāma*), which is part of the Sanskrit epic *Mahābhārata*, refers to the Lord as having one unchanging form (*sadaikarūparūpāya*). "Viṣṇu Sahasranāma" with commentary, in Parāśara Bhaṭṭar, commentator, *Bhagavad-guṇa darpanam*, p. 79.

12. On the importance of *sthala purāṇas*, see Friedhelm Hardy, "Ideology and Cultural Contexts of the Śrīvaiṣṇava Temple," especially pp. 142-149.

13. Tirupati is one of the most important pilgrimage centers in India. Its history has been related in detail in several books. See, for instance, S. Krishnaswami Aiyangar, *History of Tirupati*, 2 volumes.

14. In this connection, see Paul Younger's "Ten days of Wandering and Romance with Lord Raṅkanātan."

15. "The ammonites of the Spiti Shales known as *Saligrams* to the Hindus and considered by them as sacred objects are brought down by the Gandak and other Nepal rivers." M. S. Krishnan, *Geology of India and Burma*. I am indebted to Sri V. R. Rajagopalan, Bangalore, for this reference.

16. The best size *śālagrāmas* are the size of certain small fruits; the best color is black, and any *śālagrāma* which is not at least partly black is considered to be just passable. White *śālagrāmas* destroy wealth, and they produce a tendency to sin in their owners. A golden *śālagrāma* will bless one with a son; blue will ensure wealth; red will bring disease; and so on.

17. Srīmāṉ Kumkumam A. S. V. Varadācāriyar in "Pakavāṉ Śālakrāma Sannitya," p. 22.

18. Śrī Nāvalpākkam Yajñavarāhācārya Svāmi, in "Śālakrāma Cilaiyiṉ Perumai," recounts several stories to show how the donation of a *śālagrāma* ensures marital happiness.

19. Verses from Toṇṭaraṭipoṭiyāḻvār, Periyāḻvār, Nammāḻvār and Āṇṭāḷ are chanted. For details see *Nityānuṣṭāna kramam*.

20. Based on the number of whirls they contain, *śālagrāmas* are called Śrī Nārāyaṇamūrti, Śeṣamūrti, etc. I have heard it said that the best one to give at a wedding is the "Santana-Kṛṣṇa" *śālagrāma*.

21. I have summarized the myths concerning the origin of the *śālagrāma* from Yajñavarāhācārya Svāmi's "Śālakrāma Cilaiyiṉ Perumai" ("the glory of the Śālagrāma image"). See appendix for a full translation of the most complex of these myths.

22. The three *guṇas* in Indian philosophy are *sattva* (purity), *rajas* (passion, emotion), and *tamas* (darkness, ignorance).

23. Vēdānta Dēśika, *RTS*, vol. I, p. 60.

24. Naṭātūr Ammāḷ, *Prapanna Pārijāta*, pp. 26-27.

25. Piḷḷai Lōkācārya's *sūtras* and Maṇavāḷa Māmunikaḷ's comments are translated here:

This question [about a dvotee's birth] is more cruel than thinking of the material that comprises the *arcāvatāra*. *Śāstra* says that this is comparable to a man thinking of his mother's reproductive organ as a common sex object. *Śrīvacana Bhūṣaṇam, sūtras* 196 and 197

Commentary: The Lord graciously occupies any material that his devotee deems to be good and uses this as his auspicious body with all the desire that he has for his non-material divine form. Not knowing this glory (*vaibhavam*) a man may foolishly direct his thoughts at the material that is used to make the image (*vigraha*) and wonder what substance it is made of. Scripture puts it this way: "It is said that analyzing the material of the *arcā* or thinking of a Vaiṣṇava's birth (i.e. caste) is equivalent to examining one's mother's sexual organs." . . . due to the frequent contemplation on many women's sexual organs, one may think of one's mother in such a way. What a sin that is! Analyzing the material of the *arcāvatāra* is just as heinous!

P. B. Annangaracarya, ed., *Śrī Vacanabhūṣaṇam Viyākkiyāṉam (henceforth SVB)*, p. 109.

26. Kuruttālvān, *Varadarāja Stava*, verses 1 and 3.

27. Kuruttālvān, *Sundarabāhu Stava*, verse 119.

28 *SVB, sūtra* 39.

29. *SVB, sūtras* 34, 35 and 37.

30. Nammālvār is considered to be the "foremost" among those devotees who have taken refuge with the Lord.

31. *SVB*, pp. 39-40.

32. *SVB, sūtra* 40.

33. Vēṅkaṭēśvara literally means "The Lord of [the Hill] Vēṅkaṭa." Vēṅkaṭēśvara temples are found in many places in India and now also in Pittsburgh and Los Angeles.

34. A. K. Ramanujan, "Karma in Bhakti with special reference to Nammālvār and Basavanna," paper presented in the ACLS/SSRL Workshop on "Karma in Post-Classical texts," Pendle Hill, Pennsylvania, 1980.

35. In Śrīvaiṣṇava philosophy the Lord is considered to be the bridegroom of every human. Piḷḷai Lōkācārya sees this as one of the nine fundamental relationships between the deity and humans; Nañjīyar, a twelfth-century preceptor, speaks of this relationship in a treatise called *Ātmā Vivāha*. For further information, see V. Narayanan, "The Goddess Śrī: Blossoming Lotus and Breast Jewel of Viṣṇu," pp. 235-237.

36. *SVB*, pp. 40-42.

37. This is a translation of an origin myth found in "Śālakrāma Cilaiyiṉ Perumai" by Yajñavarāhācārya Svāmi.

4. The Devotee and the Deity.

1. Quoted in Bhaktivedanta Swami, Śrī Caitanya-caritāmṛta, Madhya-līlā, vol. 5, p. 123.

2. Robert Southey, English poet laureate from 1813 to 1843, did much to form the common Victorian idea of the festival by his depiction of it in his 1809 poem *The Curse of Kehama* (14.5).

A thousand pilgrims strain,
Arm, shoulder, breast, and thigh, with might and main,
To drag that sacred wain,
And scarce can draw along the enormous load.
Prone fall the frantic votaries in its road,
And, calling on the God,
Their self-devoted bodies there they lay
To pave his chariot way;
On Jaga-Naut they call:
The ponderous Car rolls on, and crushes all.
Through flesh and bones it ploughs its dreadful path.
Groans rise unheard; the dying cry,
And death and agony
Are trodden under foot by yon mad throng,
Who follow close, and thrust the deadly wheels along.

The Rev. William Ward remarks that "Southey's description . . . though not literally correct, conveys to the mind much of the horror which a Christian spectator of the procession of the car cannot but feel." (*A View of the History, Literature, and Religion of the Hindoos*, p. xxvii.)

3. In this paper I follow Prabhupāda's practice of using the English word *deity* to denote the worshipable form or image of God installed in the temple. Some Sanskrit terms for the deity are *arcā, śrī vigraha, śrī mūrti, arcā-mūrti*, and *arcā-vigraha. Arcā* is derived from a root meaning "shine" and "praise." *Mūrti* and *vigraha* both mean "form."

4. This achievement of Prabhupāda, and how it contrasts to other Hindu movements in the West, is discussed at length by Thomas J. Hopkins, an early observer of ISKCON, in Stephen J. Gelberg, ed., *Hare Krishna, Hare Krishna*, pp. 102-114. A. L. Basham also has some interesting comments on the uniqueness of ISKCON and Prabhupāda in the same work, pp. 163-167.

5. In fact, orthodox followers of Caitanya call themselves *rūpānugas* – those who follow Rūpa Gōsvāmī — and claim that the fault of the heterodox *sahajīyas* is that they try to follow Caitanya without following Rūpa and the other *gōsvāmīs* of Vṛndāvana.

6. This first deity installation is described in Satsvarūpa Dāsa Gōsvāmī's biography of Prabhupāda, *Śrīla Prabhupāda-līlāmṛta*, vol. 3, pp. 92-103. Here he recounts Prabhupāda's explaining to his disciples why they will begin *arcanā* specifically with Jagannātha deities:

> "Because Lord Jagannātha was very liberal and merciful to the most fallen, Śrīla Prabhupāda explained, the devotees would soon be able to worship Him in their temple. The worship of the forms of Rādhā and Kṛṣṇa in the temple require very high, strict standards, which the devotees were not yet able to meet. But Lord Jagannātha was so merciful that He could be worshiped in a simple way (mostly by chanting Hare Kṛṣṇa), even if the devotees weren't very much advanced" (p. 94).

7. Satsvarūpa Dāsa Gōsvāmī, *Śrīla Prabhupāda-līlāmṛta*, vol. 4, pp. 22-23.

8. Gauḍīya Vaiṣṇavas considers Caitanya to be an incarnation of Kṛṣṇa, or, more precisely, of Rādhā and Kṛṣṇa combined, and Nityānanda an incarnation of Balarāma, Kṛṣṇa's first emanation who appeared with Kṛṣṇa in Vṛndāvana as his elder brother.

9. According to *Caitanya-caritāmṛta*, Sanātana Gosvāmī was ordered by Caitanya to write this work, giving detailed instructions concerning Vaiṣṇava behavior and activities, including directions for *arcanā* and other rituals. See *Caitanya-caritāmṛta, Madhya-līlā* 24.324-345. S. K. De, however, attributes the work to Gopāla Baṭṭa Gosvāmī. For a brief summary of the contents of *Hari-bhakti-vilāsa* see Bhaktivedanta Swami, *Śrī Caitanya-caritāmṛta, Madhya-līlā*, vol. 1, pp. 20-21. An exhaustive summary is given by De in *Early History of the Vaiṣṇava Faith and Movement in Bengal*, pp. 448-529.

10. Diana L. Eck, *Darśan*, p. 4. Pp. 3-7 contain a detailed analysis of the notion.

11. "Interview with Srivatsa Goswami," in Stephen J. Gelberg, ed., *Hare Krishna, Hare Krishna*, p. 228.

12. Bhaktivedanta Swami, *The Nectar of Devotion*, p. 168.

13. Bhaktivedanta Swami, *Śrīmad Bhāgavatam*, Canto 9, pt. 2, p. 81.

14. William James, "Reflex Action and Theism," in *The Will to Believe and Other Essays in Popular Philosophy*, p. 122.

15. *àkatōnomastos, 'àrretos, àkatalēptos*. (*De Somniis*, 1.2.67.) Philo holds that God transcends even the form of the Good and the form of the Beautiful (*autò tò àgathòn kaì autò tò kalòn*) (*De Opificio Mundi*, 2.8).

16. Thomas Aquinas, *Summa Theologica*, Part I, Q. 3.

17. Ibid., Part I, Q. 13, art. 11.

18. James Hastings, ed., *Encyclopaedia of Religion and Ethics*, vol. 7, p. 146. Lyall is quoted from *Asiatic Studies*, London, 1907, ii 151.

19. George Thibaut, trans., *The Vedânta Sûtras with the Commentary by Śankarâkârya*, Sacred Books of the East, vol. 34, p. 62.

20. William Ward, *The Hindoos*, pp. xxxi-xxxii.

21. J. N. Farquhar, *The Crown of Hinduism*, p. 320. The quotation is from a paper read before the Ganjam Hindu Reform Association by V. Srinivasa Rao.

22. Bhakti Siddhanta Saraswati Goswāmī, trans., *Shri Brahma-samhitā.*

23. The "purpose-trees" [*kalpa-vṛkṣa*] mentioned in verse 29 are trees in Kṛṣṇa's abode that furnish any fruit desired. "Cupid" in verse 30 is Kāmadēva, the god of love (also called Kandarpa). In verse 31, "threefold-bending form" [*tribaṅga*] refers to the gracefully curved posture Kṛṣṇa assumes when he plays his flute, and "Shyamasundara," meaning "dark blue [*śyāma*] and beautiful [*sundara*]," is a name of Kṛṣṇa. According to *Caitanya-caritāmṛta* (*Madhya-līlā* 9.236-241), Caitanya discovered the fifth chapter of the *Brahmasaṃhitā* at the temple of Ādikēśava and returned to Purī with a copy. The works is said to have had originally one hundred chapters, but only the fifth is extant. It is held in very high regard by the Gauḍīya Vaiṣṇavas. Here are the quoted verses in Sanskrit:

cintāmaṇi-prakāra-sadmasu kalpa-vṛkṣa-
　　lakṣāvṛtēṣu surabhīr abhipālayantam
lakṣmī-sahasra-śata-sambhrama-sēvyamānaṃ
　　gōvindam ādi-puruṣaṃ tam aham bhajāmi (29)

vēṇuṃ kvaṇantam aravinda-dalāyatakṣam
　　barhāvataṃ samasitāmbuda-sundarāṅgam
kandarpa-kōti kamanīya vēśēṣa-śōbhaṃ
　　gōvindam ādi-puruṣaṃ tam aham bhajāmi (30)

ālōla-candraka-lasad-vanamālya-vaṃśī-
　　ratnāṅgadaṃ praṇaya-kēli-kalā-vilāsam
śyāmaṃ tribhaṅga-lalitaṃ niyata-prakaśaṃ
　　gōvindam ādi-puruṣaṃ tam aham bhajāmi (31)

aṅgāni yasya sakalēndriya vṛttimanti
　　paśyanti pānti kalayanti ciraṃ jaganti
ānanda-cinmaya-sad-ujjvala-vigrahasya
　　gōvindam ādi-puruṣaṃ tam aham bhajāmi (32)

advaitam acyutam anādim ananta-rūpam
　　ādyaṃ purāṇa-puruṣaṃ navayauvanam ca
vēdēṣu durlabham adurlabham ātma-bhaktau
　　gōvindam ādi-puruṣaṃ tam aham bhajāmi (33)

24. "He has a specific form, the concentrated embodiment of the spiritual principle of Existence, Cognition, and Bliss." Bhaktisiddhanta Saraswati, *Shri Chaitanya's Teachings*, pt. 1, p. 18.

25. "For the religious rituals of Greek and Roman paganism Christian apologists had only contempt. . . . But they took the position that while the priests and professional religionists of the nations had been perpetuating idolatrous beliefs and practices, the philosophers had begun the process of emancipation and rationalization which Christ, the eternal Reason of God, had now consummated." Jaroslav Pelikan, *The Christian Tradition*, vol. 1, p. 66.

26. Hayagrīva dāsa Adhikārī, "The Spiritual Master: Emissary of the Supreme Person," *Back to Godhead*, no. 38, p. 20.

27. *anyābhilāsitāśunyaṃ jñāna-karmādy-anāvṛtam / ānukūlyēna kṛṣṇānuśilanam bhaktir uttamā*. "One should render transcendental loving service to the Supreme Lord Kṛṣṇa favorably and without desire for material profit or gain through fruitive activities or philosophical speculation.That is called pure devotional service." (*Bhakti-rasāmṛta-sindhu* 1.1.11, quoted and translated by Bhaktivedanta Swami in *Bhagavad-gītā As It Is*, p. 387.)

28. I am here closely following an argument given by Bhaktivedanta Swami in his commentary to *Śrī Īśopaniṣad*, p. 63.

29. Alladi Mahadeva Sastry, trans., *The Bhagavad Gita with the commentary of Sri Sankaracharya*, p. 508.

30. Ibid., p. 78. Robert Minor remarks that "Śaṁkara is anxious to show that the *Gītā* teaches that the highest way rejects action, something the *Gītā* in fact does not teach, but Śaṁkara does." (*Bhagavad-gita: An Exegetical Commentary*, p. 107.)

31. *Bhakti-rasāmṛta-sindu* 1.1.12.

32. *Bhagavad Gītā* 4.18. *karmaṇy akarma yaḥ paśyēd akarmaṇi ca karma yaḥ / sa buddhimān manuṣyēṣu sa yuktaḥ kṛtsna-karma-kṛt.* "One who sees inaction in action, and action in inaction, is intelligent among men, and he is in the transcendental position [*yuktaḥ*], although engaged in all sorts of activities." (Translation by Bhaktivedanta Swami.)

33. Kṛṣṇa dāsa Kavirāja draws this distinction between *kāma* and *prēma* in *Caitanya-caritāmṛta, Ādi-līlā* 4.164-166.

34. Bhaktivedanta Swami, *Śrī Caitanya-caritāmṛta, Ādi-līlā*, vol. 1, p. 18.

35. See *Caitanya-caritāmṛta, Ādi-līlā* 2.101-104.

36. See Bhaktivedanta Swami, *Śrīmad Bhagāvatam*, Canto 1, pt. 1, p. 85.

37. Bhaktivedanta Swami, *Śrī Caitanya-caritāmṛta, Madhya-līlā*, vol. 2, pp. 158-159.

38. Letter to Jayatīrtha dāsa, November, 1975. Quoted in the ISKCON handbook, *The Process of Deity Worship (Arcana-Paddhati)*, p. vi.

39. *Caitanya-caritāmṛta, Ādi-līlā* 4.190-195.

40. Bhaktivedanta Swami, *Bhagavad-gītā As It Is*, p. 248.

41. *ataḥ śrī-kṛṣṇa-nāmādi na bhavēd grāhyam indriyaiḥ / sēvōnmukhē hi jihvādau svayam ēva sphuraty adaḥ. Bhakti-rasāmṛta-sindhu* 1.2.234. Quoted in *Bhagavad-gītā As It Is*, p. 366.

42. See Bhaktivedanta Swami, *The Teachings of Lord Caitanya*, p. 207.

5. Possession and Pottery.

1. Robert Caldwell, *The Tinnevelly Shanars ..., p. 21.*

2. Ibid., pp. 19, 20.

3. See, for example, Louis Dumont, *Une Sous-Caste de l'Inde du Sud*; Dumont, "Possession and Priesthood;" Edward B. Harper, "Shamanism in South India;" Harper, "Spirit Possession and Social Structure;" Peter Claus, "Possession, Protection and Punishment as Attributes of Deities in a South Indian Village;" Claus, "The Siri Myth and Ritual: A Mass Possession Cult of South India;" Claus, "Spirit Possession and Spirit Mediumship from the Perspective of Tulu Oral Traditions;" Marie-Louise Reiniche, *Les Dieux et les Hommes*.

4. See the discussion of this issue by Peter Claus in "Spirit Possession."

5. Information on the Vēḷār was gathered in Madurai and Ramnad Districts during 1979-80 with the support of a Doctoral Fellowship from the Canadian Social Sciences and Humanities Research Council. The community studied was a subcaste of the Pāṇṭiya Vēḷār, a caste which is spread throughout forty villages comprising two traditional territories (*nāṭu*).

6. Examples are summarized by Dumont in *Une Sous-Caste*.

7. For example, Henry Whitehead, *The Village Gods of South India*; Wilbur Elmore, "Dravidian Gods in Modern Hinduism."

8. I. M. Lewis, *Ecstatic Religion*. Tamil magicians (*mantiravāti*) who have the capability to leave their bodies and fly are known in Madurai District, but their motives and methods rarely involve the relationship to the divine commonly associated with shamanism.

9. Claus, "Spirit Possession," p. 29.

10. There are a number of variations, for example, *cāmiyāṭuvar* (Reiniche). Carl G. Diehl gives a list of names in *Instrument and Purpose*, p. 222.

11. See also Paul Younger, "A Temple Festival of Māriyamman̲," p. 516; Diehl, pp. 221-235. Dumont, and presumably his informants in Madurai District (adjoining the territory of the Vēḷār) seem to use the term *kōṭaṅki* interchangeably with *cāmiyāṭi* (*Une Sous-Caste*, p. 340).

12. Diehl, Dumont, *Une Sous-Caste*, and Reiniche.

13. Stuart Blackburn, "Oral Performance: Narrative and Ritual in a Tamil Tradition," p. 216.

14. Reiniche, p. 166.

15. Today these feats rarely include the skin piercing and hook swinging common to the large cult followings of Murukan̲ and Māriyamman̲.

16. Similar austerities among other communities are discussed in Dumont, *Une Sous-Caste*, p. 343-344 and in Reiniche, pp. 211-216.

17. Only men of the Vēḷār community participate in festivals as *cāmiyāṭis*, but in other south Indian communities, including some of those in the Madurai region, women also act as *cāmiyāṭis*.

18. Brenda E. F. Beck, "Colour and Heat in South Indian Ritual."

19. Though devotees call out the names of Kṛṣṇa and Śiva, their direct concern is not with these Brahmanical gods, but with the presence of the divine in a general sense.

20. It is most often women who become possessed in this way.

21. Although the deity Aiyaṉār sits in the main sanctum of most *kulateyvam* temples, those temples are more popularly known by the name of another powerful deity of the lineage. Aiyaṉār is, strictly speaking, never a *kulateyvam* for the Vēḷār and rarely manifests himself through possession.

22. Dumont, "Possession and Priesthood," p. 56.

23. Dumont, *Une Sous-Caste*, pp. 342, 343.

24. Reiniche, pp. 150, 179; Dumont, *Une Sous-Caste*, pp. 32, 346; Diehl, p. 40.

25. George Birdwood, *The Industrial Arts of India*, p. 84.

26. M. Monier-Williams, *Brahmanism and Hinduism*, p. 218.

27. Stephen Inglis, "Night Riders: Massive Temple Figures of Rural Tamilnadu."

28. Birdwood, p. 132.

29. Making temple images of baked clay is actually banned in the *āgamas*. K. Varma, *The Indian Technique of Clay Modelling*, pp. 192, 237.

30. Ananda Coomaraswamy, The Indian Craftsman, pp. 75-80; Edgar Thurston, *Castes and Tribes of Southern India*, vol. III, pp. 106, 192; Richard Gombrich, "The Consecration of a Buddhist Image," p. 24.

31. A Vēḷār modeller described this ritual as "naming my own child" and then "turning it over to the people."

32. A Vēḷār lineage may provide *cāmiyāṭis* only for the deities of their lineage temple, but it may provide clay images to dozens of temples under their care. The image festival usually involves a larger and more diverse gathering of devotees.

33. Reiniche, pp. 166-168.

34. The origins of central concepts in Tamil literature and mythology have been described by George Hart in *The Poems of Ancient Tamil: Their Milieu and Their Sanskrit Counterparts*, and more recently in a study by David Shulman, *Tamil Temple Myths*.

35. Jan Brouwer, cited in Claus, "Spirit Possession," p. 41.

36. See Dumont, *Une Sous-Caste*, p. 339.

6. God's Forceful Call.

1. The author conducted research in southern Koṅku from November 1979 until March 1981, with the support of a Predoctoral Fellowship provided by the Social Science Research Council. Koṅku is one of the five traditional divisions of Tamil south India, which includes the present districts of Coimbatore, Salem, Dharmapuri, Periyar, and parts of Tiruchirappalli and Madurai districts. Special thanks are due to Mr. P. Subramaniam, M.A., Lecturer in Tamil at the Paḻani Andavar College of Indian Culture for his unstinting cooperation during the period of fieldwork.

2. See especially Louis Dumont, "A Structural Definition of a Folk Deity of Tamil Nad: Aiyanar, the Lord." For more general background, the reader may refer to Louis Dumont, *Homo Hierarchicus: The Caste System and Its Implications*.

3. See McKim Marriott and Ronald Inden, "Caste Systems." Also of particular interest are McKim Marriott and Ronald Inden, "Toward an Ethnosociology of South Asian Caste Systems" and McKim Marriott, "Hindu Transactions: Diversity Without Dualism."

4. These are biological concepts exposed in various Ayurvedic treatises and widely popular among Indians. For a study of these concepts in South India and Sri Lanka, see Gananath Obeyesekere, "The Impact of Ayurvedic Ideas on the Culture and the Individual in Sri Lanka."

5. This belief is widely popular and is also reinforced by literary texts. The term *svayambhū*, "self-manifestation," is usually interpreted by informants as an expression of the territorial right of a deity. The classic Tamil text *Tirumurukāṟṟuppaṭai*, a guide to the worship of the god Murukaṉ, defines the god as "the one who has a right to reside in contentment in some places" (*uriyaṉ uraital amarntu*). See Nakkirar, *Tirumurukāṟṟuppaṭai.*

6. Manuel Moreno, "The God of Healing Poisons: Thermic complementary exchanges in two south Indian pilgrimages."

7. See Brenda E. F. Beck, "A Praise-Poem for Murugan;" A. K. Ramanujan, *Hymns for the Drowning*; Glenn E. Yocum, *Hymns to the Dancing Śiva: A Study of Māṇikkavācakar's Tiruvācakam*.

8. Informants distinguish between *aḻaippu* ("invitation") and *kaṭṭaḷai* ("command"). The call of a god upon humans is always characterized as *kaṭṭaḷai*. The fulfillment of such "call-command" gives the human recipient the quality of *adhikāra*, "competence" or "suitability" to perform the task commanded by the god.

9. For a thorough description and analysis of the Koṅku Veḷḷālar Kavuṇṭar caste, see Brenda E. F. Beck, *Peasant Society in Koṅku: A Study of Right and Left Subcastes of South India.*

10. Siddha is a medical system indigenous to south India. Although it has many similarities with Ayurvedic doctrines, it differs from the latter in emphasizing the use of poisonous substances, especially minerals. Its alchemic orientation has been discussed by Mircea Eliade, *The Forge and the Crucible: The Origins and Structures of Alchemy.*

11. The following account was translated into English with the help of Mr. Dorai Angusami and Mr. P. Subramaniam. The latter was present in the interview and recorded it in Tamil.

12. *Pēy* is a general category of powerful malevolent beings, very often "souls" (*āvi*) of departed people in search of release from a state of wandering. Girls around the age of puberty are likely candidates for possession by *pēy*. For a study of the various categories of powerful beings, see Susan S. Wadley, *Shakti: Power in the Conceptual Structure of Karimpur Religion.* For details of *pēy*-possession and exorcism, see R. Caldwell, "On demonolatry in southern India," pp. 91-105; see also Marie-Louise Reiniche, *Les dieux et les hommes: Étude des cultes d'un village du Tirunelvelli, Inde du Sud.*

13. This term is a compound of *vīṭu* ("house") and *tūram* ("distance"), and graphically conveys the notion that a menstruating woman must avoid visiting other peoples' houses.

14. These substances are considered to be highly "cooling," since they seal or bound dangerous powers generated by an excess of heat. For a study of notions of "heat" and "cold" in India, and the thermic properties of various substances, see Lawrence A. Babb, "Heat and Control in Chhatisgarhi ritual;" Brenda E. F. Beck, "Colour and Heat in south Indian ritual;" and Ruth S. Freed and Stanley A. Freed, "Shanti Nagar: The Effects of Urbanization in a Village in North India. Part 3: Sickness and Health."

15. *Paṅkuṉi Uttiram* is an important festival in the Hill Temple of Murukaṉ at Paḻani, which is accompanied by a very popular pilgrimage. See Moreno, "The God of Healing Poisons," for details on this pilgrimage. The precise deadline given by the goddess's mouthpiece seems to indicate certain rivalry between herself and the god Murukaṉ.

16. A non-Brahmin priest, garland-maker, and attendant of Kavuṇṭar temples.

17. Lineage-temples are differentiated from village-temples by the fact that in the latter all the residents in a village pay a festival tax to defray the costs of festival expenses.

18. The presence of two icons in festival procedures is very common in India. Informants would say that the anthropomorphic metal icon embodies the Dēvī (of the Great Indic Tradition), while the clay one is an icon of the *ammaṉ* (of the Little village Tradition). One can easily see a continuum of the various embodiments of the goddess (permanent stone idol, movable metal idol, clay idol which is discarded, and transitory human embodiments), in which substance and relative permanence seem to be correlated in various ways.

19. For a description of Kāḷi's difficult moods and generosity, see Bryan Pfaffenberger, *Caste in Tamil Culture: The Religious Foundations of Sudra Domination in Tamil Sri Lanka.*

20. Aspects of the territoriality and immanence of Tamil divine powers have been studied by George L. Hart, "The Nature of Tamil Devotion."

21. Giving sacred ashes is one of the prerogatives of priests and saints. Normal people can only transfer ashes which they have received from a priest or saint, but cannot give them on their own right, for they lack the *adhikāra* or competence for this task.

22. These two unbalanced states correspond at the popular level to imbalances due to an excess of phlegm (*kapam*) and an excess of bile (*pittam*), respectively, recognized in Āyurvēdic doctrine. They produce states characterized by "indolence" or "sleepiness" and "anger," respectively. For more details, see K. I. Bhishagratna, trans., *Suśruta: An English Translation of the Suśruta Saṃhitā.*

23. See Moreno, "The God of Healing Poisons," for a description and analysis of these pilgrimages.

24. Thermic qualities are not exclusive of foodstuffs, but are often attributed to people, gods, times, and even stages in the life-cycle of individuals. See below for more details on "cold" and "hot" castes.

25. This is a division typical of medieval south India. For detailed studies of this division, see Brenda E. F. Beck, *Peasant Society in Koṅku*; and Burton Stein, *Peasant State and Society in Medieval South India.*

26. These divisions are characterized in thermic values by McKim Marriott ("Hindu Transactions: Diversity Without Dualism"). The characterization is based on the respective patterns of marriage, descent, worship, diet, and temperament of the castes integrating these divisions.

27. Constellations (*nakṣatra*), or "lunar mansions," are important calendric divisions in south Indian ritual cycles. There are twenty-seven or twenty-eight constellations in a solar month, and *Kārttikai* is the third in the monthly order of succssion. Each constellation is attributed specific benevolent or malevolent influences, which are increased when the constellation appears in conjunction with other astral bodies. For details, see A. L. Basham, *The Wonder that was India.*

28. "Silence" is denoted by the term *niccalam*, which means "constant meditation" and "seclusion from social intercourse." The general Tamil term for "fasting" is *viratam*, which is variously used to denote the obligations to be followed in some religious observances (fasting or special diet, chastity, frequent baths, prayer, temple worship, among others).

29. A "golden" or "radiant" face is an expression of well-being. It also means an increase in the *sattvaguṇa*, the "cool" quality or "strand of life" responsible for goodness and knowledge. See Basham, pp. 327ff.

30. It is important to remark that the term used for "needle" means actually "beauty" or "beautiful." This euphemism brings home the notion that ascetic observances beautify the body, that is, endow it with radiance (see note 29 above).

31. *Maṇṭala* is a unit of time (forty-one lunar days in Tamilnadu) used by Siddha doctors in conjunction with their treatments. It is also the unit commonly used to compute the length of religious observances, especially viratam.

32. The third canto of Nakkirar's *Tirumurukāṟṟuppaṭai* associates Murukaṉ in his abode of *Āvinaṅkuti* (modern Paḻani) with the removal of curses (i.e., the curse inflicted on Brahmā by Murukaṉ).

33. See note 5 above.

34. For *viratam* see note 28 above. *Nōṉpu* refers to the particular occasion (such as Māriyammaṉ *nōṉpu*, Aṅkalammaṉ *nōṉpu*, and others) in which *viratam* observances are prescribed.

35. For a detailed study of the Hindu *saṃskāras*, see Raj Bali Pandey, *Hindu Saṃskāras: Socio-Religious Study of the Hindu Sacraments.* For an anthropological perspective of the Hindu *samskāra* of marriage, see Ronald B. Inden and Ralph W. Nicholas, *Kinship in Bengali Culture*, pp. 35ff.

36. See, for instance, Mariasusai Dhavamony, *Love of God according to Śaiva Siddhānta.*

37. The notion of *sātmya* ("compatibility" or "appropriateness") has been studied by Francis Zimmermann, "Ṛtu-sātmya: The seasonal cycle and the principle of appropriateness." Discussing Ayurvedic prescriptions, Zimmermann considers what is appropriate to times and seasons (*kālasātmya, ṛtusātmya*) and places or habitudes (*dēśasātmya, ōkaḥsātmya*), and the relationships between the qualities of illness and seasons and places. His analysis would seem to be directly applicable to the complementary processes involving gods and humans in which compatibility is a necessary requisite.

7. Founders, Swamis, and Devotees

1. There are many relevant studies on this subject; a few are: William Wiser, *The Hindu Jajmani System*; Kathleen Gough, "The Hindu Jajmani System;" Henry Orenstein, "Exploitation and Function in the Interpretation of Jajmani;" McKim Marriott, "Caste Ranking and Food Transactions, a Matrix Analysis;" Lawrence Babb, "The Food of the Gods in Chhattisgarh: Some Structural Features of Hindu Ritual;" and Susan Wadley, *Shakti: Power in the Conceptual Structure of Karimpur Religion*.

2. See Louis Dumont, *Homo Hierarchicus. An Essay on the Caste System*, especially pp. 184-87, 194, and 233-36. On religious leaders and founders, see note 25.

3. McKim Marriott, "Interpreting Indian Society: A Monistic Alternative to Dumont's Dualism," p. 194; see note 45. Also see Marriott's article, "Hindu Transactions: Diversity Without Dualism" in Bruce Kapferer, ed., *Transaction and Meaning*. Kapferer notes in his introductory chapter (p. 12) that Marriott shows the importance of cultural understanding of transactions, and that "transactional behavior, and the rules which occasion it, relate not only to the structure of social relationships but also to individual bodily make-up. The individual, through transactions, affects his own internal order." Kapferer further stresses the importance of not assuming transactions occur purely for "maximizing benefit" purposes (p. 8).

4. The five faces of Śiva, according to the Vīraśaiva Cennabasava's *Karaṇa-hasuge*, arose originally out of the formless Absolute (*śūnya, niranjana-brahman*, or *śūnya-liṅga*), and are manifestations of its lustre. They are the source of the five *śaktis* and five *kalās* (energies and their subtle material manifestations) from which the world as we know it is created. Each face (*mūrti, mukha*) is connected with certain qualities (see the diagram below) and syllables of the *mantra*, "Namaḥ Śivāya."

Sadāśiva

FACES:	Sadyōjāta	Vāmadēva	Aghōra	Tatpuruṣa	Īśāna
TEACHERS:	Paṇḍitārādhya or Ekōrāmārādhya	Ēkōrāma or Paṇḍitārādhya	Marulārādhya (Marula Siddhēśvara)	Rēvaṇārādhya (Rēvaṇasiddha	Viśvēśvarārādhya
	power of action	power of knowledge	power of will	power of origin (*ādī*)	highest power (*parama*)
	"Na	ma	śi	vā	ya"

Sources: Wurth, trans., *Channa Basava Purāṇa of the Lingaits*, pp. 210-211; and Nandimath, "A Handbook of Vīraśaivism."

5. R. Black Michael has written an interesting and informative article on Vīraśaiva origins, "Foundation Myths of the Two Denominations of Vīraśaivism: *Viraktas* and *Gurusthalins*."

6. Siddhaliṅgēsvara is famous for having made celibacy a *sine qua non* for his Virakta swamis; this had apparently not been the case in early Vīraśaivism. Basava, for instance, had two wives according to P. B. Desai (*Basavēśvara and His Times*, p. 180) and others. Likewise, many lower echelon Guruvarga swamis customarily marry.

7. The date and lineage order are as found in A. S. Hugara and H. C. Hulyala, *Niranjana*. This modern compilation of the Tōṇṭadārya lineage has been accepted by the swami and followers of Tōṇṭadārya Maṭh. It also concurs in general outline with oral historical lineage accounting.

8. One informant noted: "An ordinary man who is involved in *saṃsāra* and has a narrow perspective has to fulfill his own and his family's desires, get money, and purchase things. But a swami has no such attachments; he's a *sannyāsi*, always interested in the well-being of his devotees at large. The whole world is his playground where he worships *liṅga* [see note 15] for the sake of the world world." Another said: "Only swamis will get such power (*śakti*) since they have no other worries and can fully concentrate their minds on *liṅga pūje*. Our mind moves about and we can't concentrate."

9. See for example: Jan Gonda, *Some Observations on the Relations between "Gods" and "Powers" in the Veda*; Sudhendu K. Das, *Śakti or Divine Power*; Susan Wadley, *Shakti: Power in the Conceptual Structure of Karimpur Religion*; J. Abbott, *The Keys of Power*; Sir John Woodroffe, *Shakti and Shakta*; George Hart, "Some Aspects of Kinship in Ancient Tamil Culture;" Brenda E. F. Beck, "The Kin Nucleus in Tamil Folklore."

10. See chapter three of my forthcoming Ph.D. dissertation, "Renunciation, Love, and Power in Hindu Monastic Life" for comparisons and contrasts.

11. Power and purity are natural concomitants. This system seems to favor talking about power however. Also see below. S. Wadley (*Shakti: Power in the Conceptual Structure of Karimpur Religion*, p. 186) also finds purity and power to be inseparable factors of human identity.

12. "Demons in their power are attached to *māyā* and money and use their power for bad ends," according to one informant. Another said: "Demons have less *śakti* than swamis. They run away from one who has *liṅga pūje* power. They have evil intentions, and get *śakti* from those intentions."

13. As a tantalizing suggestion, I would refer the reader to Harper's claim that for Hindus purity is relatively weak and "static" compared to impurity ("Ritual Pollution as an integrator of caste and religion") and ask him/her to compare my data with Harper's. However, the issue is too complicated to treat fairly in a note; so again I must refer the reader to my forthcoming dissertation, chapters 3 and 4. See also below.

14. The *varṇa* theory of social relationships as found in *Ṛg Vēda* X.90 ("Hymn of the Primeval Man" — Puruṣa) describes four social classes arising out of his body in (it seems) fixed hierarchical order. Priests come from his mouth, warriors from his arms, traders/agriculturalists from his thighs, and servants/laborers from his feet. G. S. Ghurye (in "Class, caste, and occupation," as cited in David Mandelbaum, Vol. I, p. 7) says that by about 600 B.C. the caste system had already become crystallized to a certain extent. *Jātis* (castes) are by nature endogamous and hereditary, thus restricting the easy movement of individuals between castes. Nonetheless there have been caste and subcaste groups whose economic position and status within towns and regions have become modified. Increased wealth and modifications in occupation or lifestyle seem to be important factors in determining this social mobility. These features naturally involve changing forms of interaction or exchange with members of the other castes in the locale.

15. The *iṣṭaliṅga* is a small blue black *liṅga* which is usually worn at all times by Liṅgāyats in a casket attached to a thread and placed around the neck. This is to supercede the temple *liṅga* in importance (seen as a "static *liṅga*" separate from the human being) as a way to express the idea of "living, moving" divinity within the human saint or devotee. The *iṣṭaliṅga* is daily removed from its casket and placed in the left palm, where it is offered *pūjā* and gazed upon fixedly in meditation for a time. The goal of such meditation is to become one with the *liṅga*, as the inner *liṅga* (*ātma-liṅga*) becomes fully manifest.

16. A swami or a person with accumulated power, plus the *maṭh* where he lives, are where God always resides. This power gives protection against ghosts, sorcery, and so forth. This holy power can also attack evil power and overcome it." As another example, one of the "dēvarus" (swamis-in-training) in Tōṇṭadārya Maṭh related how he had been stricken with jaundice due to sorcery (*māṭa*). A swami gave him some holy footwash water (*pādōdaka*) and blessed food (*prasād*), and smeared sacred ash on his face. He proceeded to recover quickly. He said: "A swami's *liṅga-puje* power overcomes the power of sorcery."

17. For example: "Good man who eat the remnants of (food offered in) worship / Are freed from all sins ....' (*Bhagavad Gītā*, III.13); "Whatever thou offerest in oblation or givest/

whatever austerity thou performist, son of Kunti/ That do as an offering to Me.// ... freed, thou shalt go to Me// Those who revere Me with devotion,/ They are in Me and I too am in them." (*Bhagavad Gītā*, IX.27-IX.29) [F. Edgerton, trans.]. "A boy begotten from his father's power/ Resembles his father, can you imagine/ He looks like any other man./ When Śiva himself and Śiva's power,/ Dividing into two, became Guru and disciple, you must not say Guru and disciple are different/ ..." (from A. Menezes and S. M. Angadi, trans., *Essence of Satsthala, Vacanas of Tōṇṭada Siddhaliṅgēśvara*, vacana no. 163).

18. C. J. Fuller, "Gods, Priests, and Purity: On the Relation Between Hinduism and the Caste System."

19. *Manu* XI.176 says: "A Brāhmaṇa who unintentionally approaches a woman of Kaṇḍāla or of (any other) low caste, who eats (the food of such persons) and accepts (presents from them) becomes an outcast; but (if he does it) intentionally, he becomes their equal." *Manu* IX.243 states: "A virtuous king must not take for himself the property of a man guilty of mortal sin; but if he takes it out of greed, he is tainted by that guilt (of the offender)." Note the importance of the intentionality of both parties.

20. Equality-creating relationships are especially notable among family members. Jan Gonda notes that in the Vedas fatherhood is seen as a source of power and authority for the son, since power is part of transmitted identity (see *Some Observations* ...). Brenda Beck (in "The Kin Nucleus") mentions that power can be transferred from a young chaste girl to her father and brothers, and from a wife to her husband. Likewise, Mayer refers to witchcraft power inherited through the female line (*Caste and Kinship in Central India*, p. 205). In the *Laws of Manu* it is stated that a woman becomes like her husband and assumes his qualities like a river uniting with an ocean (*Manu* IX.22). Other major figures are also said to be able to purify others and to be unaffected themselves by impurity. For example, *Manu* V.93 and V.96-97 suggest that proper kings are never impure. *Manu* III.71 says the same thing for Brahmins who regularly perform the five great sacrifices (*yajñas*). Maintaining strong links with divinity is the key to the superior figure's ability to purify others.

21. *Liṅgaikya* refers to union with the *liṅga*, often at the time of death. One informant noted: "Siddhaliṅgēśvara is giving *darśan* even today in Eḍiyūr village."

22. The terms "subtle" and "gross" are not actually used by informants, but offer us a covenient (and standard Hindu: *sūkṣma* – "subtle" and *sthūla* "gross") way of classifying the various types of gifts. Likewise, Vīraśaiva religion mentions three *aṅgas* or bodies which correspond to the gross, subtle, and causal bodies.

23. Joachim Wach, author of *Sociology of Religion*, among others, indicated the centrality of founders, prophets, reformers, masters, and teachers to the development of spiritual communities in terms of inspirational guidance, doctrine, and structure of the group. He says that the circle of disciples is "oriented toward a central figure with whom each of the disciples is in intimate contact. The double significance of the founder as the first recipient of the new vision from which the fellowship draws its inspiration and guidance and, more generally, as the instrument of supernatural power and grace, is reflected in the reaction of his followers and variety of functions performed by them" (p. 135).

24. The *paṭṭābhiṣēka* ceremony is most well known in Indian history in connection with the installation of kings (*mahārājas, rājas*). The swami's *paṭṭābhiṣēka* is similar in that it uses traditional royal paraphernalia for the ceremony – umbrella, drum, fly whisk, flag, throne, and palanquin. In addition both king and swami are installed on the lineage or royal "seat" – the *pīṭha* – which implies the establishment of their basic authority. The swami's presence is thus considered to be like a royal presence (*mūrti*) in a number of ways. See also note 28, where he is shown to be like a temple *mūrti* in some ways.

25. Abbott in his *Keys of Power* describes a common physiological explanation of birth and inheritance and notes that food, when eaten, contributes to male semen which, through sexual contact, enters the female womb and assimilates to her blood. The child is a mixture of semen and blood and so (he says) derives soul and *śakti* from his father (p. 492). Narada in the *Bhakti Sūtras* calls the relationships between son and father, and wife and husband the most apt models for permanent absorption in God through love (*sūtra* 82).

26. Marvin Davis notes that more than any other group the family is defined by its "one physical nature" and "behavioral code" — what he calls code and substance. See "A Philosophy of Hindu Rank from Rural West Bengal."

27. The *bhēdābhēda* tradition posits both the essential unity (*abhēda*) of Godhead, and also a measure of duality or difference (*bhēda*) between the universe and God following Creation. The *viśiṣṭādvaita* position or "qualified (*viśiṣṭa*) nondualism (*advaita*)" holds that the human soul or Self (*ātman*) has a qualified identity with God — being created out of God's essence, yet always retaining some measure of individuality (e.g., in Rāmānuja's Śrī Vaiṣṇavism).

28. For instance, the Vedic *yajña* (sacrifice) and *dakṣiṇa* (ritual payment to the priest) may be thought of as gifts as the Vedic hymns themselves may be. The Fathers (*pitaras*) were offered gifts through *pitṛpiṇḍayajña*. *Prasād* may be offered in temples and homes as well as in monasteries, often involving the blessed food given by an image of God (*mūrti*). *Pādōdaka* (my informants noted) bears similarity to *tīrtha*, the holy water distributed in temples, at pilgrimage sites, and at the tombs of saints.

29. Clifford Geertz, "Religion as a Cultural System," pp. 167-178.

30. Modern education is often mentioned by informants as a prerequisite for being a swami. One could therefore argue that this statement is not referring to spiritual progress within the "traditional" swami-bhakta relationship at all. However, modern education and traditional religious education form similar prerequisite requirements.

31. Louis Dumont, *Homo Hierarchicus*, pp. 57, 72.

32. Mary Douglas, *Natural Symbols*, p. 12; also see Douglas, *Purity and Danger*.

33. Louis Dumont, *Homo Hierarchicus*, p. 185.

34. Ibid., p. 185; Dumont, "World Renunciation in Indian Religions," pp. 37-38, 60-61.

35. He says we must understand the "cognized South Asian person as permeable, composite, partly divisible, and partly transmissable." ("Interpreting Indian Society. A Monistic Alternative to Dumont's Dualism.")

36. Veena Das also holds that when *sannyāsis* are included as a part of Hindu society, series of dyadic relationships rather than fixed hierarchy form the model for Hindu society. See *Structure and Cognition*, chapter 2.

8. The Holy Man as the Abode of God.

1. Raymond B. Williams, *A New Face of Hinduism: the Swaminarayan Religion*, chapter 1.

2. Harshadbhai T. Dave, trans., *Shree Swaminarayan's "Vachanamritam,"* Gadhada II, 13, p. 380.

3. J. A. B. van Buitenen, "Akṣara," p. 183.

4. H. T. Dave, *"Vachanamritam,"* Gadhada II, 42, p. 442.

5. J. A. Yajnik, *The Philosophy of Sri Svaminarayana*, p. 100.

6. van Buitenen (trans.), p. 183.

7. H. T. Dave, *"Vachanamritam,"* Vadtal 5, p. 503.

8. Harshadbhai T. Dave, *Life and Philosophy of Shree Swaminarayan*, p. 209.

9. Ramesh M. Dave, "Ethics of the *Shikshapatri*," p. 10.

10. Raymond B. Williams, "Holy Man as Religious Specialist: the Acharya Tradition in Vaishnavism," pp. 83-86.

11. Philip Singer, *Sadhus and Charisma*.

12. M. N. Srinivas, "Prospects of Sociological Research in Gujarat," p. 33.

Conclusion

1. Friedhelm Hardy, *Viraha-Bhakti: The early history of Kṛṣṇa devotion in South India, p. 13.*

2. Ibid., p. 13.

3. Ibid., p. 13.

4. Ibid., p. 14.

5. Ibid., p. 17.

6. See Friedhelm Hardy, "Mādhavêndra Puri: a link between Bengal Vaiṣṇavism and south Indian bhakti."

7. This does *not* mean, however, that a Vīraśaivite, if scratched deeply enough, is bound to show his true colors as a Śaṅkara *advaitin*. As Lise Vail points out, the north Karnataka religious system she studies is a close relative of *bhēdābhēda* and *viśiṣṭādvaita* systems in its philosophical commitments. It is also important to keep in mind that for the Vīraśaivite, formless divinity is *śakti*, a state of being, which is quite different from Saṅkara's notion of the absolute as *jñāna*, a "state of knowing."

Contributors and Editors

Paul B. Courtright is Associate Professor and Head of the Department of Religious Studies at the University of North Carolina at Greensboro. From 1971-1976 he was a member of the Department of Religion at Williams College. He received his B.A. from Grinnell College, M.Div. from Yale University, and Ph.D. from Princeton University. He is the author of *Gaṇeśa: Lord of Obstacles, Lord of Beginnings*, to be published by Oxford University Press in Autumn 1984.

Norman Cutler is Assistant Professor in the Department of South Asian Languages and Civilizations at the University of Chicago. He received his A.B. from the University of Michigan, M.A. from the University of Washington, and Ph.D. from the University of Chicago. His primary teaching and research interests are in Tamil language and literature, especially devotional literature, and the practice of Hinduism in south India. He has published several articles on these subjects and is currently working on a book-length study of Tamil bhakti poetry.

William H. Deadwyler, III (Ravīndra-svarūpa dāsa) has been a member of the International Society for Krishna Consciousness since 1971. He received his B.A. in Philosophy from the University of Pennsylvania (1966) and his Ph.D. in Religion from Temple University (1980). He was president of the ISKON center in Philadelphia from 1971-1978. He is currently an editor for ISKON's *Back to Godhead* magazine, to which he has contributed many articles. A collection of his essays will be published in the spring of 1984 by the Gītā-nāgari Press.

Stephen Inglis is an anthropologist working as a research consultant with the National Museum of Man in Ottawa, Canada. He received his B.A. from the University of British Columbia, M.A. from Calcutta University, and is completing a Ph.D. at the University of British Columbia. His recent work has involved exhibits and publications in the field of folk and popular arts, including *Calendar Prints: Popular Art of South India*, which was presented at the Museum of Anthropology in Vancouver during 1983.

A former student of theology, ***Manuel Moreno*** obtained a *Licenciatura* in Philosophy and the Humanities in 1972 at the University of Barcelona, Spain, and subsequently taught at Jawaharlal Nehru University, New Delhi, in 1972 and 1973. He studied Anthroplogy at Vanderbilt University and at the University of Chicago where he submitted his Ph.D. dissertation on the worship of Murukaṉ at Paḻaṉi, Tamilnadu, the result of two years of fieldwork in that locality. Currently an Assistant Professor at Northeastern Illinois University, he has published articles on Gift-exchange, sociological theory, and ritual, as well as many anthropological contributions in standard Spanish encyclopedias.

Vasudha Narayanan received her Ph.D. from the University of Bombay in 1978. She taught at DePaul University from 1978 to 1982 and is currently an Assistant Professor in the Department of Religion, University of Florida. She has written articles on the Śrīvaiṣṇava tradition of south India, including "The Goddess Śrī: Blossoming Lotus and Breast Jewel of Viṣṇu" in *The Divine Consort: Rādhā and the Goddesses of India* (Berkeley: 1982) and "The Two Levels of Auspiciousness in Śrīvaiṣṇava Ritual and Literature" in *Contributions to Asian Studies*, vol. XIX (Leiden: 1984). She is presently working with Professor John Carman of Harvard University on a book entitled *Śrīvaiṣṇava Commentary: The Confluence of Tamil and Sanskrit Scriptures*.

James J. Preston is Associate Professor of Anthropology at the State University of New York at Oneonta. He received his B.A. from San Francisco State University, M.Ed. from the University of Vermont, and Ph.D. from the Hartford Seminary Foundation. He is the author of *Cult of the Goddess: Social and Religious Change in a Hindu Temple* (New Delhi: Vikas) and editor of *Mother Worship: Theme and Variations* (Chapel Hill: University of North Carolina Press). He has published articles on various aspects of Hinduism, pilgrimage, and methodology for the scientific study of religion. Currently he is conducting research on pilgrimage in America, and he is writing a book on the anthropological study of imaginative experience.

Lise F. Vail received an M.A. in History of Religions at Princeton University, and she is currently completing a Ph.D. in Religious Studies at the University of Pennsylvania and studying at Gurudev Siddha Peeth in Ganeshpuri, India. She has taught at Indiana University and Hobart and William Smith Colleges. Her dissertation, entitled "Renunciation, Love and Power in Hindu Monastic Life" is based on fieldwork conducted during 1977-79 in north Karnataka.

Joanne Punzo Waghorne has taught in the Boston area for several years and is currently Visiting Assistant Professor in the Department of Religion, Bowdoin College. She received her B.A. from Wilson College and Ph.D. from the Divinity School at the University of Chicago. Her articles have appeared in *History of Religions*, *Journal of the American Academy of Religion*, and in several volumes of collected essays. A monograph on C. Rajagopalachari is forthcoming from Chanakya Press, New Delhi and a study of sacral kingship in south India is in progress.

Raymond B. Williams is Professor of Religion at Wabash College in Crawfordsville, Indiana, where he has taught since 1965. He received his A.B. and B.D. from Phillips University and his M.A. and Ph.D. from the University of Chicago. He is the author of *A New Face of Hinduism: The Swaminarayan Religion*, published by Cambridge University Press in 1984.

Glossary

abhiṣēka. The ritual of bathing or anointing a divine embodiment; sprinkling the image with water or other fluid.

ācamana. Sipping of water, one of the sixteen traditional *upacāras* or "services" rendered to a deity during *pūjā.*

ācāram. (Tamil) A particular sequence in the rite of exorcism in drawing esoteric designs on ashes collected in a winnowing basket.

ācārya. A spiritual preceptor or teacher; the head of a *sampradāya* or spiritual lineage. In the Swaminarayan tradition it refers to the two hereditary leaders of the Ahmedabad and Vadtal dioceses of the Swaminarayan religion.

adhikāra. The authority derived from particular privileges or from powers conferred by gods.

adhikārin. A person possessing *adhikāra.*

ādhyātmika kuṭumbha. Spiritual family.

advaita-vēdānta. The school of Vēdānta founded by Śaṅkarācārya, teaching that the phenomenal world is unreal, that *brahman* alone exists and is without any distinctions, and that the individual soul is identical with *brahman* in all respects.

akṣara. The abode of the supreme person; an eternal state which is thought to have an impersonal form as a state of being and a personal form as an abode of god.

akṣardhām. The heavenly abode or state of the supreme person; equivalent to *akṣara* in the impersonal form.

akṣata. Rice grains rubbed with red powder; used frequently in conjunction with the *pūjā* to Gaṇēśa and other deities.

aḻaku. (Tamil) "Beauty"; also used in devotional contexts to designate metallic needle used to perforate the body of a votary.

āḻvār. (Tamil) "One who is immersed"; one of the twelve poet-saints of south India who lived between the seventh and ninth centuries A.D. and who composed Tamil songs in praise of the god Viṣṇu.

amṛta. "Deathless"; elixir of immortality, nectar.

aṉpu. (Tamil) Love, devotion and attachment.

anugraha. "Favor, grace."

āratī. A ritual song, performed before the image of a deity along with the waving of lamps.

arcā. "That which can be worshiped"; God manifested through a "material" image.

arcanā. "Honoring, praising"; also, the worship of the divine image in a temple.

arghya. Offering of water for sipping to the deity; one of the sixteen traditional *upacāras* or "services" rendered to a deity during *pūjā.*

Arthaśāstra. An Indian text written about the fourth-third centuries B.C. on the subject of statecraft.

aruḷcakti. (Tamil) "Grace-force"; *aruḷ* (grace) + *cakti* (power); God's grace conceived of as a powerful force.

aruvāḷ. (Tamil) A long knife or sickle used by farmers. Also an embodiment of heroic deities.

Āśādha. The Hindu lunar month corresponding to June/July.

āsana. A seat or throne for the image of the deity.

āsanavidhi. The set of ritual procedures for measuring out the seat on which the patron sits during *pūjā.*

āśīrvāda. Blessings, benediction.

aṣṭavināyaka. Eight shrines to Gaṇēśa in Maharashtra.

aṭimai. (Tamil) "Service." The term appears to be derived from the root *aṭi*, "bottom of a thing, foot, beginning, source." It indicates lowness and subservience.

ātman (*ātmā*). The soul.

āvāhana. "Invocation," one of the sixteen traditional *upacāras* or services rendered to a deity during *pūjā*.

avatāra. A "descent" or manifestation of a deity; specifically of a human or animal form assumed by Viṣṇu. The *Bhāgavata Purāṇa* identifies twenty-two, but adds that they are innumberable.

Basava. Founder of the Vīraśaiva or Liṅgāyat tradition in south India.

Bhadrapāda. The Hindu lunar month corresponding to August/September which falls at the end of the monsoon season in Maharashtra.

bhakta. "Devotee"; one who worships the deity or a spiritual teacher with love.

bhakti. "Devotion, love"; religious devotion as a way to salvation; fervent devotion to god; derived from *bhaj*, meaning "to share and participate."

bhasma. Sacred ashes. See *vibhūti*.

bhāva. Sentiment, heightened religious awareness.

bhēdābhēda. A philosophical school whose leading writer was Bhāskara. "Non-difference in difference." According to this school of thought God is neither different from nor identical with the human and the world.

Bhū. "The Earth"; a consort of Viṣṇu.

bhukti. Enjoyment of worldly pleasures.

bhūta. A class of demons or spirits.

bījā mantra. A condensed, monosyllabic *mantra* which is used at the point in the *pūjā* to Gaṇēśa when the vital power is invoked into the clay image.

bisurgan ceremony. The common custom found throughout India of dissolving mud images of the deities in rivers and ponds at the end of a festival.

brahman. The supreme creative principle; the substratum and substance of existence; frequently identified with any one of the chief gods; in Vaiṣṇava literature identified as Viṣṇu; in some Swaminarayan literature distinguished from *parabrahman* as an equivalent term for *akṣara*.

brahmapadārtha. The immortal life stuff of the deity.

calanti pratimā. A movable image of the deity associated with a shrine. This image usually substitutes for the main icon on occasions when the image is taken out of the temple and into the streets. See *utsava mūrti*.

cāmiyār. (Tamil) A holy man.

cāmiyāṭi. (Tamil) "God dancer"; the title of a specialist whose major role is to become possessed by and act as a mouthpiece for a local deity, most often as part of a hereditary responsibility to a particular social group. Usually refers to a person chosen by a god and endowed with particular powers of healing and fortune telling. Also a "dancer of god's dance."

cāmiyāṭṭam. (Tamil) "God's dance," *cāmi* (lord, god) + *āṭṭam* (dance); dance of "possession" by a god.

cāpam. (Tamil) A curse, an inordinate state of being due to negative influences.

caurang. (Marathi) The lower altar table upon which an image is placed for worship.

Citakāras. A subcaste whose duty is to paint the sacred images at Jagannāth Purī temple.

cūṭu tōṣam. (Tamil) An inordinate state resulting from an excess of heat. *Cūṭu*, "heat," especially of the body. A popular understanding of the Ayruvedic tradition of medicine, in which health is understood to be disrupted by imbalances in the natural harmony of the body's three humors (wind, phlegm, and bile).

Daitā. A subcaste of non-Brahmin priests at Jagannāth Purī temple responsible for the periodic secret carving of the wooden image of the deity.

dakṣiṇā. The gift given to a priest for performing a *pūjā* or other service.

daru. The sacred log out of which the image of the deity is carved.

Dēvī. "Goddess"; may refer to local goddesses or the consorts of the great gods.

dhyāna. "Meditation."

dīpa. "Light"; a lamp waved before the deity during *ārati.*

divya. "Divine, sacred, brilliant, wonderful."

divya dēśa. "A sacred place." The Śrīvaiṣṇava community acknowledges about 108 sacred places where Viṣṇu manifests himself.

divya maṅgala vigraha. The divine auspicious form of the deity.

Durgā Pūjā. An elaborate festival lasting one week which is particularly popular in eastern India. At this time the goddess Durgā is worshiped.

dūrvā. A kind of grass sacred to Ganēśa and used in *pūjā* performed in his honor.

Gaṇapati. A name for Gaṇēśa.

gandha. "Fragrance"; sometimes refers to sandalwood paste.

Gaṇēśa. "Lord of Gaṇas"; The elephant-headed Hindu deity, son of Śiva and Pārvatī, and remover of obstacles.

Gauḍiya Vaiṣṇavism. The Vaiṣṇava tradition founded by Caitanya, so called because it originated in *Gauḍa-dēśa*, i.e. Bengal.

gāyatrī. The Vedic *mantra* celebrating the coming of light and asking for illumination which is usually performed by Brahmins at dawn.

grāmadēvatā. The protector deity of a village.

guṇa. "Quality, attribute"; frequently refers to the three qualities of matter, *sattva* (goodness, purity) *rajas* (activity, passion), and *tamas* (darkness, inertia.)

guru. "Heavy, weight"; religious teacher, spiritual preceptor. See *ācārya.*

hārda. A technical term in Śrīvaiṣṇavism which expresses the idea that the deity is present in the soul of a human.

indriya. Sense organ.

iṣṭadēvatā. The deity a devotee chooses to worship.

iṣṭa teyvam. (Tamil) A desired or chosen god, object of a personal devotion. See *iṣṭadēvatā.*

īśvara. The lord, the gods or deities. Some Swaminarayan scholars translate it as "demigod" to distinguish it from *parabrahman*.

jagadguru. "Teacher of the world"; a title conferred on certain religious leaders, usually heads of monasteries.

Jagannātha. "Lord of the universe"; a name of Kṛṣṇa. Especially refers to the unusual wooden image of Kṛṣṇa worshiped originally at Jagannātha Purī.

jaṅgama. (Kannada) Members of the priestly class in the Liṅgāyat tradition.

jīva. Living creature, soul.

jñāna. "Knowledge"; particularly the attempt to understand the absolute truth by philosophical discrimination between matter and spirit, issuing in an impersonal concept of God.

kāla. "Time"; a basic element of change and destruction.

kalaśa. A ritual water vessel.

kalyāṇa utsava. "Auspicious celebration"; a ritual performed in Śrīvaiṣṇava temples in which Viṣṇu is married to his consorts Śrī and Bhū.

kāṇikkai. (Tamil) Alms given for the maintenance of temple worship.

kānti. "Beauty; brilliance"; a double strand of 108 wooden beads worn by Swaminarayan devotees; the necklace given to the person at the time of initiation into the tradition.

karma. "Work"; in particular that materially motivated work which causes rebirth in the world.

Karnataka. A state in south India.

karuṇā. Compassion"; pity, tenderness.

Kavuṇṭar. (Tamil) "Lord of the territory"; the caste title of the Koṅku Veḷḷāḷar caste.

kirāmacānti. (Tamil) Rites performed before a festival to pacify the powers residing within a territory.

kīrtanā. "Praise, glorification", especially the glorification of God through singing or chanting.

kōlam. (Tamil) Designs made by women with rice flour on ground plastered with cowdung, to express auspiciousness and joy and also to avert malevolent powers.

kṛṣṇapakṣa. The "dark half" of the Hindu month when the moon is waning.

kuladēvatā. The particular deity worshiped by a family as its ancestral protector.

kuṇḍalinī. "Coiling like a snake." In the tantric tradition, it denotes the latent power that is made manifest through meditation.

kurukkaḷ. (Tamil) A priest of a "Sankritized" temple. See *guru*.

kuśa. Sacred grass used in sacrifice.

līlā. "Play, sport"; used to characterize the activities of God.

liṅga. The "sign" or "emblem" of Śiva. Śiva worshiped in the form of a stone or marble column which generally rises out of the *yōni* or symbol for the female sexual organ.

Liṅgāyat. "One who wears a *liṅga*"; a Śaiva sect of south India.

mahant. The ascetic appointed or elected as head of a temple and as leader of the ascetics resident there; a religious leader and preacher for the devotees of the villages associated with the temple.

mahāprasād. The food offered to the deity in a temple, then distributed among the people as a sacrament. Sometimes this food is distributed many miles away in temples associated with a major deity at a pilgrimage shrine. The *mahāprasād* of Jagannāth Purī, usually in the form of dried grains, is distributed among small Jagannāth shrines throughout coastal Orissa. See *prasāda.*

Mahārāna. A subcaste of carpenters responsible for cutting down the trees used for the construction of the images of the three deities at the Jagannāth Purī temple.

mañcaḷnīr. "Yellow Water"; turmeric water; a substance used in rituals of cooling and ceremonies concluding lengthy rituals.

manṭalam. (Tamil) A variable measure of time (forty-one or forty-eight lunar days) in Ayurvēdic and Siddha medicine, as well as in devotional observances, particularly fasting.

mantra. A sacred formula or word in ritual worship and meditation; words or phrases which possess power; a sacred phrase or chant which is given in the initiation ritual.

māyā. "Illusion, wondrous power." In the Swaminarayan tradition, it refers to the flux and change in which all existence, apart from Puruṣōttam and *akṣara*, is bound.

māyāvāda. The doctrine (*vāda*), taught in *advaita-vēdānta*, that the world as well as the personal form of God are illusory (*māyā*).

mōdaka. A sweet wheat-flour ball, especially favored by Gaṇēśa and offered to him during *pūjā.*

mōkṣa. "Release"; freedom from suffering and rebirth, the highest spiritual goal in Hinduism.

mṛdaṅga. A two-headed, clay drum, suspended from the neck by a strap, used in *kīrtanā.*

mukurttakkāl. (Tamil) Literally "auspicious time"; but refers popularly to a bamboo pole inserted in the northeast corner of a temple entrance to indicate the beginning of a festival, or in the front of a house at the time of a marriage celebration.

mūlavar. (Tamil) "The primary one"; the immovable image of a deity.

mūlikai. (Tamil) Herbs in general, and particularly certain herbs thought to have medicinal qualities.

mūrti. "Form, likeness, image" of a deity.

naivēdya. Food offered to a deity.

namaskāra. Honorific greeting; bowing in reverential salutation.

nambike. (Kannada) Belief.

Navakalēvara ceremony. The elaborate ritualization of the burial, carving, and renewal of the deities at the Jagannāth Purī temple.

navapaśanam. "Nine poisons" or nine metaloids often used in indigenous medical practice; the constituents of Murukaṉ's physical embodiment.

nērttikkaṭaṉ. (Tamil) The fulfillment of a vow or repayment of a debt (*kaṭaṉ*) contracted with a deity.

nirguṇa. "Without qualities"; a characterization of divinity in the most abstract sense.

noṉpu. (Tamil) Particular domestic observances in which deities are worshiped with *pūjā* and fasting, particularly by women.

Nṛsimha. The man-lion incarnation of Viṣṇu.

paccarici. (Tamil) "Raw rice"; rice which has not been parboiled.

pāda pūjā. "Worship of holy feet" usually done to a religious teacher.

pādōdaka. Sacred water obtained by washing the feet of a religious teacher.

pādya. Worship of the deity's feet.

Pañcācāryas. A Vīraśaiva sub-group that reveres five teachers who are regarded as founders of the sect.

pañcāmṛtasnāna. Bathing the images with five sacred "nectars": milk, curd, clarified butter, honey, and sugar.

pañcāṅga. The Hindu almanac.

pañcāyatana. The five deities worshipped by Smārta Brahmins in their homes.

Paṅkuni Uttiram. (Tamil) An important Śaivite festival, celebrated in the month of Paṅkuṉi (March-April), when the full moon intersects with the Uttiram constellation.

paṇṭāram. (Tamil) A class of non-Brahmin priests, temple guides, or florists.

para. "High." In Śrīvaiṣṇava theology it refers to the manifestation of Viṣṇu in heaven.

parabrahman. The supreme *brahman*; equivalent to *puruṣōttama* in Swaminarayan tradition.

paramātman. "Supreme Soul"; usually refers to God.

paramparā. "Successive, a regular series, lineage"; usually refers to a lineage of *gurus*.

pātre. (Kannada) Vessel.

paṭṭābhiṣēka. Coronation, consecration.

pavitra. "Pure, sacred."

pēy. (Tamil) A kind of powerful malevolent being; wandering ghost.

phala. "Fruit"; the consequences of ritual performance for devotees.

Piḷḷai Lōkācārya. A thirteenth century Śrīvaiṣṇava theologian.

piṇḍa. A ball of rice offered to deceased ancestors.

piracātam. (Tamil) Transvalued left-over food or washings of a deity. See *prasāda*.

piśāca. A class of demons.

pīṭha. "Seat"; a seat of the deity or the traditional seat of authority in a monastery.

poṅkal. (Tamil) Boiled rice; milk-rice.

pradakṣiṇa. Circumambulation, keeping the sacred object on one's right side.

prāna, Vital breath, life-force.

prāṇapratiṣṭhā. The establishment of vital breath in the image of the deity by which it is brought to animating power; the central sequence in some forms of *pūjā*.

prāṇayāma. Breath control exercise.

prarthanā. Prayer.

prasāda. "Favor, clarity"; grace; also refers to offerings (usually food) made to the deity and then distributed among devotees.

pūcāri. Non-Brahmin priest, usually a hereditary specialist who administers worship (*pūjā*) at local temples.

pūjā. Worship, formal act of devotion to deity.

pūje. (Kannada) See *pūjā.*

pulunkalarici. (Tamil) Parboiled rice, thought to be "hotter" than raw rice.

purāṇa. "Old, ancient"; a sacred book, often considered to be one of the eighteen collections which contain Hindu mythology and stories of the principal Hindu deities.

purōhita. The priest who oversees the performance of *pūjā.*

Puruṣasukta. *Ṛg Vēda* 10.90, a hymn celebrating the sacrifice of the cosmic person. An important hymn for many *pūjās.*

puruṣōttama. "The supreme person"; the highest divine reality; equivalent to *parabrahman* in Swaminarayan tradition.

Rāmadāsa. A seventeenth century poet-saint of Maharashtra.

Rāmānuja. An eleventh century religious leader and theologian of the Śrīvaiṣṇava community.

ratha-yātra. "Chariot procession"; a festival in which the divine image is taken out of the temple and pulled through the streets on a hand-drawn cart or chariot.

rasa. "Flavor, extract, concoction"; a term used in medicine, poetics, and cooking.

Śabara. A tribal group of uncertain origin (probably from south India) related to the Daitās and other non-Brahmin temple priests in Orissa.

ṣaḍaṅganyāsa. The set of gestures purifying the six limbs of the patron's body and thereby identifying them with those of Puruṣa; the cosmic man.

sādhane. (Kannada) Spiritual practice.

sādhu. A Hindu ascetic; one who has renounced the world; sometimes refers to one who has received initiation (*pārvati dīkṣā*) and taken the vows of the Swaminarayan ascetics.

saguṇa. "With qualities"; an attribute of divinity in manifested form.

śakti. "Power, energy"; also refers to the active power of Śiva, sometimes personified as his wife.

śālagrāma. The ammonite fossil of a fish found in the Himalaya mountains which is revered as a manifestation of Viṣṇu.

saṃkalpa. The announced intention of the rite.

saṃkaṣṭacaturthī. "Dangerous fourth," the fourth day of the dark half of the month, understood to be inauspicious. Ritual acts of a renunciatory nature are performed on this day.

sampradāya. A tradition handed down from a founder through successive religious teachers which shapes the followers into a distinct fellowship with institutional forms.

saṃsāra. The stream or flow of life. In the Vīraśaiva tradition, it refers to areas where darkness and impurity dominate.

saṃskāra. Hindu rites of passage or transition; sacraments marking stages of the life cycle.

Śaṅkara. Ninth century scholar and philosopher, associated with the spread of non-dualistic (*advaita*) Vēdānta philosophy.

sannyāsa. "Renunciation."

sannyāsī. A member of the renounced order of life.

śāstra. A Sanskrit text containing political, legal, and moral codes.

sāttvik. Pure.

sātmya. Appropriateness, compatibility.

siddha. A sage endowed with miraculous powers; an alchemist; an indigenous doctor who uses metaloid substances in his treatments.

siddhi. "Accomplishment, perfection, completion"; a power which can be obtained through ascetic practices.

śiṣya. Student, disciple.

Śiva. "Pure, auspicious"; one of the important Hindu gods.

smṛti. "Remembered"; post-Vedic classical Sanskrit literature, to be distinguished from the more authoritative *śruti* or "revealed" literature. The epics, *purāṇas*, and codes of *dharma* fall in this category.

sōma. Sacred drink used in Vedic sacrifices, believed to have special probably hallucinatory, powers when consumed.

Śrī. "The auspicious one"; the most important consort of Viṣṇu.

Śrīgaṇēśa Atharvaśīrsa. A text celebrating Gaṇēśa as the incarnation of the ultimate principle *brahman.*

Śrīvaiṣṇava. A community that worships Viṣṇu and his consort Śrī. It reveres Rāmānuja as its most important preceptor.

śruti. The sacred Vedas heard by the ancients and transmitted through the generations; the most sacred religious texts; to be distinguished from *smṛti* or "remembered" texts.

sthala purāṇa. A book giving the myths legends and history of a holy place.

Stambeśwarī. Wooden pillars worshiped by tribal people as their tutelary goddess.

sthāpana. Rites by which an image is set up in a place of worship.

Sthapati. A subcaste of image makers.

śuddhikaraṇa. Gestures of purification.

śuklapakṣa. The "bright half" of a Hindu lunar month when the moon is waxing.

Sūrya. The sun god.

svāmi (swami). "Master, lord"; a term applied to the deity or to a religious teacher.

svayambhū. "Self-existent"; an image that is not carved or fashioned by an artist, but appears naturally and is taken to be particularly potent in its religious power.

Tai Pucam. (Tamil) An important Śaivite festival, celebrated in the month of Tai (January-February), when the full moon intersects with the Pūcam constellation.

Tāraka. A demon who was defeated by Śiva.

tīrtha. "Crossing"; a sacred spot in a river where ritual bathing is done; a place of pilgrimage.

tīrttam. (Tamil) Sacred water.

tōppu. (Tamil) A grove; often refers specifically to a coconut or palm grove.

ugra. The "furious" manifestation of a particular deity.

upacāra. "Way of service," a ritual gesture performed during *pūjā,* e.g., *ācamana,* sipping of water. Traditional ritual texts enumerate sixteen *upacāras.*

upavastra. A garment worn over the shoulders, a shawl.

Uṭaiyavar. (Tamil) "He who owns"; a title of Rāmānuja.

uttarapūjā. The concluding *pūjā*; the ritual sequence in which the deity is immersed in water.

vaikuṇṭha. Heaven; the celestial realm of Viṣṇu.

Vaiṣṇava. "Of or relating to Viṣṇu." A member of one of the traditions which are devoted to Viṣṇu (and the Viṣṇu-incarnations such as Kṛṣṇa or Rāma) as the supreme Godhead.

varam. (Tamil) A boon, a gift from a god.

vastra. A garment clothing the body.

Vēḷār. (Tamil) An ancient honoriphic title used by potter castes in several regions of Tamilnadu.

vēṇṭutal. (Tamil) "That which is needed," from *vēṇṭu* "be necessary, be wanted." A term indicating a type of worship which is undertaken to make a request.

vēr. (Tamil) Root, usually with medicinal properties.

vibhava. "Manifestation, appearance"; usually refers to an incarnation of the deity on earth.

vibhūti. "Wealth"; sacred ashes used in worship to mark devotee's forehead, arms and often also chest.

Vināyaka. A name of Gaṇēśa.

vināyakacaturthi. The fourth day of the bright half of the Hindu month, an especially auspicious day.

vipūti. (Tamil) See *vibhūti.*

Virakta. A Vīraśaiva sub-sect that reveres Basava as its founder.

Vīraśaiva. "Heroic Śiva worshiper." See Liṅgāyat.

viratam. (Tamil) A type of religious observance characterized by fasting, celebration of *pūjā*, and other devotions.

visarjana. "Sending forth"; the point near the conclusion of the Gaṇeśa festival (and other Hindu festivals) when the images are immersed in water.

viśiṣṭādvaita. "Qualified non-dualism"; the philosophical school whose main spokesman was Rāmānuja. According to this school, the primary reality, *brahman*, is qualified by spirit and matter.

Viṣṇu. "All pervasive"; an important deity in Hinduism.

viśvāsa. "Trust, confidence."

Vṛndāvana. A village in what is now Uttara Pradesh, where Kṛṣṇa is said to have manifested fested his divine *līlā* on earth. Also the name for the transcendental abode of Kṛṣṇa in the kingdom of God.

vyūha. "Form, manifestation"; in Śrīvaiṣṇava theology, the quadruple manifestation of Viṣṇu as Vāsudēva Saṃkarṣaṇa, Pradyumna and Aniruddha. Usually portrayed as Viṣṇu reclining on the Sea of Milk.

yajamāna. The patron of the *pūjā.*

Bibliography

Abbott, J. *The Keys of Power: A Study of Indian Ritual and Belief.* London: Methuen and Company, 1932.

Alston, William P. "The Elucidation of Religious Statements." In *Process and Divinity: Philosophical Essays presented to Charles Hartstone.* Edited by William L. Reese and Eugene Freeman, pp. 429-443. LaSalle, Ill.: Open Court Publishing Co., 1964.

Annangaracariyar, P. B., ed. *Nālāyira tiviyap pirapantam.* Kāñcīpuram: n.p., 1973.

Appadurai, Arjun. *Worship and Conflict Under Colonial Rule: A South Indian Case.* Cambridge: Cambridge University Press, 1981.

Appadurai, Arjun and Carol Appadurai Breckenridge. "The South Indian Temple: Authority, Honor and Redistribution." *Contributions to Indian Sociology*, vol. 10, no. 2 (July-December 1976), pp. 187-211.

Aquinas, Thomas. *Summa Theologica.* Translated by Fathers of the English Dominican Province. New York: Benziger Brothers, 1947.

Babb, Lawrence. "The Food of the Gods in Chhattisgarh: Some Structural Features of Hindu Ritual." *Southwestern Journal of Anthropology*, vol. 26, no. 3. (Autumn 1970), pp. 287-304.

__________. "Heat and Control in Chhattisgarhi ritual." *Eastern Anthropologist*, vol. 26, no. 1 (January-March 1973), pp. 11-28.

__________. *The Divine Hierarchy*. New York: Columbia University Press, 1975.

Banerjea, Jitendra Nath. "The Hindu Concept of God." In *The Religion of the Hindus.* Edited by Kenneth W. Morgan. New York: The Ronald Press, 1953.

Basham, A. L. *The Wonder that was India.* 2nd ed. New York: Grove Press, 1959.

Beck, Brenda. "Colour and Heat in South Indian Ritual." *Man* (NS), vol. 4, no. 4 (December 1969), pp. 553-572.

__________. *Peasant society in Koṅku: A study of right and left subcastes in South India.* Vancouver: University of British Columbia Press, 1972.

__________. *"The Kin Nucleus in Tamil Folklore."* In *Kinship and History in South Asia* (Michigan Papers on South and Southeast Asia, no. 7). Edited by Thomas Trautman, pp. 1-28. Ann Arbor: University of Michigan, 1974.

__________. "A praise-poem for Murugan." *Journal of South Asian Literature*, vol. 11, nos. 1 & 2 (Fall and Winter 1975), pp. 95-116.

__________. "The Goddess and the Demon: A local south Indian festival and its wider context." *Puruṣārtha* (Paris), no. 5 (1981), pp. 83-136.

Bhaktisiddahānta Sarasvatī Gosvāmī, trans. *Shri Brahma-samhitā with Commentary by Shri Shrila Jeeva Goswāmi.* 3rd ed. Madras: Sree Gaudiya Math, 1973.

__________. *Shri Chaitanya's Teachings.* Part 1; Madras: Sree Gaudiya Math, 1967. Part 2; Mayapur: Sree Chaitanya Math, 1974.

Bhaktivedanta Swami Prabhupāda, A. C. *Bhagavad-gita As It Is.* Complete Edition. New York: The Macmillan Company, 1972.

__________. *The Nectar of Devotion: The Complete Science of Bhaktiyoga.* "A Summary Study of Śrīla Rūpa Gosvāmi's *Bhaktirasāmṛta-sindhu*." 2nd ed. Los Angeles: The Bhaktivedanta Book Trust, 1982.

__________. *Śrī Caitanya-Caritāmṛta of Kṛṣṇadasa Kavirāja Gosvāmī.* 17 vols. New York and Los Angeles: The Bhaktivedanta Book Trust, 1974-1975.

__________. *Śrī Īśopaniṣad.* 2nd ed. New York and Los Angeles: The Bhaktivedanta Book Trust, 1974.

———. *Śrīmad Bhāgavatam*. Cantos 1-10. 30 vols. New York and Los Angeles: The Bhaktivedanta Book Trust, 1972-1980.

Birdwood, George. *The Industrial Arts of India*. London: Chapman & Hall, 1880.

Blackburn, Stuart. "Oral Performance: Narrative and Ritual in a Tamil Tradition." *Journal of American Folklore*, vol. 94, no. 372 (April-June 1981), pp. 207-227.

Bolles, Kees W. "Speaking of a Place." In *Myths and Symbols: Studies in honor of Mircea Eliade*. Edited by Joseph M. Kitagawa and Charles H. Long, pp. 127-139. Chicago: The University of Chicago Press, 1969.

Brubaker, Richard L. "The Ambivalent Mistress: A study of south Indian village goddesses and their religious meaning." Ph.D. dissertation, University of Chicago, 1978.

Bühler, Georg, trans. *The Laws of Manu*. New York: Dover Publications, 1969.

Caldwell, Robert. *The Tinnevelly Shanars*. Vepery: Reuben Twig, 1849.

Carman, John *The Theology of Ramanuja*. New Haven: Yale University Press, 1974.

Claus, Peter. "Possession, Protection and Punishment at Attributes of Deities in a South Indian Village." *Man in India*, vol. 53, no. 3 (July-September 1973), pp. 231-242.

———. "The Siri Myth and ritual: A Mass Possession Cult of South India." *Ethnology*, vol. 14, no. 1 (January 1975), pp. 47-58.

———. "Spirit Possession and Spirit Mediumship from the Perspective of Tulu Oral Traditions." *Culture, Medicine and Psychiatry*, vol. 3, no. 1 (March 1979), pp. 29-52.

Coomaraswamy, Ananda. *The Indian Craftsman*. London: Probsthain & Co., 1909.

Copleston, Frederick. *A History of Philosophy*. vol. 1: *Greece and Rome*, Rev. ed., New York: Image Books, 1962.

Crooke, William. "Images and Idols (India)." In *Encyclopaedia of Religion and Ethics*. Edited by James Hastings, vol. 7, pp. 142-146. New York: Charles Scribner's Sons, 1915.

Das, Sudhendu Kumar. *Śakti or Divine Power*. Calcutta: University of Calcutta, 1934.

Das, Veena. "On the Categorization of Space in Hindu Ritual." In *Text and Context: The Social Anthropology of Tradition*. Edited by Ravindra Jain, pp. 9-27. Philadelphia: Institute for the Study of Human Issues, 1977.

———. *Structure and Cognition: Aspects of Hindu Caste and Ritual*. 2nd ed. Delhi: Oxford University Press, 1982.

Dave, Harshabdhai T. *Life and Philosophy of Shree Swaminarayan*. London: George Allen & Unwin, 1974.

———, trans. *Shree Swaminarayan's 'Vachanamritam.'* Bombay: Bharatiya Vidya Bhavan, 1977.

Dave, Ramesh M. "Ethics of the *Shikshapatri*." In *Swaminarayan Magazine* (April 1978). Ahmedabad: Akshar Purushottam Sanstha, pp. 9-10.

Davis, Marvin. "A Philosophy of Hindu Rank from Rural West Bengal." *Journal of Asian Studies*, vol. 36, no. 1 (November 1976), pp. 5-24.

De, Sushil Kumar. *Early History of the Vaisnava Faith and Movement in Bengal*. 2nd ed. Calcutta: K. L. Mukhopadhyay, 1961.

Desai, P.B. *Basavēśvara and His Times*. Dharwar: Kannada Research Institute, Karnataka University, 1968.

Deutsch, Eliot. *Advaita Vedānta: A Philosophical Reconstruction*. Honolulu: East-West Center Press, 1969.

Dhavamony, Mariasusai. *Love of God according to Śaiva Siddhānta*. Oxford: The Clarendon Press, 1971.

Diehl, Carl. *Instrument and Purpose*. Lund: G. W. K. Gleerup, 1956.

Dobbin, Frank S. *Error's Chains: How Forged and Broken*. New York: Standard Publishing House, 1883.

Douglas, Mary. *Natural Symbols*. New York: Pantheon Books, 1970.

__________. *Purity and Danger.* Hammondsworth: Penguin Books, 1970.

Dumont, Louis. *Une Sous-Caste de l'Inde du Sud.* Paris and The Hague: Mouton, 1957.

__________. "Possession and Priesthood." *Contributions to Indian Sociology* (Paris), no. 3 (July 1959), pp. 55-74.

__________. *Homo Hierarchicus: An Essay on the Caste System.* Chicago: University of Chicago Press, 1970.

__________. "World Renunciation in Indian Religions." *Contributions to Indian Sociology* (Paris), no. 4 (April 1960), pp. 33-62.

Eck, Diana L. *Darśan: Seeing the Divine Image in India.* Chambersburg, Pa.: Anima Books, 1981.

Edgerton, Franklin, trans. *The Bhagavad Gītā.* New York: Harper and Row (Harper Torchbooks), 1965.

Eliade, Mircea. *Patanjali and Yoga.* New York: Funk and Wagnalls, 1969.

__________. *Yoga: Immortality and Freedom.* Princeton: Princeton University Press, 1969.

Elmore, Wilbur. "Dravidian Gods in Modern Hinduism." University of Nebraska Dissertations, vol. 4. Lincoln: 1915.

Eschmann, Anncharlott. "Hinduization of Tribal Deities in Orissa." In *The Cult of Jagannāth and the Regional Traditions of Orissa.* Edited by Anncharlott Eschmann, *et al*, pp. 79-97. New Delhi: Manohar Publications, 1978.

__________. "The Vaiṣṇava Typology of Hinduization and the Origin of Jagannātha." In *The Cult of Jagannāth and the Regional Traditions of Orissa.* Edited by Anncharlott Eschmann, *et al*, pp. 99-117. New Delhi: Manohar Publications, 1978.

Farquhar, J. N. *The Crown of Hinduism.* London: Oxford University Press, 1915.

Frazer, James G. *The New Golden Bough.* Edited and abridged by Theodor G. Gaster. A Mentor Book. New York: The New American Library of World Literature, 1959.

Freeman, James M. *Scarcity and Opportunity in an Indian Village.* Menlo Park: Cummings Publishing Company, 1977.

Fuller, C. J. "Gods, Priests, and Purity: On the Relation between Hinduism and the Caste System." *Man* (N.S.), vol. 14, no. 3 (September 1979), pp. 459-476.

Geertz, Clifford. "Religion as a Cultural System." In *Reader in Comparative Religion: An Anthropological Approach.* 3rd ed. Edited by William Lessa and Evon Vogt, pp. 167-178. Evanston, Ill.: Row and Peterson, 1958.

Gelberg, Stephen J. ed. *Hare Krishna, Hare Krishna: Five Distinguished Scholars on the Krishna Movement in the West.* New York: Grove Press, 1983.

Gombrich, Richard, "The Consecration of a Buddhist Image." Journal of Asian Studies, vol. 26, no. 1 (November 1966), pp. 23-36.

Gonda, Jan. "Pratiṣṭhā." *Studia Indologica Internationalia*, vol. 1 (1951), pp. 1-37.

__________. "The Indian Mantra." *Oriens*, vol. 16 (1963), pp. 247-97.

__________. *Some Observations on the Relations between "Gods" and "Powers" in the Veda à propos of the Phrase Sunuḥ Sahasaḥ.* The Hague: Mouton and Company, 1957.

Gough, Kathleen. "The Hindu Jajmani System." *Economic Development and Cultural Change*, vol. 9, no. 1 (October 1960), pp. 83-91.

Gould, Harold A. "The Jajmani System of North India: Its Structure Magnitude, and Meaning." *Ethnology*, vol. 3, no. 1 (January 1964), pp. 12-41.

Gosvāmī, Satsvarūpa Dāsa. *Śrīla Prabhupāda-līlāmṛta: A Biography of His Divine Grace A. C. Bhaktivedanta Swami Prabhupāda.* vol. 1: *A Lifetime in Preparation: India 1896-1965.* vol. 2: *Planting the Seed: New York City 1965-1966.* vol. 3: *Only He Could Lead Them: San Francisco/India 1967.* vol. 4: *In Every Town and Village: Around the World 1968-1971.* vol. 5: *Let There be a Temple: India/Around the World 1971-1975.* vol. 6: *Uniting Two Worlds: Around the World/Back to Vṛndāvana.* Los Angeles: The Bhaktivedanta Book Trust, 1980-1983.

Green, Garrett. "Reconstructing Christian Theology: A Review of Gordon D. Kaufman's *The Theological Imagination: Constructing The Concept of God*." *Religious Studies Review*, vol. 9, no. 3 (July 1983), pp. 219-222.

Hardy, Friedhelm. "Mādhavêndra Puri: A link between Bengal Vaiṣṇavism and South Indian bhakti." *Journal of the Royal Asiatic Society*, 1974, pp. 23-41.

__________. "Ideology and Cultural Contexts of the Śrīvaiṣṇava Temple." *Indian Economic and Social History Review*, vol. 14, no. 1 (January-March 1977), pp. 119-151.

__________. *Viraha-Bhakti: The early history of Kṛṣṇa devotion in South India.* Delhi: Oxford University Press, 1983.

Harper, Edward. "Shamanism in South India." *Southwestern Journal of Anthropology*, vol. 13, no. 1 (Spring 1957), pp. 267-287.

__________. "Spirit Possession and Social Structure." In *Anthropology on the March*. Edited by Bala Ratman, pp. 165-177. Madras: Social Science Association, 1963.

__________. "Ritual Pollution as an Integrator of Caste and Religion." *Journal of Asian Studies*, vol. 23 (June 1964), pp. 151-193.

Hart, George L. III. "Some Aspects of Kinship in Ancient Tamil Literature." In *Kinship and History in South Asia* (Michigan Papers on South and Southeast Asia, no. 7). Edited by Thomas Trautman, pp. 29-60. Ann Arbor: University of Michigan, 1974.

__________. *The Poems of Ancient Tamil: Their Milieu and Their Sanskrit Counterparts.* Berkeley: University of California Press, 1975.

__________. "The nature of Tamil devotion." In *Aryan and Non-Aryan in India.* (*Michigan Papers on South and Southeast Asia*, no. 14). Edited by M. N. Deshpande and P. Hook, pp. 11-33. Ann Arbor: University of Michigan, 1979.

Hayagrīva dāsa Adhikārī. "The Spiritual Master: Emissary of the Supreme Person." *Back to Godhead*, no. 38, pp. 16-21.

Hopkins, Thomas J. *The Hindu Religious Tradition.* Encino, California: Dickenson Publishing Company, 1971.

Hugara, A. S. and Hulyala, H. C. *Niranjana.* Dharwar: Karnatak University, 1974.

Hume, Robert E., trans. *The Thirteen Principal Upanishads*. London and New York: Oxford University Press, 1971.

Inglis, Stephen. "Night Riders: Massive Temple Figures of Rural Tamilnadu." In *Festschrift for for Professor M. Shanmugam Piḷḷai.* Edited by V. Vijayavenugopal, pp. 297-307. Madurai: Madurai University Press, 1980.

International Society for Krishna Consciousness. *The Process of Deity Worship (Arcana-Paddhati)*. Los Angeles: The Bhaktivedanta Book Trust, 1978.

James, William. "Reflex Action and Theism." In *The Will to Believe and Other Essays in Popular Philosophy*, pp. 111-144. 1897; reprint ed., New York: Dover Publications, 1956.

Javadekar, A. Y. *Now Begins the Worship and Story of the Fourth Lunar Day of the Lord of Troops.* 2nd Edition. Edited by McKim Marriott. Chicago: University of Chicago Press, 1969.

Jindel, Rajendra. *Culture of a Sacred Town*. Bombay: Popular Prakashan, 1976.

Jośī, Nārāyanaśāstri. *Śrī Gaṇeśa Ārādhanā*. Bombay: Śrimayureśa Prakāsan, 1969.

Kane, P. V. *History of Dharmaśāstra.* 1930-1962; reprint ed., Pune: Bhandarkar Oriental Research Institute, 1974.

Kapferer, Bruce, ed. *Transaction and Meaning: Directions in the Anthropology of Exchange and Symbolic Behavior.* Philadelphia: Institute for the Study of Human Issues, 1976.

Kapoor, O. B. L. *The Philosophy and Religion of Śri Caitanya: (The Philosophical Background of the Hare Krishna Movement).* New Delhi: Munshiram Manoharlal, 1977.

Kaw, R. K. *The Doctrine of Recognition.* Hoshiapur: Vishvesvaranand Institute, 1967.

Kinsley, David R. *Hinduism: A Cultural Perspective.* Englewood Cliffs, N.J.: Prentice Hall, 1982.

Kramrisch, Stella. "Traditions of the Indian Craftsman." In *Traditional India: Structure and Change*. Edited by Milton Singer, pp. 18-24. Philadelphia: The American Folklore Society, 1959.

Krishnan, M. S. *Geology of India and Burma*. Fifth Edition. Madras: Higginbothams Publications, 1968.

Krishnaswami, Aiyangar S. *History of Tirupati*, 2 vols. Madras: Tirumalai-Tirupati Devasthanam, 1940-1941.

Kulke, Hermann. "Early Royal Patronage of the Jagannāth Cult." In *The Cult of Jagannāth and the Regional Traditions of Orissa*. Edited by Anncharlott Eschmann, *et al*, pp. 139-155. New Delhi: Manohar Publications, 1978.

Kūrattāḻvāṉ, "Śrī Varadarājastavaḥ and Sundarabāhustavaḥ." In *Stotramālā*. Edited by P. B. Annangaracarya, pp. 27-41. Kāncipuram: Granthamālakaryālaya, 1969.

Lannoy, Richard. *The Speaking Tree*. New York: Oxford University Press, 1971.

Lewis, I. M. *Ecstatic Religion*. Middlesex: Penguin, 1971.

Mandelbaum, David. *Society in India*, 2 vols. Berkeley: University of California, 1970.

Marriott, McKim. "Caste Ranking and Food Transactions, a Matrix Analysis." In *Structure and Change in Indian Society*. Edited by Milton Singer and Bernard Cohn, pp. 133-172. Chicago: Aldine, 1968.

__________. "Hindu Transactions: Diversity Without Dualism." In *Transactions and Meaning: Directions in the Anthropology of Exchange and Symbolic Behavior*. Edited by Bruce Kapferer, pp. 109-142. Philadelphia: Institute for the Study of Human Issues, 1976.

__________. Interpreting Indian Society: A Monistic Alternative to Dumont's Dualism." *Journal of Asian Studies*, vol. 36, no. 1 (November 1976), pp. 189-195.

Mayer, Adrian C. *Caste and Kinship in Central India*. Berkeley: University of California Press, 1970.

Menezes, Armando and Angadi, S. M., trans. *Essence of Satsthala, Vacanas of Tōṇṭada Siddhaliṅgēśvara*. Dharwar: Karnataka University, 1978.

__________. *Vacanas of Basavanna*. Chitradurg: Sirigere Math (Annana Balaga), 1967.

Michael, Blake. "Foundation Myths of the Two Denominations of Vīraśaivism: Viraktas and Gurusthalins." *Journal of Asian Studies*, vol. 42, no. 2 (February 1983), pp. 309-322.

Minor, Robert. *Bhagavad-gītā: An Exegetical Commentary*. New Delhi: Heritage Publishers, 1982.

Mishra, K.C. *The Cult of Jagannātha*. Calcutta: K. L. Mukhapadhyay, 1971.

Monier-Williams, M. *Brahmanism and Hinduism*. New York: MacMillan, 1891.

Moreno, Manuel. "The appropriation of order in a Hindu festival: Rituals of Māriyammaṉ in the hot season." Manuscript, 1982.

__________. "The god of healing poisons: thermic complementarity and cexchanges in two south Indian pilgrimages." Manuscript, 1982.

Müller, Max F. *Lectures on the Origin and Growth of Religion as Illustrated by the Religions of India*. 1878; reprint ed., Varanasi: Indological Book House, 1964.

Nandimath, S. C. "A Handbook of Vīraśaivism." In *Commemoration Volume*, Part III. Edited by S. C. Nandimath, S. S. Baswanal, and K. R. Srinivasa Iyengar. Dharwar: The Literary Committee of the Lingayat Education Association, 1941.

Narayanan, Vasudha. "The Goddess Śrī: Blossoming Lotus and Breast Jewel of Viṣṇu." In *The Divine Consort: Rādha and the Goddesses of India*. Edited by John S. Hawley and Donna Wulff, pp. 224-237. Berkeley Religious series, Graduate Theological Union, 1982.

Naṭāṭūr Ammāḷ. *Prapanna Pārijāta*. Madraṣ: Viśiṣṭadvaita Pracharinī Sabhā, 1971.

Nityānuṣṭānakramam. Edited by Śrī Stalacāyaṉattūraivar Svāmi. Madras: The Little Flower Company, 1979.

Noss, John B. *Man's Religions*. 6th ed. New York: MacMillan Publishing Company, 1980.

Orenstein, Henry. "Exploitation and Function in the Interpretation of Jajamani." *Southwestern Journal of Anthropology*, vol. 18, no. 4 (Winter 1962), pp. 302-315.

Östor, Ākos. *The Play of the Gods*. Chicago: University of Chicago Press, 1981.

Parāśara Bhattar. *Viṣṇu Sahasranāma bhāṣyam. Bhagavadguṇadarpaṇam*. Edited by P. B. Annangaracarya. Madras: Pathnam Press, 1964.

Paz, Octavio. *The Bow and the Lyre*. Translated by Ruth Simms. Austin: University of Texas Press, 1956.

__________. "Foreword." In *Quetzalcoatl and Guadalupe* by Jacque Lafaye. Translated by Benjamin Keen, pp. i-xxii. Chicago: The University of Chicago Press, 1974.

Pelikan, Jaroslav. *The Christian Tradition: A History of the Development of Doctrine*. vol. 1: The Emergence of the Catholic Tradition (100-600). vol. 2: *The Spirit of Eastern Christendom (600-1700)*. vol. 3: *The Growth of Medieval Theology (600-1300)*. Chicago and London: The University of chicago Press, 1971-1978.

Philo of Alexandria. *Philo*. Translated by F. H. Colson, G. H. Whitaker, and Ralph Marcus. The Loeb Classical Library. 12 vols. Cambridge: Harvard University Press, 1949-1962.

Piḷḷai Lōkācārya. "Artapañcakam." In *Aśtādaśa Rahasyam*. Edited by Che. Kriṣṇamācāriyar. pp. 24-33. Madras: Ananda Press, 1911.

__________. Śrī Vacaṉa Bhūṣaṇam. Edited by P. B. Annangaracarya. Kāñcipuram: P. B. Annangaracarya Publications, 1966.

Piḷḷāṉ, Tirukkurukai Pirāṉ. "Āṟāyirappaṭi." Commentary on the *Tiruvāymoḻi*. In *Śrī Bhagavad Viṣayam*, 10 vols. Edited by S. Krishnamacary. Madras: Noble Press, 1925-1930.

Piṉpaḻakiya Perumāḷ Jīyar. *Āṟāyirappaṭi Guruparamparaprabhāvam*. Edited by S. Kiriṣṇasvāmi Ayyaṅkār. Tirucci: Puttūr Agrahāram, 1975.

Preston, James J. *Cult of the Goddess: Social and Religious Change in a Hindu Temple*. New Delhi: Vikas Publishers, 1980.

__________. "The Goddess Chandi as an Agent of Change." In *Mother Worship: Theme and Variations*. Edited by James J. Preston, pp. 210-226. Chapel Hill: University of North Carolina Press, 1982.

__________. "Goddess Temples in Orissa: An Anthropological Survey." In *Religion in Modern India*. Edited by Giri Raj Gupta. New Delhi: Vikas Publishers (in press).

Preston, James J. and James Freeman. "Two Urbanizing Orissan Temples." In *Transformations of a Sacred City: Bhubaneswar, India*. Edited by Susan Seymour, pp. 97-117. Boulder: Westview Press, 1980.

Rajagopala Ayyangar, trans. *Rahasyatraya Sāra of Vedānta Deśika*. Salem: The Literary Press, 956.

Ramanujan, A. K. *Speaking of Śiva*. Baltimore: Penguin Books, 1973.

__________. "Karma in Bhakti with Special reference to Nammāḻvār and Basavanna." Paper presented in the ACLS/SSRC Workshop on "Karma in Post-Classical Texts." Pendle Hill, Pennsylvania, October, 1980.

__________. *Hymns for the Drowning: Poems for Viṣṇu by Nammāḻvār*. Princeton: Princeton University Press, 1981.

Reiniche, Marie-Louise. *Les dieux et les hommes: Étude des cultes d'un village du Tirunelveli, Inde du Sud*. Collection "Cahiers de l'Homme." Paris and The Hague: Mouton, 1979.

Sadānanda Yogīndra. *Vedāntasāra*. Translated by Swami Nikhilananda. 3rd ed. Calcutta: Advaita Ashrama, 1949.

Śaṅkarācārya. *The Vedânta Sûtras with the Commentary by Saṅkarâcârya*. Translated by George Thibaut. Sacred Books of the East, vols. 34, 38. 1904; reprint ed., Delhi: Montilal Banarsidass, 1962.

__________. *The Bhagavad Gita with the Commentary of Sri Sankaracharya*. Translated by Alladi Mahadeva Sastry. 1897; reprint ed., Madras: Samata Books, 1977.

Saraswati, Baidyanath. *Kashi: Myth and Reality of a Classical Cultural Tradition*. Simla: Indian Institute of Advanced Study, 1975.

__________. "The Śaiva Component in the Early Evolution of Jagannātha." In *The Cult of Jagannāth and the Regional Traditions of Orissa.* Edited by Anncharlott Eschmann, *et al*, pp. 119-124. New Delhi: Manohar Publications, 1978.

Shulman, David. *Tamil Temple Myths.* Princeton: Princeton University Press, 1980.

Singer, Milton. "Changing Craft Traditions in India." In *Labor Commitment and Social Change in Developing Areas.* Edited by Wilbert Moore and Arnold Feldman, pp. 258-275. New York: Social Science Research Council, 1960.

__________. *When a Great Tradition Modernizes.* New York: Praeger Publishers, 1972.

Singer, Philip. *Sadhus and Charisma.* Bombay: Asia Publishing House, 1970.

Sinha, Nandlal, trans. *The Bhakti Sūtras of Narada.* The Sacred Books of the Hindus Series, vol. 7, pt. I. New York: AMS Press, n.d.

Southey, Robert. "The Curse of Kehama." In *The Poetical Works of Robert Southey.* vol. 8. Boston: James R. Osgood and Company, 1875.

Srinivas, M. N. "Prospects of Sociological Research in Gujarat." In *Journal of the Maharaja Sayajirao University of Baroda*, vol. 2 (1953), pp. 21-35.

Stanley, John M. "Special Time, Special Power: The Fluidity of Power in a Popular Hindu Festival." *Journal of Asian Studies*, vol. 37, no. 1 (November 1977), pp. 27-43.

Stietencron, H. von. "The Advent of Viṣṇuism in Orissa." In *The Cult of Jagannāth and the Regional Tradition of Orissa.* Edited by Anncharlott Eschmann, *et al*, pp. 1-30. New Delhi: Manohar Publications, 1978.

Thurston, Edgar. *Castes and Tribes of Southern India.* Madras: Government Press, 1909.

Tripathi, G. C. "Jagannātha: The Ageless Deity of the Hindus." In *The Cult of Jagannāth and the Regional Traditions of Orissa.* Edited by Anncharlott Eschmann, et al, pp. 477-490. New Delhi: Manohar Publications, 1978.

__________. "Navakalevara: The Unique Ceremony of the 'Birth' and the 'Death' of the 'Lord of the World'." In *The Cult of Jagannāth and the Regional Traditions in Orissa.* Edited by Anncharlott Eschmann, *et al*, pp. 223-264. New Delhi: Manohar Publications, 1978.

Turner, Victor. *The Ritual Process.* Chicago: Aldine Press, 1968.

Tylor, Edward B. *Anthropology.* Abridged by Leslie A. White. Ann Arbor: The University of Michigan Press, 1960.

Vail, Lise. "Renunciation, Love and Power in Hindu Monastic Life." Ph.D. dissertation, University of Pennsylvania (forthcoming).

van Buitenen, J. A. B. "Akṣara." In *Journal of the American Oriental Society*, vol. 79, no. 3 (July-September 1959), pp. 176-187.

Van Gennap, Arnold. *The Rites of Passage.* Translated by Monika Vizedom and Gabrielle Caffee. Chicago: University of Chicago Press, 1960.

Varadācariyar, Śrīmān Kumkumam A. S. V. "Pakavān Śālakrāmā Sannitya Mahimai." *Śrī Ranganātha Pāduka*, vol. 14, no. 12 (March 1978), pp. 22-23.

Varma, K. *The Indian Technique of Clay Modelling.* Santiniketan: Proddu, 1970.

Vēdānta Dēśika. *Rahasya traya sāram.* 2 vols Edited by Śrī Rāmatēcikācāriyar. Kumbakonam: Oppilliappan Sanniti, 1961.

__________. *Catuḥślōkibhāṣyam, Stōtraratnabhāṣyam, gadyatrayabhāṣyaṃs ca.* Madras: Śrī Vedānta Deśika Seventh Centenary Trust, 1968.

__________. *Cillarai Rahasyaṅkaḷ.* Edited by Śrī Rāmatēcikācāryar Svāmi. Kumbakonam: Oppilliappan Sanniti, 1972.

Vidyarthi, L. P., *et al. The Sacred Complex of Kashi.* Delhi: Concept Publishing Company, 1979.

Wach, Joachim. *Sociology of Religion.* Chicago: University of Chicago Press (Phoenix Books), 1944.

Wadley, Susan. *Shakti: Power in the Conceptual Structure of Karimpur Religion* (The University of Chicago Studies in Anthropology Series in Social, Cultural, and Linguistic Anthropology, no. 2). Chicago: University of Chicago Department of Anthropology, 1975.

Walker, Sheila. *Ceremonial Spirit Possession in Africa and Afro-America.* Leiden: E. J. Brill, 1972.

Ward, William. *A View of the History, Literature, and Religion of the Hindoos: Including a Minute Description of Their Manners and Customs, and Translations from Their Principal Works.* 5th ed. abridged. Madras: J. Higginbotham, 1863.

Whitehead, Henry. *The Village Gods of South India.* Calcutta: Oxford University Press, 1921.

Williams, Raymond B. "Holy Man as Religious Specialist: the Acharya Tradition in Vaishnavism." *Encounter*, vol. 43, no. 1 (Winter 1982), pp. 61-97.

__________. *A New Face of Hinduism: The Swaminarayan Religion.* Cambridge: Cambridge University Press, 1984.

Wiser, William. *The Hindu Jajamani System.* Lucknow: Lucknow Publishing House, 1936.

Woodroffe, Sir John (Arthur Avalon). *Introduction to Tantra Shastra.* Madras: Ganesh & Company, 1952.

__________. *Shakti and Shakta: Essays and Addresses on the Shakta Tantra Shastra.* Madras: Ganesh & Company, 1951.

Woods, James H., trans. "Channa Basava Purāṇa of the Lingaits." *Journal of the Bombay Branch of the Royal Asiatic Society*, vol. 8, no. 24 (1863-1866), pp. 98-215.

Yajñavarāha Svāmi, Śri Nāvalpākkam. "Śālakrāma Cilayiṉ Perumai." *Śrī Nṛsimha Priya*, vol. 34, no. 12 (April 1976), pp. 42-48.

Yajnik, Jayendrakumar Anandji. *The Philosophy of Sri Svaminarayana.* Ahmedabad: L. D. Institute of Indology, 1972.

Younger, Paul. "A Temple Festival of Māriyammaṉ." *Journal of the American Academy of Religion*, vol. 18, no. 4 (1980), pp. 493-517.

__________. "Ten days of Wandering and Romance with Lord Raṅkanātan: The Paṅkuṉi Festival in Śrīraṅkam Temple, South India." *Modern Asian Studies*, vol. 16, no 4 (October 1982), pp. 623-656.

Zimmerman, Francis. "Ṛtu-sātmya: The seasonal cycle and the principle of appropriateness." Translated by McKim Marriott and John Leavitt. *Social Science and Medicine*, vol. 14B (1980), pp. 99-106.